With Compliments...

Please accept this copy of *We Were in the Big One: Experiences of the World War II Generation* edited by Mark P. Parillo, Kansas State University, with our compliments.

This collection of diary entries, letters, photographs, and other documents for the World War II era were carefully selected by Mark P. Parillo from the Eisenhower Library's World War II Participants Collection and other archives. These documents show how the war affected Americans across gender lines, across social and political spectrums, on the home front, and on the battlefield.

With a concise introduction and headnotes that introduce each document, Professor Parillo provides an interpretive framework that puts the selections in context for students.

From:
SR Books (an imprint of Scholarly Resources)
104 Greenhill Avenue
Wilmington DE 19805

PHONE: 800-772-8937
FAX: 302-654-3871
INTERNET: www.scholarly.com
EMAIL: sales@scholarly.com

We Were in the Big One

WE WERE IN THE BIG ONE

EXPERIENCES OF THE WORLD WAR II GENERATION

Edited by Mark P. Parillo

A Scholarly Resources Inc. Imprint
Wilmington, Delaware

Scholarly Resources Inc.
104 Greenhill Avenue
Wilmington, DE 19805-1897
www.scholarly.com

Library of Congress Cataloging-in-Publication Data

We were in the big one : experiences of the World War II generation / edited by Mark P. Parillo
     p. cm.
  Includes bibliographical references and index.
  ISBN 0-8420-2796-3 (alk. paper) — ISBN 0-8420-2797-1 (pbk. : alk. paper)
    1. World War, 1939–1945 — United States.   2. World War, 1939–1945 — Personal
narratives, American.   I. Parillo, Mark, P., 1955–

D769.A2 W4 2002
940.54'8173'0922—dc21

                                                                    2001049093

To my father—
Who taught me how to apply the Secret of Capablanca's Combination to life

ABOUT THE EDITOR

MARK P. PARILLO is an associate professor of history at Kansas State University and a faculty member of the KSU Institute for Military History and Twentieth Century Studies. He earned a B.A. from Notre Dame University and completed his Ph.D. at Ohio State University. He serves as secretary-treasurer of the World War II Studies Association and editor of H-War, the international electronic discussion list devoted to the scholarly study of military history.

The son of a U.S. Marine Corps veteran of World War II, Parillo grew up with an insatiable interest in matters related to the great global conflict. His other publications include *The Japanese Merchant Marine in World War II* (1993) and several articles, essays, and book chapters on various aspects of the war. He is currently undertaking analytical studies of the Burma Road and Japanese and U.S. utilization of railroads during the Second World War.

CONTENTS

TWO

AT THE FRONT

55

THREE

HEALING

101

FOUR

SO THAT OTHERS MAY FIGHT

121

FIVE

SINCE YOU WENT AWAY

163

SIX

THE ARSENAL OF DEMOCRACY

191

SEVEN

IN THE WAR'S SHADOW

211

EIGHT

COMING HOME

231

ACKNOWLEDGMENTS

As much as authors are loathe to admit it, a book is never the product of one person's thoughts or efforts. And for this volume especially many hands have been at work. It is only proper to recognize some of the people and organizations that have enriched it, though I alone must bear the responsibility for its shortcomings, as no one has been better served by his collaborators.

My first thanks must go to Matt Hershey of Scholarly Resources, who had the original idea for this work, labored tirelessly on its behalf, and always placed the quality of the end product above all else, including my penchant for missing deadlines. His patience and wisdom have, I hope, been well served.

Also deserving much praise are the staff members at the Eisenhower Library in Abilene, Kansas, whose efficiency was exceeded only by their courtesy and unfailing good humor. Dan Holt and Mack Teasley direct the operations of a facility unrivaled in the quality of its collections, working conditions for the researcher, and graciousness of staff. Special mention must also be made of the incomparable Dave Haight, whose knowledge of the impressive holdings of the library quite literally surpasses that of any computer.

I can go no further without thanking Professor Emeritus Robin Higham of Kansas State University. He always found time to discuss the work, make suggestions, and offer encouragement, despite a schedule in his "retirement" that would overwhelm two scholars half his age. I would also like to offer special thanks to James Ehrman of Kansas State University, whose expertise with all things cybernetic is matched only by the outstanding generosity with which he dispenses his remarkable knowledge and his precious time.

I wish also to thank the members of the World War II generation whose works were used in this volume. They and their family members who opened their treasured links to their own personal past to public inspection have demonstrated a true love of knowledge and respect for our collective, shared past. There can be no greater legacy to bequeath future generations.

Finally, I reserve my deepest and most fervent gratitude for my family. My brother Steven assisted with the research, and my father, a veteran of the Marine Corps in the World War II era, proved to be a living resource. Donata, Sunny, Allie, and Taryn, my daughters, abided my late nights and weekends at the "family" computer and incessant discussions of "the book" at the dinner table. And special thanks, as always, go to Marcella, my favorite editor.

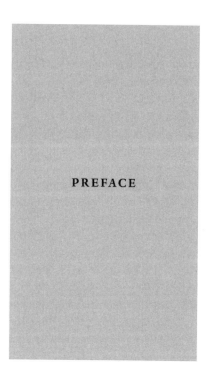

PREFACE

Why in the world do we need another book on World War II? Surely the world has enough literature on this subject, yet more continues to pour forth from authors and publishing houses every month. Oral histories of the World War II generation are receiving special attention now because only recently has it become broadly recognized that these people are disappearing from the population at a rapid rate. So, more and more books and articles are appearing about this group of Americans who participated in the great global conflict. To add to the blizzard of material might appear to be a pointless exercise.

There are, nevertheless, good reasons for undertaking the task. World War II was an event of huge proportions and implications for the United States, as it was for all of humankind. Even the tens of millions of deaths it caused, tragic though those were, cannot begin to measure its impact on the planet. Minor powers were caught in its currents and eddies, and the major belligerents were forced to transform their very fabric in order to wage this greatest of all wars. For no nation is this statement truer than for the United States, where there is plenty of reason to label the Second World War the "Big One."

Furthermore, we Americans tend to give short shrift to our wars. We view them as aberrations amid the relatively lengthy stretches of peace when our focus has been on economic concerns, slavery and civil rights, automobiles and movies and the rest of our popular culture, scientific and technological developments, gender equity issues, law and order, our health and health costs, and the activities of our celebrities and politicians. When our wars are over, we try to forget them and turn our attention once more to all our peacetime pursuits. For Americans, watching the Super Bowl or studying our stock market investments is a far more natural pursuit than dealing with our military past.

And yet, our wars, as much as any other kind of event in our past, have shaped who we are today. Although most Americans will grudgingly concede this truth if pressed, we give it little thought as we carry on our daily lives. Yet we do recognize the impact of our military past even in our language and thought patterns, albeit only half-consciously. For instance, we tend to date events by our wars, as in, "I haven't seen anything like that since before Vietnam," or "They stopped making that model before Pearl Harbor." We use references such as "the antebellum South," the "interwar years," or "post-Vietnam." Our wars have been watersheds not only because of their obvious political consequences but also because we, as a society, polity, and culture, have often been changed by the pressures of wartime. Or, more precisely, we have often reshaped ourselves to meet the exigencies of war.

If these words are taken as a plea for more recognition of the value of military history, then so be it, for few events can rival military activity in their revelations about a nation's social values, collective psychology and worldview, economic philosophies, and cultural expression. In sum, we can learn more about human beings, as individuals and as members of social groups, from war than from virtually any other kind of event.

World War II is the best example. It was not just the biggest war, in terms of participation by the American public, of all the wars in U.S. history, but also it is unlikely to be matched in its scale by any conflict in the nation's future. It was a unique ordeal experienced by a unique generation.

The rush to record the testimony of the generation who waged this great struggle is thus a worthwhile endeavor, for it is wise to harvest this tremendous historical resource while the World War II generation's day on earth still lingers in its twilight. But, for all its value, oral history has its limitations. The memory's penchant for trickery, amply demonstrated in recent psychological research, can be magnified by the passage of several decades. By checking the verifiable facts of a given interview, the diligent researcher can assess the general reliability of the witness. Some aspects of the story, however, never can or will be substantiated. We cannot expect the recollections of septuagenarians and octogenarians across a half-century to be precise, comprehensive, and accurate in every respect. So, some events will be recalled correctly but at the wrong time or in the wrong place. Some people and incidents will be merged, corrupted, or completely forgotten. And, inevitably, there will be factual errors.

There are other factors that may taint memory. Some people, from embarrassment, fear, jealousy, egotism, shame, or a half dozen other motives, will be, quite simply, dishonest about their past. More commonly, it is human nature to exaggerate, glamorize, or embellish. Also, an interviewer may, intentionally or not, prompt a certain response by the way a question is posed or by the choice of vocabulary or the sequence of questions asked.

Perhaps the most profound yet subtle influence on memory, however, is our own philosophy of life, which can cause us to remember things not so much as they happened but as we *need* them to have happened. To avoid the violation of or an attack upon our heartfelt convictions and conceptions of how the world works, our psyches can sometimes insist that certain events could have transpired only in certain ways. Thus, we can, without even realizing it, remember past events as we want them to have happened. This danger grows with the passing of the years, as our ideas become more fully formed and ingrained in our subconscious minds. We cannot, for example, see World War II without peering through the window of Vietnam. Although that window might be quite differently constructed for one person as opposed to another, there is no denying its presence as well as the possibility, indeed likelihood, that it will affect our reconstruction of the past. In short, remembering events precisely the way we perceived them when they happened is not only unlikely; it would scarcely be human to do so.

After reading these arguments, one might wonder why it is worthwhile to pursue oral history at all, but the weaknesses of this type of source should not hide its great value for our understanding of the past. By direct questioning the interviewer can, for example, elicit testimony on topics or events for which there simply is no other evidence, thus making the twentieth-century historian the envy of his profession. Nevertheless, it is important to recognize the shortcomings of oral history if we are to appreciate what the documentary evidence can do to balance the picture.

Documents can lie. They can present a version of events just as influenced by dishonesty, misperception, or an agenda as oral history. They are, after all, written by humans, with the same failings and weaknesses of the humans who give oral testimony about past events. One should not, therefore, expect a diary entry or letter to be "the truth" any more than the reminiscences of an aging participant might be.

Documents, photographs, and other materials generated in response to the historical events themselves, however, have the considerable benefit of reflecting the particular mindset of people who produced them *at the time they were produced*. That is, they manifest the views and philosophies of a society at the moment in which the events under study actually occurred. The practical effect is that we can glean a great deal about the attitudes of the World War II generation toward matters such as gender, political creeds, race, religion, social and cultural beliefs, and personal values from what they wrote during the war, which, in their oral testimony decades later, might be altered or otherwise obfuscated. Therein lies the prospective contribution of this volume.

To keep the flavor of the original documents in this collection, grammar, spelling, and punctuation mistakes have been retained, aside from typographical or other errors hampering the clarity of the writing. Letters and diary entries, with very few exceptions, have been included in full to obviate the feeling of reading disjointed document excerpts. However, this practice occasionally results in retention of passages of idle chitchat or references to persons or events unknown to the reader. It is hoped that they will enhance the establishment of context for the portions of more interest or moment.

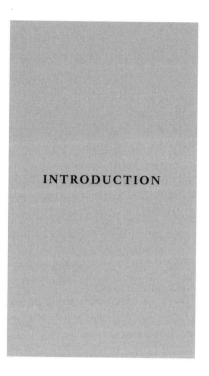

INTRODUCTION

T O THE GENERATION WHO LIVED THROUGH IT, W ORLD W AR II WOULD ALWAYS BE the "Big One." The expression became a common, informal reference understood by all Americans who experienced the war, and it still carries meaning among them today. In the war's immediate aftermath, the phrase was intended to distinguish the recently concluded global conflict from the "Great War" of 1914–1918, in which U.S. participation had been considerable but not nearly as extensive, materially, geographically, or chronologically, as it would be in 1941–1945. As time wore on, the expression took on new meaning as a way to differentiate World War II from the more limited conflicts in Korea and Vietnam. "I was in the Big One, Double-ya Double-ya Two," Archie Bunker would proudly proclaim to his pacifist son-in-law on the popular 1970s television comedy *All in the Family,* and in doing so he intoned the creed and apologia of his generation.

It is difficult to argue convincingly against Archie's claim, for, on almost any scale, World War II was the largest and greatest conflagration in U.S. history. Although not as lengthy as the Revolutionary War or the clash in Vietnam, World War II exceeded all other wars in the nation's past in almost any other quantifiable category. Americans spent more tax dollars, joined the armed forces in greater numbers, fought in more places and climates, and waged war as part of a grander alliance than in any other war in their history.

Five million Americans wore a military uniform in World War I, but nearly three times that many saw service in the four years after Pearl Harbor. The

United States spent $32 billion to underwrite its war effort in 1917–18 but near-
ly twelve times as much in 1941–1945, with the automotive industry by itself
producing $29 billion worth of war matériel, so that, even allowing for infla-
tion, the scale of expenditures in World War II dwarfed that of the earlier conflict. In World War I, 1.3 million U.S. soldiers fought in France, of whom more
than 50,000 died, yet in World War II, the army alone sent 3.1 million men
overseas, and U.S. battle deaths in Europe topped 170,000, with an additional
120,000 killed in other theaters. Americans launched three million tons of shipping in 1919, its single best year in the World War I era, but in 1942 alone the
United States built eight million tons and added forty-six million deadweight
tons more in the next three years. In no other war did Americans toil and fight
in deserts, jungles, plains, mountains, wheat fields, coral atolls, tundra, swamps,
and forests on every continent except Antarctica. Linked in arms with Indians,
Poles, Australians, Frenchmen, Russians, Jews, Canadians, Scots, Gurkhas,
Dutchmen, Chinese, Brazilians, Englishmen, Kachins, New Zealanders, and
countless other peoples, the United States helped forge a victorious alliance
that survived the war as the United Nations. By any standard, on anyone's
terms, among America's wars World War II was truly the Big One.

It was more than chance or fate that made it so. World War II in fact epit-
omized warfare in the industrial age, its parameters shaped by historical forces
that had been at work for centuries. The rebirth of nationalism coupled with
the flowering of the industrial revolution had been making national military
forces ever larger and more complicated since the latter part of the seven-
teenth century. Industrialization brought more efficiency and profitability to
basic production processes, allowing societies to spare more manpower for
martial activities and contributing a much more fertile and predictable tax
base to underwrite the newly expanded armies and navies. Nationalism provided the motivation for men to join the colors, which they did by the tens of
thousands in the eighteenth century and by the millions by the early twentieth. Albrecht von Wallenstein's one-hundred-thousand-strong army was a
marvel in the 1620s, yet by century's end a strong economy and improved fiscal and administrative methods allowed France to maintain standing forces of
four hundred thousand. A hundred years later Revolutionary France, fortified
by the first phases of industrialization and a vibrant surge of patriotism, field-
ed eight hundred thousand troops to withstand the reactionary onslaught of
the rest of Europe. By the time of the Great War of 1914–1918, the combination of industrialization and nationalism enabled more than eight million
Frenchmen to fill out the ranks.

World War II demanded yet more manpower from its belligerents. For
one thing, armies were getting ever larger. Three and a quarter million
German servicemen died in World War II, for example, more than the Kaiser's

government had mobilized for the outbreak of hostilities in August 1914. Indeed, in June 1941, more than three million German soldiers launched Operation Barbarossa, and this figure excludes the forty divisions supplied by Hitler's allies. Even in the final days of the war, the *Wehrmacht* numbered five million, facing approximately nine million Allied soldiers. Although only in the United States has World War II earned the informal epithet of the Big One, the designation could be fairly applied by all the war's major participants. Never before or since has so much of humanity been under arms.

Consider for a moment what military forces numbering in the millions require for their daily sustenance. Every soldier, sailor, and airman needed uniforms, somewhere to sleep, bathroom facilities, accommodations for personal possessions, and, of course, a well-balanced diet to support a hard day of physical activity. The United States boasted twelve million men and women in uniform by 1945, necessitating the production and distribution of mountains of blankets, kitchen utensils, razor blades, socks, fresh produce, shoe polish, and toilet paper. If every person in the U.S. armed forces drank one cup of coffee a day, it would have taken a fleet of one thousand tank trucks to keep the caffeine percolating. Hauling enough sugar for every American serviceman to sweeten his or her morning beverage with a teaspoon of sugar would have tied up two thirty-ton railroad boxcars.

These ruminations include only life's daily necessities. We should also bear in mind the other basic services and facilities necessary for maintaining a fit and spirited military machine. Military personnel periodically need telephone exchanges, barbers, recreation facilities, dental care, laundry service, and dependable mail delivery. The sick and wounded require a complete medical system capable of treating every sort of mundane and exotic malady as well as all the traumatic injuries inflicted by combat. In short, military bases should be seen as not just places for training soldiers but also as independent communities providing all the amenities necessary to keep men and women healthy, disciplined, and reasonably content. During World War II, these "GI towns" dotted the American landscape.

Consider also what the main business of these "towns" was: the equipping and training of forces capable of defeating the Axis enemies. Rivers of machines, tools, weapons, and other equipment, from silk parachutes to bulldozers, flowed into the camps to outfit America's legions for battle. To cite but two examples, U.S. factories turned out more than a quarter million artillery pieces (exclusive of antiaircraft guns) and 2.4 million motor trucks of myriad varieties. Every radar set, LST, and machine gun produced was testament to American industrial might, but we should not lose sight of the fact that instructing the personnel necessary to use each piece of equipment was an equally impressive undertaking. Schools and training courses of all sorts, up to and including a railroad line operated exclusively for the training of U.S. Army transportation specialists, were a major national enterprise.

These prodigious feats of production and education enabled the United States to assemble a mighty war machine, yet there is still more, much more, to the story of the American war effort. Consider, for example, the tremendous distances that separated this emerging military behemoth from its targeted adversaries. Germany lay across the Atlantic Ocean, with Berlin as far from Washington as Washington is from Los Angeles. The Japanese military forces were even more remote from American shores, and any U.S. battalions intent on tangling with the emperor's samurai had to cross five thousand miles or more of ocean first. Bear in mind that these forces, whether in Europe, Africa, or the far reaches of the Pacific Ocean, needed not only an initial lift to close with their foes but also a dependable and ever-flowing logistical network to support them in the field.

The daily and operational needs of armies, navies, and air forces in the 1940s were staggering. A look at a single commodity, fuel oil, illustrates this point. A typical U.S. armored fighting vehicle expended one gallon of fuel per mile, meaning that it consumed about fifty gallons for every normal operational day. So numerous were U.S. armored forces in northwest Europe, exclusive of troops in the British Isles, that by September 1944 the U.S. ground troops were burning an average of over fifty-five hundred tons of motor fuel a day, or about four large tanker loads a week. The high performance of aircraft engines demanded prodigious quantities of high-grade fuel. A single squadron of single-engine fighters drank nearly ten tons of fuel per mission, and bombers such as the B-17 and B-24 consumed six times as much. Mammoth warships swallowed fuel oil by the barrel. A battleship of the *Iowa* class required 8,000 barrels for twenty-four hours of steaming at an operational speed of thirty knots. In the first month of the Pacific War, the U.S. Navy consumed over 800,000 barrels of fuel oil, and in the war's final months the figure was ten times as high. No serious operations could be undertaken without a vast system of transportation just for these oil needs; thousands of people used tankers, pipelines, oilers, tank trucks, and packaged oil, such as in drums or smaller cans, to provide the single, indispensable article of liquid fuel.

Thus, the manning, equipping, training, moving, and sustaining of the awesome U.S. war machine involved massive amounts of manpower, materials, and managerial expertise. And yet even this quick sketch of requirements does not give the whole picture of the U.S. war effort. The United States, in the end, lived up to the title of "arsenal of democracy" that Franklin Roosevelt had claimed for it. That is, American resources and production helped underwrite major portions of the Allied war effort. For example, a partial list of Lend-Lease aid sent to the Soviet Union during the war includes 14,000 aircraft, 5.5 million pairs of boots, 433,000 trucks, and over 100 merchant vessels, including 36 Liberty ships. The United States shipped 3,700 railroad locomotives and 33,000 freight cars overseas as part of the Lend-Lease program, totals that do not include the 2,000 locomotives and 10,000 cars the U.S. Army brought with it.

The military, industrial, and transportation achievements of the United States in World War II are unparalleled in human history. But besides bringing victory in a titanic conflict, these activities had a tremendous economic and social impact on the nation. The terrible oppression of unemployment, poverty, and despair that had characterized the 1930s gave way to bustling factories, swollen paychecks, and disrupted family life. Men went off to the service, women went off to the war plants, and children grew up quickly. African Americans, women, "okies," Latinos, and other groups long discriminated against in the labor market suddenly found lucrative employment in the burgeoning steel mills, shipyards, arsenals, and airplane factories. People poured into cities in the Northeast, the upper Midwest, the West Coast, and along the Gulf, as the nation experienced its most vigorous internal migration. Urban services groaned under the strain, rents and meal prices ballooned, and finding a seat on streetcars and buses became next to impossible.

The impact, however, extended beyond the laborers in the factories and offices to all Americans. Necessities became scarce and luxuries unobtainable. "Roses are red / Violets are blue / Sugar is sweet / Remember?" was pointedly humorous to a generation learning to live with shortages and rationing. The government imposed gasoline rationing, despite the existence of sufficient motor fuel stocks, to save wear on tires that could not be replaced for the duration because of the dire shortage of rubber. Scrap and paper drives occupied spare hours, not to mention air raid and blackout drills, aircraft identification classes, and first aid lessons.

Added to these constant reminders of the war were the difficult personal circumstances that most families had to learn to endure. Sons and brothers left, to return, if they survived, as changed men. Young women spread their wings, too, in ways unthinkable before Pearl Harbor, whether it be to don a military uniform or to gain a taste of financial and emotional independence conferred by well-paying jobs. Husbands and wives were separated for months or even years.

The war was everywhere. Bombs may not have rained down on U.S. cities, and no enemy tanks rolled into town squares, but the war was nevertheless inescapable. Relatives and friends were gone, some forever. Newspapers, movies and the theater, radio, and magazines all dealt with the war or with its consequences. Street corners, train stations, and other public places were dotted with young men and women in uniform. Gold stars adorned many a living room window. One could not walk down a street in any city or town without encountering some reminder of the war.

No war before or since touched so many Americans and so many aspects and facets of their lives. That generation would always thereafter conceive of it as the ultimate experience of sacrifice, hard work, and accomplishment.

ONE

BECOMING A SOLDIER

A s a war of attrition in the industrial age, World War II made tremendous demands on the belligerents for military manpower. The United States obliged by enacting a draft and beginning the delicate task of balancing the needs of the armed forces with that of industry. Yet, of the fifteen million Americans who served in uniform in the years between Pearl Harbor and the Japanese surrender in Tokyo Bay, the vast majority never saw combat. They drove trucks, typed orders and requisitions, loaded ammunition, built roads and ports, cooked meals, and patrolled waters and guarded outposts from Alaska to Calcutta.

But every soldier, sailor, airman, WAC, and WAVE underwent the experience of military training. This process was as much psychological as it was physical, for recruits learned military bearing and culture even as they hardened their bodies for the anticipated ordeals of modern war. For some, military training was the beginning of an

exciting and unanticipated career, for others it was a nearly unen-
durable affliction of lost freedom, but for most it was only an interlude,
an intermission between acts in the long arc of their civilian lives. For
better or worse, however, it was an experience shared, to a degree
unmatched before or since, by an entire generation of Americans.

While all service men and women underwent basic military training,
most also proceeded on to more specialized schools or programs.
Whether it was learning engine repairs, typing and filing, or gunlay-
ing, the troops spent weeks or months after their basic training course
acquiring specialized skills. Induction and training thus usually took
several months, during which time the fledgling soldier or sailor
might be stationed at a few or several different camps all over the
United States. Moving from camp to camp meant long train rides,
extended separations from family and friends, and exposure to
strange new peoples and places.

It also meant new social experiences. Recruits learned to eat, sleep,
and wash with dozens of other people, to personalize the impersonal
world of the military, and to appreciate the precious few days or
hours away from the base on a pass or furlough. Residents of any
town near a military camp or school became accustomed to the
intense and often raucous outpourings of pent-up emotions and
desires of soldiers and sailors spending their limited time and money.
Exciting to some, frightening to others, this new life was nevertheless
shared by millions.

TO DRAFT OR NOT TO DRAFT?

VIEWS OF THE AMERICAN LEGION

In a war being fought by millions of men on a side, would the draft
be necessary for American success? This question was one of the
first the nation faced during the crisis of World War II.

"A Catechism on Universal Draft"[1]

Observers of military events recognized from the outset that victory in this war would require millions of men, and perhaps
women, in uniform. Even before Pearl Harbor, the U.S. Congress
enacted legislation that reestablished the draft. Although the

Roosevelt administration supported the peacetime draft, Congress was also reacting to growing public pressure for preparedness. Here is a call for conscription from the American Legion.

All authorities, even those opposed to enacting a universal draft law before war is actually declared, agree that manpower must be drafted in modern warfare. The age when a few thousand, or even a million, volunteers could fight, alone, a big nation's war is past. . . . Modern war demands the employment of . . . vast numbers of men and amounts of equipment.

Petition to President Roosevelt[2]

Despite the calls for the reinstatement of selective service and the actions of Congress, not everyone favored the draft. Before Pearl Harbor, there were groups who opposed conscription and worried about involvement in another European war.

President Roosevelt:

We the undersigned American Citizens insist that you keep your oft-repeated campaign promise that you will not send American boys to fight in foreign wars.

Please keep our ships for our own defense and not out in belligerent waters where they will be targets for foreign gun powder and thereby involve us in this devastating war.

Return at once to:
Mothers' Mobilizing Against War,
2673 N. 60th St. or Room 5197 Plankinton Arcade
Milwaukee, Wisconsin

Petition to the American Legion[3]

Some of the antidraft groups attempted not only to persuade those neutral on the question of a draft but also to win over their opponents.

To the Legionnaires

We, the undersigned American mothers, fathers, sisters, and brothers, appeal to you and beg you, fathers and brothers, in the name of our dear Lord and your own sweet mothers, to exercise your mighty strength and influence to stop this country from helping to prolong and spread this war.

"What you have done to the least of My brethren you have done unto Me."

You have the might and power to save America and America is in deadly danger. The war party wants us to believe it is our fight for humanity and brotherhood. The last war was a war to end all wars. Twenty years from now, when your baby boys are of soldier age, they will offer another cry.

Remember, those who are crying for war are not the ones who will do the fighting and dying.

Yes, you Legionnaires can do it and God will be on your side.

Please fill out this form and return at once.

2461 W. Center St.

Membership over 100,000

2673 N. 60th St.

THE AVERAGE SOLDIER

"YOO-HOO," COMIC CORPORATION OF AMERICA, "THE AVERAGE SOLDIER"[4]

Conscription was enacted nonetheless, and then the bombs fell on Pearl Harbor. The soldiers poured into the induction centers and training camps in great numbers. They were, however, not super-men or even professional soldiers but just average Joes. Here is the statistical composite soldier and some of the costs to produce him.

THE AVERAGE SOLDIER

The average young man starting service in the United States Army is 5 feet 8 inches tall, weighs 144 pounds, has a chest measurement of 33 1/4 inches, a 31-inch waistline, wears a 9 1/2-D shoe and a size 7 hat, according to figures compiled by the War Department. The data is based on records of the Army Quartermaster Corps, which has directed the measuring and clothing of more than 1,500,000 men.

After a few months in the Army, however, the recruit has gained in weight on Army food, wears shoes one-half size larger and has an expanded chest measurement. This is indicated by sample test, although complete examination comparable to that given upon induction is not routine.

To keep this average soldier in fighting trim for the first year, the Quartermaster Corps spends $404.65, of which $175.20 is for his food; $162.05 for clothing; $15.79 for individual equipment; and $51.61 for barracks equipment. Weapons, ammunition, pay and other expenses incurred during his training are not included in these estimates.

At an accelerated rate, and in some instances contrary to the expressed will of Congress, the various agencies of the government are taking over the land of the United States. The government owns or is acquiring 395,978,724 acres. That amounts to the combined land areas of Maine, New Hampshire, Vermont, Rhode Island, Massachusetts, Connecticut, New York, New Jersey, Pennsylvania, Delaware, Maryland, West Virginia, Virginia, North Carolina, South Carolina, Georgia, Florida, Alabama, Ohio, Illinois and Indiana, with enough left over to make 32 Districts of Columbia. It is about one fifth of the total area of the entire United States.

—Harry F. Byrd, U.S. Senator (Dem.) from Virginia, in 1943

THE CITIZEN SOLDIER

POEM BY LT. LENHARDT E. BAUER, "THE RECRUIT"[5]

The young men flooding the induction centers and training camps had little military experience among them. They were true "citizen-soldiers," idealized and even mythologized later. But contemporaries, too, were inspired by the tradition of average citizens taking up arms in defense of their beliefs.

THE RECRUIT

He ain't from the Regular Army . . .
He just "joined up" today,
An' he wasn't long on his reasons . . .
Just said he was "going away."
His pa was right smart of worried,
But just brimmin' over with pride,
An' ma, with her flustered apron,
Wiped tears she was tryin' to hide.

He'd never been given to fightin'
No soul had he ever done harm . . .
'Bout all that he know'd was workin',
An' helpin' to tend the farm.

He ain't got the slightest notion,
How an Army's s'posed to be run;
But you can bet that he's willin'
To help with the job to be done.

Don't think 'cause his shirt is too skimpy,
An' nothin' fits him just right,
That he ain't the kind of a soldier
To be counted upon in the fight.
In his veins flow the blood of freedom;
He will perform as he should . . .
As his daddy did before him
At Argonne, and Belleau Wood.

Tho' the Army ain't his profession,
He wasn't cut out for to roam;
He'll fight in the best of tradition,
Get the job done, and go home;
And that's where he'll head, when it's over,
Both happy and willin' to cease
The strife and the struggle of battle
To tend to the fruits of the peace.

An' when cuts 'cross the pasture,
Down the old and well-worn track,
There'll be souvenirs of his glory
In the duffle swung on his back;
An' the future writers of hist'ry
Thru their pages will give a salute,
To this hero, civilian soldier . . .
Today's just "joined-up" recruit.

Lt. Lenhardt E. Bauer

INSTRUCTIONS FOR THE RECRUIT

AMERICAN LEGION PUBLICATION, "FALL-IN"[6]

The citizen-soldiers in the training centers now had to learn not only the arts of making war—shooting, wielding bayonets, marching, siting guns, laying mines—but also the manner, methods, and rhythms of the military life. Here is some of the advice proffered recruits by the American Legion. It involved more than just learning to rise before dawn.

Army private washing clothes in bucket behind tent. (Courtesy of the Dwight D. Eisenhower Library, William B. Glover Collection.)

This booklet could properly be titled, "Letters from a veteran father to his son in service." It is a welcome to comradeship from the members of The American Legion to those young men who are just now entering upon the greatest experience of their lives. They have become Service Men in the Armed Forces of the United States. . . .

Three million copies of this booklet "Fall-In" have been printed and distributed. . . .

FALL-IN

First, you are an individual worthy to defend liberty and freedom. You have chosen to preserve that for which many have died to obtain and to defend. You are to wear the uniform and the insignia of the grandest organizations on earth, the armed forces of the United States.

Second, you are now a comrade of every man and woman who has served, or is serving, under the flag of the United States; of Washington, Jackson, Grant, Lee, Farragut, Custer, Shafter, Roosevelt, Dewey, Funston, Pershing, and all the rest. After your service is completed, you will find no rank or preference among your comrades.

Third, you are going to have a lot of new experiences, many of which will seem very hard and burdensome as you pass through them but which will appear some time later as interesting and amusing experiences.

Fourth, you are entering upon a new life, and it will be somewhat difficult to make adjustments. The Service has its regulations and traditions. They are "sacred to the Service," so do not try to change them. They are older than you, and each regulation exists for some good reason. Their worth has been proven by experience—and hard experience at that. So accept them as they are and conform yourself to them.

"The Service is just what you make it," so perhaps a few *"don'ts"* will save you some trouble.

Do not criticize your officers because you think they know less about military and naval affairs than you do. Remember they have spent hours, days and months, perhaps years, in study before you came into service. Let the General Staff do the worrying; it's not your job.

Do not set yourself up as a loud-mouthed authority on any one subject. You may know all about it, but the other fellow does not like to be told that such is the case.

Do not try to be tough and want to show it. There's always someone who is just a little tougher and it's embarrassing when you run into him.

Do not repeat rumors you may hear. Many of those rumors are started just for the benefit of those who are willing to repeat them. Much damage is done by repeating rumors. If you do not know something is true, do not repeat it. The tales that start out with "They said" are generally pure gossip. No one has ever found out who "They" are anyway.

Do not invent stories about yourself, your family, your sweetheart, the army or the navy. Your comrades will appreciate good stories but not the kind that are created to gather sympathy or to aggrandize yourself.

Do not, when you are invited to a civilian home for an entertainment or a meal, tell of the hardships or privations you think you are suffering. They may appear to be interested, but they only seem so to be polite. Your looks belie your statements, and they know differently. After all, they are the taxpayers who are paying the war bill, and they do not appreciate being criticized indirectly. Tell them the funny things—it will make the food taste better.

Do not threaten to or actually "go over the hill" or "jump ship." A desertion charge will stick to you for the rest of your life. It will deprive you of privileges and benefits until death and then transfer itself to your dependents and loved ones. It will appear in all cases of compensation and pension claims, in proving citizenship and in so many other ways. It may even deprive you of your liberty.

Things are never as hard as they seem. Grin and take it in your stride. Talk it over with the Chaplain, but don't "go over the hill." That is perhaps the most important "don't" of them all. However, there's another that is a close second.

Do not allow yourself to become involved with the other sex in such a way as to impair your health and future. A "G.O. 45" (ask your officers about it), like a desertion charge, will stick to you for life. "Willful misconduct" is a serious charge in the service and on a service record. It will show up at times that will be embarrassing, and it will be very expensive. A few thoughtless moments may wreck an entire life.

Do not borrow, appropriate, or take government property such as automobiles, trucks, motorcycles, pistols, rifles, clothing, blankets, etc., unless ordered to do so. Regulations are very strict, and what may seem to be "just laying around" is not to be taken. Government prisons contain many men who "just borrowed" government property.

Do not be a borrower or a "gimmie" among your comrades. If you do not have the money to pay for things, do without them. The man who continually repeats "gimme a cigarette," "loan me your brush," "lemme have a dollar till pay day" is always unpopular. The other fellow needs his own possessions, too.

Do not bring criticism or disgrace upon the uniform you wear. To be arrested by civilian authorities, to be intoxicated, to be in tough or improper places such as "dives," "juke joints," cheap dance halls, houses of ill fame, or even in close proximity of such places, will bring criticism and harm to the entire service. In uniform, you are the personal representative of the service to which you belong. Treasure that trust.

Do not act, imply or pretend to be better than any of your comrades. The very man you criticize or scorn may be the one who later saves your life.

But there are *"do's"* which are as important as the *"don'ts."*

Do obey the orders of your officers, whether it be Admiral, General, Corporal, or a Private in command. There is nothing personal about orders.

Remember as long as you obey orders the responsibility rests on those who give the orders. If you disobey, the aftermath becomes your responsibility.

Do value the traditions of your outfit. If your ship, company, regiment, division or squadron has distinguished itself in some past engagement, battle, or war, it is your duty to keep that spirit alive. Remember, there are those who have died to create that tradition.

Do be careful regarding the "clique" or "gang" with whom you associate. Remember the old adages about "Poor Dog Tray" or the "rotten apple." You will be classified by the company you keep.

Do salute your officers as if you really mean it. The salute is not an act of servility, it is a courteous salutation exchanged by members of the armed forces of our country. The officer returns your salute in the same spirit. The service man is the only person entitled to use it from a military standpoint. It is an honor to give the salute, an honor to return it.

Do keep your uniform and equipment clean and in good order. A carelessly dressed soldier or sailor is a poor representative of the service. There are no exceptions to that rule. A dirty rifle may not fire when it is most needed; a pack, poorly packed, is harder to carry than one carefully packed. If you are to be a soldier, be a good one.

Do write home as often as you can. Those at home are interested in everything you do. They are not interested in made-up stories of supposed hardships. Make your letters truthful, and they will be interesting.

Do read your Bible, prayer book or other volume of your church. Attend church services in camp and in nearby communities. You may find, as others of us found, that there are times when no other thing is as important as your faith in the Deity. Know how to call upon Him when you need Him. . . .

SOME SUGGESTIONS

ARTICLES YOU'LL NEED
Remember you will have to carry anything you have, so don't take unnecessary things. You will be glad you have: A good pair of sun glasses, a good cigarette lighter (matches are hard to get overseas), fountain pen and pencil, razor blades, sewing kit, small flashlight, a good can opener, playing cards, an extra pipe, waterproof tobacco pouch, extra socks and large handkerchiefs, and a good wrist watch. Don't forget your Bible or prayer book.

YOU WON'T NEED
Extra clothing, fancy toilet kits, alarm clock, medicines or fancy first-aid kit, folding drinking cups, folding bathtub, and fancy gadgets.

HAVE THE FOLKS SEND YOU
After you get settled in camp and know you'll need certain things, have

them send the radio, musical instruments, camera, needles for a record player, etc.

The Home Folks Can Also Send

There are a lot of things those at home can send from time to time: Cigarettes, tobacco, camera films, playing cards, letter paper and envelopes, cookies (but no soft or iced cakes). Air mail stamps are always handy to have.

Power of Attorney

Every person entering the armed service of the United States is urged to give serious consideration to giving a power of attorney to some person that can be trusted to carry out that trust in case of death, capture, or serious disability. This should be done before leaving home, and a trusted attorney should be consulted before such power is completed. If this has not been done before leaving home, the service man should do so at once in order that his interests and those of his dependents may be conserved during his absence. This power of attorney must be acknowledged before some official authorized to administer oaths. . . .

AU REVOIR

You are on your way.

Be a good soldier, sailor or marine.

Write home as often and whenever the opportunity presents itself.

Attend church and read your Bible or Prayer Book. Pray for the folks at home as they will pray for you.

Keep your mind and body clean.

When the time comes, fight and fight hard. Yes, you will be scared, but so will everybody. Remember, there are no Marquis of Queensbury rules in battle.

We wish we were with you. Maybe we will be.

We'll be seeing you later.

Good luck and God bless you.

The American Legion

DIARY OF A RECRUIT

NAP GLASS, "A GOLDBRICK IN THE USA"[7]

At times bewildering, at times funny, at times tedious, at times frightening and disorienting, induction and training embraced millions of Americans unacquainted with military life and ways. The details varied by service, but the basic elements remained the same

for all the civilians-turned-soldiers. The "newbies" adapted and
adjusted, but some did so more willingly or skillfully than others.
Here, Nap Glass, a self-proclaimed "goldbrick," gives us a view of
the process, along with a few tips on how to avoid serious work.

Sunday, 12/7/41

I just about managed to get up yesterday morning at seven in order to have time to dress and have Pop drive me to the railroad station. We made it with about a minute to spare and found the station jammed with young fellows waiting for the Hartford train, which would take us on the last step toward army life. Tickets were handed out to us for the ride up and back.

The train ride was uneventful except for a little more noise than is usual on a train. I talked with a couple of fellows I didn't know, even though there were a couple of Jewish boys I knew. One of the boys I talked to was Italian and as dumb as they make them. This was his first train ride, which gave him plenty to be excited about. The other was Polish and seemed to have a little more brains. Both were laborers, according to their questionnaires. The only comment they had about going into the army was that they would be unable to keep up with their women and their drinking.

At Hartford we were met by regular army officers from the Hartford Recruiting center, who marched us two abreast down a couple of blocks to the examination center. From this point on, we were aware of the fact that we were in the army, for the first speech given us by one of the officers was bawling us out for making noise, and he told us he would have the room patrolled if we didn't quiet down. The noise was nothing unusual when you consider that there were about 150 of us seated in a room about 15 feet wide and 30 feet long.

Our names were then called, not in any particular order, and we were handed a few forms which would be filled out by each of the examining officers. Next we passed on to a desk at the back of the room, where we had to sign a register and were handed a number to be put on our wrist for identification during the examination. From there, we went on to a typist who took down a few facts about birth, education and employment. I noticed that most of the typists used the two-finger system, so that when I get in, I might be able to get in an office doing typing. When asked what I did, I said I was general manager of the Feldman Glass Co., which of course gave him an opportunity to make some crack about being Mr. Glass of the Feldman Glass. Then when I told him I was being paid $35.00, he said, "They don't pay very well. It's probably just a title you have." I let it pass without remarking that I didn't think the army rate was much better.

The next stop was in the locker rooms, where we were told to take off all our clothes with the exception of our pants and shoes, and to carry our shirts. Our hanger numbers were the same as our identification numbers. We then passed into the x-ray room and met the first officer who had a sense of humor. Incidentally, this x-ray was the only addition to the examination given in New Haven previously, as all the following exams were given before. That is, we were checked for reflexes, for sugar, etc. Our teeth were looked at, our ears and our eyes were checked. Height, weight and chest measurements were taken. Heart and pulse were listened to. After all of these check-ups, I found that the only comment made by any doctor to me was, "You know, you need a shave." On the whole this exam was simpler than the last and could have been done away with, saving the state a lot of money in transportation costs to and from Hartford, as well as a lot of time.

After all these medical examinations, we were fingerprinted and were then seated in a large hall awaiting final results on the medical reports. While sitting there, we were handed pamphlets as well as a pep talk by a recruiting officer who outlined the advantages of signing up with the regular army rather than being a draftee. "More pay." "Better positions." "Travel." "Only three years of training without any further call, whereas being a draftee you are on call for ten years." Not one of us made a move to sign up, but in looking through the pamphlet I did note a few positions which I could fill while I am in the army. These are: Finance, Auditing, Motion Pictures, Teletype Operator, Stenography, Typist. I am going to make it a point to mention I am qualified for all these positions when I hit Fort Devens.

Finally a few of us were called up to the front desk and were told, "You are qualified," and told to go out and get dressed again. This brought us back to the small front reception hall. We were told we would have to wait for our x-ray report, after which we could go home. It was stuffy in the hall, so I started to walk out with the idea of getting some air as well as some food, as it was near twelve and I hadn't eaten since the night before. I was stopped at the door by an officer who said no one could go out and furthermore we would be their guests for lunch. Lunch arrived about a half hour later. We were lined up like convicts and handed paper cups. We marched past a large coffee container, which was poured into the cups already mixed. I asked if there was any sugar and the wise officer asked, "One lump or two?" but I didn't answer, as he was ready to put the lumps on my head.

Along with the coffee, we were handed a bag containing the lunch consisting of one ham sandwich, one cheese sandwich, a cupcake, and two apples. It took us no time to finish this, taking care of our appetites for a while. I then tilted back my chair and put another chair under my feet and dozed off for a while. A little after one, the barking voice of an officer woke me up. He was reading a list of numbers of those who could leave for home. About half of us had to wait around, as our reports hadn't come in yet. After those whose names had been called off left, the officer walked to the middle of the room and told all those in front of him to go into the next room. Seeing a few brooms brought in, I tried to sneak around him to get into the other room but was called back. We were then told to clean up the room, putting magazines away, straightening out the chairs, and sweeping the floor. Of course I kept to the back of everything and managed to do very little, as I felt I was not in the army yet and under no compulsion to do it.

When the room was cleaned up, they came out with a second list of numbers, among which was mine. I checked out and found I had just missed a train to New Haven, so I had to sit around for over an hour for the next train. I got back to New Haven late in the afternoon full of ideas of what I had to do during my temporary deferment till the first call the early part of January. . . .

Tuesday, January 20, 1942

It's been quite a long week since I changed from Nap Glass the man to Nap Glass the soldier but I certainly think it has been for the best. We started out by arriving at the railroad station at 8:15 and found one of the biggest crowds I had ever seen I think even at Grand Central. I saw quite a few fellows I knew or had met when I was last at Hartford at the examination. We boarded the train, which had three extra cars for us. I sat with Dave Horowitz a friend of Norman's. We took two seats and made ourselves comfortable, as we expected it to be for the last time. A short while later we were hungry, so we walked down to the dining car, expecting to get breakfast. The dining car was pretty well crowded, and after waiting quite a bit and placing our order, we didn't get it because we were arriving in Hartford and the dining car was being taken off there. So we went hungry and spent the next three hours throwing the bull with two other Jewish boys we picked up, Moe Steinberg and Murray Alpert.

Finally we arrived at Fort Devens, the train pulling right into camp. We all were told to fall out and line up in columns of three with any bags we might have. I didn't have any. We were marched over to one of the warehouses which had been converted into a reception center. We stood outside in the cold for quite a while before we were called in. Once inside, our names were called out, and we had to line up in that order and were marched over to the barracks, where we were assigned beds. From there we were again marched over to the supply house, where we were given quite a speech by the supply sergeant about getting orders and instructions straight and then were given three blankets, two sheets, and a pillow case.

Again we were marched back to the barracks and were shown how to make up a bunk by placing one sheet over the mattress and making square corners and then placing the second sheet with a blanket over it, then folding down one end of this second sheet and blanket in eight inch folds. The two other blankets were placed folded at the head of the bed on which you placed the pillow. My bed was in the center aisle, which would mean I was approximately in the middle of the 25 beds. After everyone fooled around with this, some of them getting pretty queer beds, our sergeant informed us we were members of Company M, Barrack 5.

We were then allowed to rest and wait for the next call. None of us could leave, so we stretched out, doing nothing and wondering what it was all about. A couple hours later we heard a whistle and had to line up outside the barracks ready to march over to the mess hall. Once there we were at the end of the line, so had to stand there in the cold until everyone else was in. Once in, we had to line up and pass by the counters with the regulation trays, which I saw pictured in Life sometime ago. They filled one section of the tray with beef stew, which didn't look too appetizing, another section with jam, another with some salad, a cup of coffee and the last with bread and butter. Being hungry, we ate but didn't relish it much. After finishing we had to pick up our tray and carry it over to the kitchen and march out.

Then line up again and march again back to the barracks. Again we sat around and did nothing and just bulled. Some played cards, and one fellow who had a mandolin played a few melodies for us.

Again the whistle, line up and this time a long march over to the other end of camp, where we had first arrived. We had to stand, as the place was crowded with a couple hundred fellows. Our names were called, and we were marched over to the dispensary for a physical check up, which took a couple of minutes, but we all had to wait till everyone was through. We waited in the corridor, which was filling with smoke rapidly, and when it was almost unbearable, we had to be marched back to the warehouse and placed in another room there which was filled with rows of benches. We were told to sit, so we sat and sat from nine that evening till two thirty the next morning. During all this time everyone smoked and bulled, bulled and smoked and just filled the room to bursting. As the time passed some of the fellows tried to sleep on the hard benches, on the floor or on the wooden pieces, tables or anything. One fellow fell asleep on a table and rolled over on his face, cutting it so that he had to have a few stitches. He was sent home the next day to rest up for a few weeks. Another fellow couldn't stand it any longer and took a fit on the floor and was foaming at the mouth. He had to be carried out. On the whole, the only thing wrong with me was that I was tired and missed my two usual evening steak sandwiches. However, as luck would have it, a couple of the boys stationed at Devens who had been giving us a few pointers had to drive into town, so they offered to bring in a few sandwiches. They came back later, and the one sandwich I had was just an appetizer.

Hurray, a call to line up. We were then marched to a building across the street, where we went to a fellow with a typewriter who took down a few facts about us, and persons to be notified in case of death, etc. From there we passed into the next room to be fingerprinted, and then into another room where we were handed a raincoat, towel, shaving kit, tooth brush, shaving brush. We sat once more, waiting for everyone else to catch up with us. At last we were marching back to the barracks for sleep, and did we run. I hit the bunk and stretched out without taking off my clothes, but just my shoes. We expected to be waked in a few hours. It was now 3:30, so we didn't want to muss the beds or have to waste time getting dressed. I fell asleep the minute I hit the bed.

Wednesday, January 21 [1942]

One and a half short hours later, the whistle blew. Rise we did, and fast. I, being all dressed, just had to wash my face and was ready for the next day. Line up again, march again, over to the mess hall. Same procedure and handed breakfast on a tray. This time it was eggs that looked as though they had been through a compressor, they were packed down so hard. I struggled with a bit of it but decided it would be better to just go hungry. Since I came in, I had my eye out for Marvin Smirnoff, but as we couldn't leave the barracks except when marched, I didn't have much chance and didn't see him.

After breakfast we were marched back to the barracks and stood there a few minutes and then turned around and marched right back past the mess hall over to the other side of the tracks into a large room filled with tables and chairs. We sat at these tables and were given an I.Q. test. Everyone of us was very sleepy, but we had to do the best we could. It was a simple exam which anyone having gone through grammar school could answer. It was one of those exams in which you check the correct answer out of three or four possibilities. We had forty minutes for this.

This completed, we were marched over to another large building, seated and waited to be called upon. We were then given an interview with a technical sergeant, who asked what work you had done, what hobbies you did and especially questioned those things you did which were important in an army, which in my case was teletyping, motion pictures. He also put down that I was interested in theatricals.

From there we moved on to another desk where we could take out insurance, which was about 70¢ per thousand to be taken out monthly from your $21.00. I turned this down, as I have plenty of insurance. Next we went on to another desk where our answers were checked again and a classification number placed on the card, and the entire file was then turned over to the captain, who looked over each card personally. He offered no comments.

Marching again. This time to the clothes mill. Each was handed a blue denim bag into which you put all your clothes, everything, including personals. And then a race for time started. You started at one end of the mill, given a box with a number on it, mine being 33. This box was pushed along a very long counter, and you went along with it, men would look at you, holler out sizes and throw clothes at you or into the box. First John L. Sullivan underwear. Try it on for fit. Then a shirt. Test the collar, then a pair of socks, how are the toes? Then pants, too long, okay roll them up. How's the waist? Not bad. Put this belt on. Then a jacket. They call it a blouse. Tight, but it straightens out the shoulders. Then a cap, one too large, okay hits the fit. Next climb up on this table. Measure your feet. Size 8. I never wore larger than 7 1/2. Never mind, here's size 8-D. How do they fit? They seem large. Forget it, your feet will spread. Off the table, down the line. Try on the overcoat. Good fit. You're at the end of the line. Your box into which they had been throwing extras of everything was dumped out and counted as it was put into the blue bag. In addition they threw in a few odds and ends such as ties, handkerchiefs, mess kit, water bottle, etc. Grab the bag over your shoulder and stand on this platform. Turn around, you look fine, step outside. This took less than a half hour, and I never was fitted so fast in my life completely from head to foot. Once outside, we started to button all the clothes we had thrown on and tied our shoe laces and were allowed to go back to the barracks. At the barracks we began to pull off tags, which kept piling up as you pulled stuff out of the bag. Success at last, everything ready. Then I took out all my own clothes and rolled them all into a compact bundle, with the exception of my shoes and shorts. I thought these might come in handy later. I then took them over to Railway Express, packed them up and sent the clothes home, as we have no use for them at all. As a matter of fact, you can't even wear white shirts any longer in the army. Then back to the barracks for a much needed rest. We loafed around till dinner time.

Once lined up for dinner, some of the boys were called out and sent off elsewhere. We learned later they had gone down for injections and were being shipped off to Virginia. After dinner, which was lousier than the rest, we were back at the barracks for more rest. Dave Horowitz, who had been with me up to this time, came back for his clothes and left us to go to Virginia. After this bunch left, we were marched over to one of the small theatres in the camp area where the captain gave us a very boring lecture on venereal diseases as well as the articles of war, which tell you what you can't do in the army without punishment. His was such a droning voice that most of the fellows, being tired, fell asleep. When he finished, the chaplain gave a short lecture, but his was interesting and quite frank, coming from a member of the church. Then a motion picture was shown giving the results of diseases, etc. It was supposed to make the boys sick, but it wasn't as bad as all that.

Still on the march, we were back at the barracks for a little more rest, but of course we couldn't leave the barracks. When the mess call came, we lined up, and some of us were assigned to duties for the next day. I was to do warehouse duty, whatever that is. At the mess hall, I bumped into Sam Faiman and sat with him. He had come in the previous Thursday, and since he was on K.P. the day his group left, he had to remain at camp a few more days for another group to be shipped out wherever he was supposed to go, I think Missouri. After supper we were back at the barracks and told to sweep up and clean up. As this wasn't to be a permanent camp for me, I didn't care, so stretched out to sleep and after a while the sergeant came over to me and asked if I was sleepy, answering "yes," he said, "Well, go to bed." About three minutes later, someone came running up asking for "Glass." I answered, and they said the orderly wanted me down at the day room. This was down the end of the street, so I had to put on my blouse and my coat and run down there. On arriving, I walked into the orderly's room, and he said he hadn't sent for me. It must have been the sarge pulling a fast one.

I came back and found Cinque, our oil man, who was in camp looking up anybody he knew. He gave me a few pointers, which I stuck in the back of my head, and after he left, about eight o'clock, took off my clothes and got into bed for the first time since I left home.

Thursday, January 22 [1942]

About five someone shook me, the whistle had blown but I didn't hear it. It was crowded in the washroom, but I managed to get room to shave in and then took a shower. These camps are very well equipped. They have running hot and cold water. Flush toilets, mirrors over each sink. But these are metal ones, so you can't see unless you are very close. The showers are the needle-point kind and certainly wake you up. It was pretty crowded, and, not having much time, I was among the last to get out, as I was taking a shower. The mess whistle blew, and I ran with all buttons unbuttoned, tie off with my coat over everything buttoned so it looked as though I was fully dressed. While standing in line, I managed to make myself presentable. From this line a few of us were called out, and this time I was called. We were told to turn in our blankets, get our breakfast and report back. Doing this, we were sent over to a large room again where we had to strip to the waist ready for three injections, one in the left and two in the right arm. One of Miller's boys, the clothier, was one of those giving the injections. While coming through this lineup, I saw Archie Aarons across the hall in a lineup of new recruits just arriving. Back to the barracks to pick up our belongings, and then we were packed into trucks like sardines. In one of these small trucks we had 19, so it was a good thing the ride was only two miles to the Ayer railroad station. At the station we had quite a wait for our train, which we finally learned was to take us to Fort Knox in Kentucky.

In the train we were assigned three to a section. As it was a pullman, it meant that two would have to sleep in the lower with one in the upper. I was with Benny, an Italian fellow I knew from New Haven, and with the "Rebel," who was a southerner living in the north. Boy, was this a lousy ride. The train just dragged. About lunch time they handed us a couple sandwiches, dish-water coffee, tomato juice in a bottle, a hard boiled egg, and a cake turnover. As yet we haven't had a decent meal. The ride was uneventful except for quite a poker game, which I didn't enter as the stakes were five-and-five. At Troy, N.Y. we made a short stop, and some Red Cross workers came on board with baskets of fruit, magazines, cigarettes and post-cards. I took some of the cigarettes, these being the first I had since Monday night. I also took a couple of post cards to send home. The ride was boring, but it was tiresome. The "Rebel" and Benny kept things going with jokes and arguments, and it seems our section of the car which was down at one end was always crowded with fellows.

At last a dining car was put on, and we had our first good meal. It began with a salad plate, then veal, stuffing, and trimmings, then dessert and coffee. This was with porter service and all. Also, the government was paying for it. After dinner we kidded around and passed the time until nine, when the lights were put out, same as they would be at camp. The "rebel," being odd man in a coin toss, had the upper, so I slept with Benny. Being tired, I didn't mind and slept right through.

Friday, January 23 [1942]

At six we were waked and again had a good breakfast in the dining car. We began to meet characters now in the way of paper men, magazine and sandwich peddlers. The sandwich man was about sixty, toothless and with one of those movie comic faces. He was eating one of his own sandwiches, so I picked up a bar of candy from his basket and refused to pay, kiddingly. He began to get sore and finally turned around with tears in his eyes and said "Ef you pay me, at's al' rye," and walked away. We called him back and when we handed him the nickel, he was still sore.

We arrived in Cincinnati, where we changed our watches back an hour and were allowed to get off the train and stretch. The poker game began again, but I still was an onlooker, which was okay, as the final result was that one of the boys won $20.00 and some of the others lost quite a bit. At Cincinnati we had to switch engines, and we began backing up, going forward and backing up. At last we made it and got into Louisville a few hours later, where the same thing began in backing up and going forward in switching engines. Finally we were on our way for the 30 mile trip to Fort Knox from there. This was the most tiresome part of the ride, as we didn't go much over 25 miles, and most of the time stopped to wait for other trains to pass. We made it, we rolled right into Fort Knox, which looked like a city larger than West Haven. We were put into trucks again and taken through part of this city over to the barracks and were assigned to beds in Co. B, 10th Battalion of the Armoured Force Replacement Training Center. Blankets and sheets were issued, and we made our beds. We hadn't eaten since breakfast, so we asked and were ushered in to the mess hall. Here things were different. Plates were set out on the tables with silverware. Serving plates with steaming food were set on the tables, and at the sign of a whistle you just helped yourself. If the plate was empty, you asked for more and got it. The food here was good. After eating, we had to make about 90 beds for some recruits who were expected sometime during the night.

When this was completed we were on our own, and so Benny and I, who were bunked next to each other, went over to the Post Exchange to buy locks for our lockers so that nothing could be taken, as we are responsible for every piece of clothes issued to us. Once back at the barracks, we rolled into our own beds and fell off to sleep.

So ended Glass's first few days in the U.S. Army. He went on to serve three years in communications, including a tour in the European theater. Aside from a court-martial for showing up for roll call in slippers because of back pain, he managed to avoid many of the unpleasant aspects of army life.

First Rookie: "Did you know that my sergeant talks to himself?"

Second Ditto: "So does mine, but he doesn't know it. He thinks someone is listening."

ANOTHER VIEW

LETTERS HOME FROM WILLIAM H. HERBERT[8]

Although for some, induction and training were a succession of inconveniences and labors to be minimized or avoided altogether, for others life in the military offered opportunities, excitement, and rewards.

December 3, 1942

Dear Mother:

This is just a note to let you know I'm getting along fine and am crazy about this camp and the officers in it.

I haven't gotten an answer to my first letter, but I imagine it will reach me soon. There is not much to tell you except I have been drilling all day and am pretty tired. I've gained *five* pounds and haven't needed any medicine since I've been here.

I'm here sitting on the side of my bunk, and you will have to excuse my writing. When a guy gets low on dough, he usually writes home for more. So if you can take a hint, you can send me some by Special Delivery, because I need it bad.

For one thing, I need some cleaning and pressing done, and I want a little to take to Houston over the week-end when I go to see Daddy and Manganel.*

Tell everybody "hello" and write soon.

Love,
Your Son,
Billy

Sunday—[May] 23 [1943]

Dear Mother,

Well, I arrived at Fort Bliss safe and sound. The outfit, the 821st C.A.BN, that I was first assigned to has not activated yet, so I was transferred and asgnd. to the 111th C.A.BN. I am in Headquarters Battery, and I like my work very much. As of yet, I haven't gotten my rating because my orders haven't come through yet. It will take a little time, but I will get it before long.

You haven't heard the worst part yet, though, so I'll tell you now.

The 11th C.A.BN., *and I,* are stationed in the middle of the Oragrande Desert in New Mexico. We are living in tents and have sand in our food, sand in our bed, and in everything we have. You ought to see some of the sand storms we have out here. Boy, is this place "Hell." In the daytime the sun beats down, and you burn up, and at night a cold wind blows off of the mountains that completely surround us, and you practically freeze. Your wildest imaginations could not fulfill the reality of this place. We are miles and miles from any civilization of any kind, and just as far as you can see are mountains and desert. A mail truck goes to Fort Bliss every day, and our letters are mailed and picked up there. From what I understand, we will be here about three months or longer. They may be preparing us for North Africa, who knows?

---

*Herbert's stepmother.

If I had been assigned to any other outfit I would have had an excellent chance of getting a furlough. But here chances are small, but I am going to put in an application as soon as possible and just hope.

There is not much more to tell you, and this candle is burning pretty low, so I guess I'd better close. By the way, I'm writing by candlelight, so please excuse my writing. Please don't try to write yet, because I haven't been assigned to permanent quarters, and your letter might never reach me.

Tell every body at home "hello," and I'll write again tomorrow night.

Love,
Billy

A WOMAN'S VIEW

LETTERS HOME FROM JEANNE E. BETCHER[9]

The Women's Army Auxiliary Corps (WAAC) presented one of the first opportunities for women to serve in uniform, and young women responded in great numbers to the call. Here is an extensive accounting of a WAAC's first week in the armed forces, interesting for the similarities as well as the contrasts to the basic training being experienced by so many young men at the same time. This woman, from New Jersey, served for three years and eventually was decorated for her overseas service.

November 19, 1942

9:00 P.M.

Well, here it is again, the end of another busy day.

The lights are turned on in the morning at 6:00 o'clock, at which time we arise, wash and dress—at 6:30 the sergeant blows a whistle, and we "fall out" "on the double" (this means running), for reveille—when the roll is called—then we return to the barracks, make our bed—(we received new mattress covers this morning)—then are called out for breakfast, of which they have a variety—then back to our barrack, clean around our cot, and the barracks. We are then called out for drilling. We always have to be on the alert, as we do not know when we are to be called, or for what.

Today we received more clothing at the warehouse—raincoat, red corduroy bath robe, khaki panties, woolen cap, woolen gloves, dress hat, sneaks, stockings, flannel pajamas, girdles (pink).

We also had tests today (mental and mechanical) and were interviewed.

This evening we marched to the theatre for a lecture on Army rules.

Have just had a shower, and am writing this letter sitting on my foot locker.

Please do not worry about me, and you can write to the address as I have it on my envelope.

The weather has been perfect—this morning was just like a spring morning—and very warm today.

We get very good food, so you do not have to worry, and are well taken care of.

We were warned not to have any portions of our letters given out for publication to the newspapers—they stressed this several times.

It is almost "lights out" time again (9:30), and will have to hurry to end this letter.

Hoping that both of you are in the very best of health, and do not worry about me. I am kept busy, but it is different, and interesting.

Love and kisses to you both, and let me hear how everything is.

> With love and kisses
> your daughter
> *Jeanne X X X X X X X*

P.S. Do not even know how the war is going, or even if there is still one.

November 20, 1942

7:20 P.M.

Dear Mother and Father,

This is the first day the weather has not been nice. It was misting all day. We drilled on the parade ground this morning, and were ordered to put on our galoshes before we left. We then had a lecture on military courtesy, and this morning we had a physical examination, almost similar to th one we had in New York, and were vaccinated for smallpox, and had injections, which did not affect me. Am well and strong—One of the woman doctors said—"There is nothing wrong with me." We marched to the theatre this afternoon to hear a lecture concerning the reasons leading to this war. A woman spoke, and her lecture was very interesting—we did not have a hard day today.

We are moving to "Boom Town" tomorrow at 11:00 A.M. We are packing tonight. My packing is now completed, and I have a barracks bag full.

Today I received a lovely, genuine leather handbag (they call it a utility bag), which hangs from the shoulder so your hands can be free. Also received the insignia buttons we wear on our uniform, and one for my dress hat, which is not worn as yet because we do not have the full uniform.

It has been like Christmas all week with receiving "G.I." (Government issue) clothing.

They are now having an informal party, as we are leaving this barrack to go to another tomorrow. We each contributed $.10 for it.

Saturday, November 21, 1942

9:00 P.M.

Am now in the new barrack. We moved here at 1:00 o'clock, right after lunch. A truck took our baggage over, and we marched here—which is about a 10 minute walk from the old barrack building in which I was located (Stable Row). They call this "Boom Town" because the barrack buildings sprung up like mushrooms, similar to the ones on top of the Belleville Pike. All the new buildings are made of red tile bricks about 5" x 12", and the buildings are quite nice. Am very fortunate, being in a room with two other girls from Michigan. The building holds 50 auxiliaries. They are two stories high, and I am on the second floor in a corner room. The main room outside of mine holds 24 beds. I was to be in one of those beds, but as one girl was sick in the hospital, and the girl who was to be in this room wished to go to another barrack, I switched with her; therefore I am in this room.

Went to the Mess Hall in this area this evening at 5:15. At the other Mess Hall, where we were this week, it was cafeteria style. At this Mess Hall, the food is placed on the table, and the platters passed around. The meals have all been excellent so far. We have the heavy meal at noon, and a lighter one in the evening. This evening they had nice tender lamb, peas, baked potatoes, raw carrots, and hot chocolate, and vanilla custard. I really prefer the cafeteria style though in a group like this, as it is much quicker to be served.

Wednesday noon we had chicken and ice cream—good.

The two girls with me are named May and Marguerite, both from Michigan, the one named May being from Detroit. We did not have very much time to become acquainted as we were all busy unpacking.

How do you like this fancy letterhead? Went to the Post Exchange (a store here where you can buy almost everything), and bought this paper for $.20, a box of 24 sheets and envelopes. Also bought a small spiral notebook for $.04, a wooden coathanger with a rod, which is necessary to hang my face cloth and towel, and a box of Ivory Snow Flakes. Had hoped to launder this evening after taking my shower, but the laundry room was full of clothes already, so will have to wait until tomorrow sometime.

3:40 P.M.

Dear Mother and Father,

They just were collecting the mail, and I hurriedly finished the letter I was writing to get it to you—and this is in continuation.

As I was saying—I slept well, and at 6:00 A.M. the lights were turned on, and we had to get up. It was not too bad. Washed myself in a private tub room, and then dressed—There are private shower rooms, and private rooms with tub. At 6:30 they blew a whistle for reveille. The Lieutenant called the roll; we then reported to the barracks; were shown how to make our bed, which we did. At 7:13 we were called out for breakfast. They served bacon, toast dipped in eggs, regular toast, a dry cereal, milk, and coffee. I had toast. We returned to our barracks; then were called to a supply building where we were issued (temporarily) regular soldiers' overcoats, as they do not have on hand any to give to the new Waacs coming in. Mine fits me, although it is quite bulky. At the same time we were given a raincoat (regular soldiers) for temporary use. These are to be returned when we receive our regular issue. At the same time they gave us a pair of galoshes, which we keep—(they are made by the Hood Rubber Co.—very nice). We had some drilling then in our soldiers' overcoats.

We then went to another supply house, where I received a pair of cotton stockings, and was measured for shoes, and received two pairs for myself, two seersucker dresses with fine green and white stripes and bloomers to match. They are to be worn when we have kitchen duty, and such. Was also measured for a uniform. They do this by trying samples on you. At another time this morning we went to a supply house and were given three large white bath towels, two ties, a black comb, with the words "U.S. Army," a toothbrush, having the same wording, and four plain white handkerchiefs. I have a trunk, and put all these things into it.

At the time I received my shoes and dresses, also received a barracks bag, into which we had to put our new issue of clothing, and marched back to the barracks. We must have looked very cute.

For lunch today I had steak, peas, hashed potatoes, Waldorf salad, pudding, and milk. We march into the Mess Hall, take our silver (of which there is a shortage, as they had no teaspoons or knives left), take a tray, upon which they put the food in the different partitions (cafeteria style), and we eat directly from the tray. The Mess Hall, I should judge, holds about 500 people.

The weather has been very good—not too cold at all. In Chicago the temperature was 64°.

Am enclosing a form letter we were just given. We did not have a hard day today.

Hoping you are both well, as I am,
Love and kisses

Your loving daughter
Jeanne X X X

It is now 8:30 and am going to take a shower, and go to bed.
Am going to bed now as it is 9:45.
Love and kisses,
Jeanne

9:45 A.M.

Sunday morning

Got up about 8:30 this morning—they do not have reveille on Sunday. Am now going to see if I can find the Post Office and mail this letter, and then go to the Church.

There was a flurry of snow this morning, and now it is dreary looking, and the wind is blowing.

Hoping that both of you are behaving yourselves—and, most important, that you are perfectly well—as I am.

Avec beaucoup d'amour

Your Wacky daughter
Jeanne
X X X X X X X X X X X X X X X X X X X X X X X X X X X X X X X X X

November 24, 1942

9:15 P.M.

Dear Mother and Father,

Received your letter Sunday afternoon, and was very, very happy to receive it.

Am just jotting down these few words before "lights out." Believe we are having Thursday as a holiday, and then will be able to write a long letter telling you just what our day consists of. And then I will be able to do the little odds and ends that take time, such as darning one pair of stockings that have a hole in each toe, and sewing my name tags on my clothes.

The weather has been beautiful today. Sunday we had drizzling rain and snow, just enough to cover the ground, and the Southerners were all excited about it. The rain made the ground around here very muddy, and we have had to wear galoshes until this evening. Have never seen such mud—it sticks, and when you lift your feet up, more mud sticks to that, and we have to scrub our galoshes with a brush to get it off.

Am in the very best of health, and will answer your long and beautiful letter Thursday, I hope.

Avec beaucoup d'amour

Your Wacky daughter

Jeanne

Keep well X X X X

> Husband to wife considering WAAC service: "I don't think you'd like it, dear. It's strictly noncombat duty."

TRAINING FOR THE SEA

LETTERS HOME FROM HERBERT EUGENE BOOK, JR.[10]

The U.S. Navy had its own training centers, including some in places as unlikely as Idaho. But neophyte sailors had the same sorts of triumphs, concerns, and problems as trainees in the other branches. These selections provide a vivid example of how much mail from home meant to the boys in the camps. There is also some interesting insight into the vexing problem of the normal appetites of healthy young men.

March 16, 1943

Herbert Eugene Book, Jr., A.S.
Company 176-43, Camp Hill
U.S.N.T.S.
Farragut, Idaho.

Dear Folks,

Well, we finally got here. We left K.C. at 5:15 Friday and got here at 2:30 Monday morning. We didn't sleep at all Sunday nite and had a hard day today. We cleaned up a barrack and washed all the windows in it in the morning. After dinner we all had our physical—worse than Leavenworth or K.C.—and then were issued our uniforms. We all have our bunks assigned now. All the boys who were in Abilene were in my Company and barracks. John Switzer is in the lower bunk, and I am in the upper. The rest of them are right across the aisle. I really like our Co. commander. All the boys I have talked to say he is the best one in camp, so I can't kick. I haven't spent any money yet, and it don't look like I will for a while. Tell Verna happy birthday and tell her she can have that 17 shoe stamp for her birthday present. Both my arms are so stiff from shots that I can hardly write. It's typhoid shots that really make your arm sore. They gave us one in each arm at the same time—wow! The food is fine, and if they feed us like they have been, I will gain some weight. I saw George and Earl Fouse after supper tonite and talked to them for a while. They live just 2 barracks down from us. They are in 8, and we are in 10-lower. It might not hurt to put that on the address when you write. They issued underwear and hankies, so I sent mine home. We came thru mountains all day Sun. and thru some of the best that night after dark. They aren't so high as the ones in Colo., none of them are above timberline. Tomorrow we learn to roll our clothes. From the looks of things, it will take us the 12 weeks to learn to roll our clothes. Carroll says the laundry service around here is awful, too. Ho-hum. If you can sell my brown shoes or anything else, you'd just as well. I've got enough clothes to last me for a long time. Well, we turn in at 9:00, and I want to take a shower and shave. None of us have had a bath since Friday, and after that long train ride we are just a little strong. Everybody is about half sick tonite after those typhoid and yellow fever shots, so they're a pretty sober bunch. Well, time to quit. Write, and tell everyone hello.

Love,
Gene

March 17, 1943

Dear Folks,

Well. How is Chapman* now with all the young men gone? There sure are a lot of them around here. In my company there are 140 men, most of them 19 or 20. Nearly all of them are from Kansas and Missouri. When we took our physical, the eye man said he never saw a bunch with such good eyes. I guess they raise them good in Central U.S. I don't know of any of the boys who flunked the physical up here. Yesterday morning we all got our haircuts. Are we a pretty looking bunch now. They really clipped us. It cost us 15¢ each, too. Nothing is free around here. I'm glad I had my hair cut. The ones with real long hair, waves, and "slick back" pompadours got clipped about an inch shorter than the rest of us. I went over to ship's service last night. That's the same as a P.X. I got some laundry soap, black shoe polish, and some cigarettes.

---

*Book's hometown, about one hundred fifty miles west of Kansas City.

This afternoon we had our pictures taken, complete with numbers, for our identification tags. We really get plenty to eat. All well balanced and stuff. Every dinner and supper we have soup of some kind along with the regular meal. They issued us 3 pair of Nunn Brush shoes, so I don't need to worry about that. Also we got underwear, hankies, sox, and all the fixins. John and I finished all our rolling of clothes tonight, so everything is shipshape and all secured. I was on guard duty last night, but I get to sleep tonight. Everyone takes his turn at that in alphabetical order. Say, if you can make a bag out of blue denim, Mom, about 6" in diam. and 8 or 9 high with drawstring in the top, I could sure use it. We worked all day yesterday, 'cause today was admiral's inspection. We have to wear our rubbers all the time (issued) 'cause it's awful wet. Still snow but it thaws in the aft. It snowed all the way up and the morning we got here. About 4 or 5 in. How's the weather at home? Well, I'm about out of paper, so I'll quit. I want to take a shower tonite. Write, and tell everyone hello.

Love,
Gene

March 19, 1943

Dear Folks,

Well, I haven't got any mail yet but I'm going to expect some Monday. Today was field day. Field day in the navy is general cleanup. We're scared to even walk on the floor. Tomorrow is captain's inspection, so we really have to have things clean, including ourselves. I washed last nite. Imagine me leaning over a washboard. I've got my clothes all clean now anyway.

We've really got a good bunch of boys here in this barracks. The Co. commander says it is the likeliest looking bunch he has had for a long time. I sure hope we do good 'cause the sooner we learn all the stuff, the quicker we graduate. Some of the boys have graduated in 8 wks. I saw George this morning. He said a wrist watch disappeared in his company. For 3 nites straight, the whole company had to do double time 2 times around the camp. (2 1/2 mi) Then the watch showed up on the Co. commander's desk. The Navy really gets things done. Some of the boys got smart in drill today, and now they are out running. I'm going to be a good boy. I don't want any of that. We signed up for insurance today. I am now carrying $10,000 worth of insurance. It costs me $6.50 each month. Not bad. I'll never miss the money. We don't have any place to spend it here. I've been writing letters to everybody in my address book. Say, I would like to have Wilmer's address. Have you heard from him yet? I feel right at home here. It snows one day and all melts the next. Just like Kansas. One thing I could use is a whisk broom. I have a good one somewhere in my stuff. These blue wool uniforms really collect the lint. Well, I've about run out of something to say, so I had better go clean out my sea bag (not to be confused with Waves). So long.

Gene

March 26, 1943

7:00 P.M.

Dear Folks,

Well, in an hour I have to go to work again, so I will just write a few lines. I washed my leggings tonite. Getting ready for Admiral's inspection tomorrow. Our Commandant here has been promoted to Admiral. I passed my 75 yd. swimming test today. Only 10 out of 140 didn't pass it. If we get 100% swimmers, we get an extra weekend liberty, maybe. Everybody is in quarantine now. Spinal meningitis and scarlet fever. There is an armed guard on every corner.

We got our new haircuts again today. Every 10 days while we are in boot camp. It's been raining hard all day, so we can't go outside today. They sure kept us busy inside. They've just about cut out everything here. No more muster for colors in the morning, no more picture shows, we can't go to ship's service, no nothing. Some fun.

Two days have gone by and no mail. What's holding up production back there? I don't have much time with washing, working from 2000 to 2100 and then turning in. Somebody write me every day or I'll have to start writing someone who will. It makes me feel like a heel not to get any mail when everybody else does. I'll see you some day.

As Ever,
Gene

April 16, 1943

Friday nite

Dear Folks,

Well, I've been so darn busy that I haven't had time to write. I haven't written a letter for 4 days. I'm really behind time. Now to start with the news. We took all our tests. I made these grades. General Classification Test 99, Arithmetic 100, English 92, Spelling 96. Average of 96 ³/₄. That was the highest average in the Company. One fellow I have been running around with was the only one who beat me on the G.C.T. test. A kid from San Francisco. He made 100. Smart guy. With grades like I have, it is almost certain I will go to school. They gave us 4 choices. I put down Motor Machinist (Diesel), Aviation metalsmith (sheet metal work), Radioman, and Electrician mate. Which one of those schools I go to is entirely up to the selection officer. It doesn't make much difference to me. Any one of them will be O.K.

Out of the clear sky Wednesday night they told us that we would have a liberty on Thursday. Boy, was there some rushing around that night. I got up at 4:00 A.M. Thursday morning and really shined myself up. We had a personal inspection by the regimental commander before we could go. Some had to stay here 'cause they had little spots on their coats or their shoes didn't shine quite enough. We got on the bus about 10:00 and got into Spokane at 12:30. We ate a great big turkey dinner. I drank 3 glasses of milk with mine. I think the waitress thought I was crazy. I don't get enough milk up here to satisfy me. We all had our pictures taken. 3 for 20¢. I won't spend any more money on pictures till I get a dress jumper with some stripes on it. I am sending the pictures, and you can see they are of the 3 for 20¢ quality. Also notice—no hair showing. We wear those flat hats only when we are on liberty. Around here we wear the little white ones. After dinner we went to a show. Dorothy Lamour and Bob Hope in "They've Got Me Covered." It was really good. The first show that I have seen since we went to one in Kansas City. After the show we just fooled around—drank 3 choc. malts, played 2 games of snooker, ate candy and did all the things we couldn't do in camp. We caught the bus at 7:15 back to Coeur D'Alene. We wasted about an hour there and caught the 9:30 bus back to camp. A fine time was had by all. This morning everybody was as tired as a dog.

Oh—one thing that I forgot to tell you. We have to check in at the Regimental Headquarters. There we turn in our liberty pass and write "yes" or "no" on the back of it. That means—did you make any contacts above and beyond the line of duty? Of course "no" was unanimous. What a nice bunch of sailor boys.

Spokane and Coeur D'Alene are both very nice, clean, quiet towns. The people treat us human, very friendly. I expected something like J.C.*

This week we are a work company. This morning we policed the whole regiment. Picked up a truck load of paper. This afternoon we landscaped around our barracks. They leave that up to the companies. There are really some nice jobs around camp. We have to carry dirt in buckets to cover the rocks so we can plant some grass. We have to go out in the timber and dig some trees and plant them.

---

*Junction City, a town near Book's hometown and situated near Fort Riley, Kansas.

Tomorrow we go on mess detail. That means we wear a white uniform and a clean one every day. Wash every night. There's no K.P. Here. The whole company has the detail. That will last a week. That also means that we won't have any Sunday.

A boy had $20 stolen today. I was on guard duty, and I took a list of the names of the 8 men who were in the barracks at the time. The C.O. sent them all to their bunks with envelopes and had them seal them. He took them all up, and the bill was in one envelope. It's sure a good thing it was. When something like that happens, the whole company catches hell till it shows up.

We can go to ship's service now, but next week we probably won't have time. I got the razor today and also the latest papers. I also got a letter from Miss Woods. Well, time to quit.

Love,
Gene

THE M1

WAR DEPARTMENT BASIC FIELD MANUAL 23-5, U.S. RIFLE, CALIBER .30, M1 (1940)[11]

Every U.S. infantryman in World War II came to know well the M1 Garand rifle. Indeed, more soldiers became familiar with that weapon than with any other piece of ordnance in American history. The following is an excerpt from an army field manual.

DESCRIPTION OF RIFLE

The U.S. rifle, caliber .30, M1, is a self-loading shoulder weapon. (See Fig. 1.) It is gas operated, clip fed, and air cooled. It weighs approximately 9 pounds and the bayonet an additional pound. The ammunition is loaded in clips of eight rounds. Bandoleers of ammunition for this rifle have six pockets with a total of 40 rounds and weigh 3 1/4 pounds each.

> The new army rifle weighs 8.69 pounds. After it has been carried a few hours, the decimal point drops out.

ADVANCED TRAINING

LETTERS HOME FROM RICHARD CIPRA[12]

Basic training was an assembly-line process, but most troops had advanced training in one specialization or another. The advanced courses in the combat arms featured especially rigorous physical exercises, so much so that accidents and even some loss of life were accepted as part of the price for combat readiness.

Nov. 26, 1942

Camp Hood, Texas

Dear Eleanor,*

Was awful glad to hear from you so soon, we got the day off so I'll answer your letter.

I am sending you a little birthday present along with this letter. Let me know if you get it O.K.

School still goes on!! Our first week we had the .30 cal. carbine, and the Thompson Sub machine gun (Tommy gun), then we had hand grenades, we also made a small demolition Bomb, and a Molotov cocktail for use against tanks. Also we've had a week of T/D** Tactics and Tank identification, this week we had the .30 cal machine gun. After we learn all about a gun, the nomenclature, care and cleaning, we take them out and fire them. We were out on the range yesterday and fired 250 rounds of ammunition in the machine gun, sure was fun.

All of our shooting here is a lot different from what we were used to, it used to be all of our shooting was done for the record, but here all firing is done in combat positions, as it would be done in actual combat. We shoot the carbine, Tommy gun and pistol from the hip, with a little practice a guy can really get good.

We've had 5 graded tests already, and got 3 of them back, so far I've got an "S" (satisfactory) in all of them, I am kind of worried about one of them, but I think I passed yesterday's test O.K.

I am really enjoying the course here though, even though the camp isn't much and lacks entertainment. I sure miss you kids, I wish they had this school in Los Angeles!!!

---

*Cipra's sister.

**Tank destroyer, an armored vehicle with a large antitank gun but with no movable turret.

"Company Street" (row of tents), Camp Barksdalte, Texas. (Courtesy of the Dwight D. Eisenhower Library, Loren Fred Collection.)

Tell Joe I am sending his stripes this time. If you take his picture I sure want one.

We put in about 9 hrs a day in school, we get up at 5:30 AM and fall out for school at 8, school till 12, an hour off for noon, then from 1 till 5, and we have an hour study hall from 7:30 to 8:30 in the evening (the rest of the night is ours) (till 10 o'clock!!!). But on week ends we can get from about 4 Sat afternoon, until eleven Sunday nite, but the catch is we have to be off the streets of any town at eleven at night. Saturday night you can be out until 2:AM. Sure isn't anything like L.A., I hear there is a bunch of Negroes in our barracks now, and "B" and "C" Co. have moved to Pasadena.

How is Bud?* Is he still working on that big plane? Maybe they got it up in the air, huh?

Well, I guess I better quit now, so let me know if you get your present O.K. and I hope you like it.

Love,
Cotton

---

*Eleanor's husband.

March 8, 1943

Camp Hood, Tex.

Dear Eleanor,

Guess I better be writing, or you are going to think we have died off—and we almost did!!

Last week I put in the roughest, toughest 5 days I ever put in in my life.

Our Battalion went out in the woods on one of the roughest commando courses in the country. It about killed us off!! We walked out about 6 or 7 miles, stayed out there for five days and then walked 5 miles back in 65 minutes. We had an obstacle course about half of a mile long, we ran it 3 times a day, and when we were not running the course we were having classes in different subjects such as night firing, woods fighting, street fighting, Ju Du, woodcraft, Tank Hunting, Tank Ambush, etc. We never had a moment's rest, and cold, it turned awful cold and we liked to froze to death!!

We also ran an infiltration course, we ran 25 yards and then crawled 75 yards on our stomachs! We had to crawl thru holes and barbed wire entanglements and all the time they were throwing small bombs at us and firing a machine gun 16 or 18 inches over our heads, that was to keep us down low.

We went into camp Friday afternoon and came out here Sat. morning. We are now about 10 or 12 miles from camp, out in the woods, we will be here for possibly 6 weeks. We don't have a thing out here, no lights, no water, no nothing. I am writing this by candle light, I hope you can make it out!!

We got out of measles quarantine for 1 day, and then right back in again, some one else got 'em!

I got a letter from Geo. Unruh, and he's at Camp Santa Anita, Arcadia, Cal. He's in the Ordnance. He don't seem to mind it much.

Bud sure must be busy, is he working overtime now? How does he like Welding School, is it electric or acetylene welding?

So it has really been raining? We don't get much rain here, but it sure has been cold the last week.

What have you and Kathryn and Joe been doing? Tell Joe and Kathryn hell-o for me.

Well, guess I better quit for now. Be sure to write soon and I'll write more next time and *Better*—we are trying to get hold of a gas lamp for our tent so we can see!!

Love
Cotton

May 12, 1943

Tues. Eve.,

Dear Eleanor,

I'm ashamed of not answering sooner, I'm out of excuses so I hope you will forgive me.

I got the package and everything was okay. Say, there was nothing wrong with that cake, that's the kind you used to make when I was at Burbank, isn't it? I think since then it has been my favorite cake. I'll tell you one thing, it sure didn't last long, I almost had to hide the box so I would have some for myself!!

We have really been busy lately. We have had 2 24-hour problems in the last week. They start in the afternoon and last all night and continue on until the next afternoon.

We had a terrible accident last night. A fellow from Hq Co. was sleeping on the ground, and about 3 this morning we pulled out and somebody ran over him with a half-track. I've heard all kinds of stories, but no one knows for sure how bad he was hurt. I also heard he had died. A half track weighs almost 10 tons, so it seems improbable that if it did run over him he has much of a chance. Some seem to think that maybe just a gun ran over him. Even at that, one of those 3 inch guns is pretty heavy. It's a wonder there aren't more accidents, the way we tear around thru the woods at night with no lights on, it's all black out.

The problem we had last night is supposed to be our last one. It was in the way of a proficiency test, and according to A.U.T.C., the problem went off excellently.

I don't know what we will do now, probably have inspection after inspection. I can almost see them coming!!

We should be leaving here before long if we are going, there has been some rumor about furloughs, but I think that that is about all it is, I sure hope we get them.

Our original 6 weeks we were supposed to be out here in the field sure have been long ones. Already we have been out here over 8 weeks.

I did get super ambitious and go to town with Maynard Saturday night, we came back Sat night, and went back to Temple Sunday and took in a show, my first for about two months. We are out of quarantine now, you know.

Did I tell you we have shot our new guns? They are really honeys. After we got thru shooting, I got to go out and hunt for projectiles. I did find one. They weigh 15# each, you see they are armor piercing.

I've got mine all polished up, and I am going to have my gun section's names printed on it.

I also found a 37 M/M projectile. This was the gun the T/D's originally started out with, they have really come a long way. You should see the difference in the two shells.

Dog gone you know I can't think of any more news, so I am going to have to quit. I want to thank you again for the small cake and stuff, also the cigarettes, they sure come in mighty handy. Be sure and write soon and let me know all the news and what Bud is doing. Tell Joe and Kathryn Hello for me.

Love
Cotton

NEW PLACES, NEW ADVENTURES

LETTERS HOME FROM BRUCE CARSON[13]

A young soldier from the greater Chicago area writes home about his first days of cavalry training at Fort Riley, Kansas.

Sunday March 30th [1941]

Fort Riley, Kansas,

Dear Family:

So this is Kansas!

The wind outside my barracks is whipping up a miniature sand storm and all in all, I am feeling that the army is training me for a Blitzkrieg campaign in the Sahara. Anyway, I think I know now what the newspapers mean when they talk of a dust bowl.

This is Fort Riley, product of the last World War,* white barracks, green roofs, gravel roads, sand filled ditches, sand filled soldiers, biggest Cavalry Replacement Center in America, and the apple of the eye of cavalrymen everywhere. The draftees (5000 of us) are barracked in the section so new that the Canteen sells fountain pens but no ink, sells shoe polish but no polishing cloths, and the drinking fountains, toilets, and wash bowls still have their manufacturer's tag on. The officers tell us that three months ago there wasn't a stick of wood above ground. I believe them!!

What we do have here, completed and occupied, is all excellently built, comfortably laid out, and the fixtures, windows, blankets, and clothing seems all designed for good solid comfort. The food, too, is well prepared and dished out in quantities that add inches to my waist line just thinking about it.

---

*In fact, Fort Riley was established in the nineteenth century.

However, cups, plates, knives and forks have not arrived as yet, so we are all using our field mess kits, which, if you ever tried to eat out of an aluminum skillet with a collapsible handle, you would realize is no small feat.

This may sound funny, but soldiers' dispositions seem to depend on coffee. At Camp Grant* the coffee was like medicine. Everyone was guessing whether the chef was putting saltpeter, garlic, castor oil or garbage in it, or whether he just whipped up a batch on January 1st and dished out a bit of it each day during the year. Consequently we groused 24 hours a day.

Here at Fort Riley, where the work is harder, hours are longer and facilities less complete, any time we get to thinking about the hours of drilling on the cursed wind-blown sand, we all console ourselves by thinking "anyway, we've got darned good coffee here." It works like a charm.

I suppose right now you are all laughing at the thought of my being in the Cavalry. I don't blame you, I'm laughing too. Of all the States in the Union I might have been sent to, Kansas was the last State I ever dreamed of arriving at. Of all the thirty-seven branches of the Army I might have gotten into, horse *cavalry* was farthest from my thoughts. But I'm here (God help me), and I'll learn to ride a horse if it means I can't sit down for the rest of my life.

I won't deny that there was plenty of weeping, wailing, cussing, and what have you, at Camp Grant, when our Sergeant announced we were to be sent to Kansas. We all believed those fairy stories about California, and we were already basking on nice sunny beaches surrounded by a bevy of Hollywood beauties, or gazing through crystal pure mountain air at the blue Pacific rolling in and out below. I was in the "gazing-at-the-Pacific-rolling-in-below" group, but it was just as big a blow to me as to the "sandy-beach-and-Hollywood-beauties" group. However, we are all recovering rapidly, and are looking forward with considerable agitation to the day we have to mount a horse.

There are some 3000 horses here, and if one could believe the rumors flying about, they are 3000 man-hating, man-killing, blood-thirsty, bucking broncos. (I've got my fingers crossed and am trying hard to be an unbeliever.)

Maybe you'd like to hear more about our barracks? They are rectangular buildings, white with green roofs, wooden, and as identical in appearance as newly minted pennies. If you stay too far away from your home stamping ground, you're likely to be lost for half an hour. All evening long, newly arrived recruits march into a building, climb the stairs, go down to their bed, open their locker, take out their toilet articles, look about, and find they're in the wrong barracks. I know. I've done it.

---

*The induction center where Carson had spent a few days before being sent to Fort Riley.

The heating system is surprisingly good, and beds are comfortable. One barrack holds about 64 men, 32 to a floor. There are showers, all new plumbing, and once in a while there's hot water.

Canteens sell a variety of miscellaneous goods, including 3.2% beer, but as I said they are usually just out of whatever you're looking for. Down the block, a theatre is being completed and 20¢ shows will soon be given twice an evening. Haircuts are 30¢ army style, and tend to destroy a good many illusions. I'm going to hold off as long as possible if the haircuts I've seen so far are really representative.

Buses come through the camp many times during the day, and take one either to Junction City (Pop. 2000) 2 miles away, or Manhattan (Pop. 12000) 18 miles away. Topeka is 75 miles away, and that's where the soldiers here head for, when they're feeling extra prosperous.

Kansas, unfortunately for a good many here, is a dry state (in that it is at least consistent). It doesn't rain here, and they don't sell liquor either. I understand the bootleggers are fattening up daily, and human nature being what it is, they're likely to keep right on fattening up.

My day begins at 5:00 A.M. with reveille, which is a fancy name for roll call, and ends at 5 P.M. with retreat. That is, of course, unless I'm one of those lucky birds who get stuck on K.P. (Kitchen Police), which means my morning begins at 4:30 A.M. and ends at 8 P.M. Back at Camp Grant, I was put on K.P. my second day there, and then proceeded to work so well, the kitchen staff couldn't do without me, so I got a repeat call. The first time, I worked in the butcher shop quartering big slabs of bacon, scraping the floor, sanding, mopping, and finally loading and unloading big quarters of beef. My second visit with the K.P. was spent in the dining room. Here I mopped, scrubbed, mopped, scrubbed till well past eight. As a little reward for services well rendered, I received two nice red apples from the Sergeant as I left.

At Fort Riley we have K.P. duty but also S.P. duty (Stable Police). On S.P., one spends the day midst horses and a general smell of ammonia. I'm looking forward to that little sojourn with thrilled anticipation as you can imagine.

We are still using the uniforms issued us at Camp Grant. Long overcoats, slacks, wool shirts, overseas cap, and such miscellaneous items as long woolen underwear, ankle high shoes, and blue overalls for "fatigue clothes" for K.P. or S.P. duty. Before long we will get either boots or their equivalent, breeches, and other riding gear.

And here comes some very important news. We will be at Fort Riley just 13 weeks, while we are being trained in the fundamentals of drilling, shooting, and riding. At the end of the 13 weeks, we will be sent to the Cavalry Divisions at California, Ft. Bliss Texas, or Virginia for the rest of the year. Probably we will go somewhere else late in the summer for general Army maneuvers. Of course, happenings in Europe or a declaration of war by the United States would upset that schedule, and no one even tries to guess what would happen to our training in that event, or wherever we would be sent.

Actually there are two Ft. Rileys, and I'm afraid we draftees got the short end of the deal. The old Ft. Riley has the advantage of being 30 years older than ours is, and has the grass, trees, sidewalks, stone buildings, and hills that add so much to one's mental satisfaction. I doubt if the barracks there are as nice or if the plumbing compares with ours, but there isn't a soldier in our camp that wouldn't give half his wages for those rolling hills and forests that just seem to have missed our camp, and all rushed down to the older fort. Actually there's no basic physical difference between the camps, and as I write now, I can look out the windows on any side and see a low ridge of hills surrounding our camp, the same hills that add so much to the older fort. Some day soon I'm going to walk to those hills and climb them, and rush up one and down another, till I'm so sick of hills, I'll be glad to come back to my sandy flats and sleep.

Before I finish this letter, I ought to mention the people here, whom I seem to have neglected in all this talk of windows, hills, over seas caps and food. Very few of the draftees I started out with at Camp Grant are still with me. We are scattered from barrack to barrack, and many are in the mechanized cavalry (I'm in horse cavalry of course), which is barracked half a mile down the road. One meets the usual percentage of natural comedians, sneak thieves, office boys, country boy "slickers" (who know all the gambling tricks and petty vices considered fashionable in their backwoods bailiwick), ex-bank clerks, preacher's sons, truck drivers, school teachers, and just plain tramps that one might find in any cross section of the country. On the whole, they are as clean, considerate, and human a bunch as one would find anywhere, and the fact that we're all in the "same boat," and all have the same worries, the same jobs, the same pleasures helps a lot to make living together easier.

The top sergeants around here are the most distinctive group. I can tell one at a glance now. They've got a crotchety "Wish I were on a horse" look, are usually lean, short, tough, with a dried up wrinkled face, but are sometimes surprisingly big and over-balanced so that one wonders how they even stay on a horse. Ours has been in the Army 24 years, and in spite of a look that would sour two hour old cream, is universally well liked.

This letter must come to an end. If I write any more there won't be anything left to write about later on. That's why I'm writing so much now, so I won't have to write so often. But it's well on toward 11 o'clock now, I've got to wash and shave for dinner (so I can eat out of an aluminum skillet), and I must also get a ton or two of this good Kansas sand out of my hair and teeth.

Write soon, please. I like letters even if this Army is making me too lazy to write any.

As ever
[*signed*]

Sunday, April 6th [1941]

Dear Family:

Sunday in the Army is really a day for rest. The one day of the week, in fact, when one has that comforting feeling of being able to shave, shine shoes, or what have you, with never a glance at the clock.

So today I'm tossing time right out of my barracks window, and for the next few eons, I shall concentrate my thoughts on all the people, places, times and happenings I've left so many million miles behind. Looking down the line of bunks, I see six rookies sleeping. Two more are reading magazines, Life and the Saturday Evening Post, I'd say as a guess. A radio in the Corporal's room is playing a Viennese Waltz. From somewhere down stairs, I hear the buzzing of an electric razor. So now, with no distractions, perhaps I shall be able to write. I know I won't be able to completely put out of my mind all the drilling, scrubbing, eating that makes up my daily routine, but I shall think of them and talk of them as might some tourist from another world, who finds things on this earth very, very queer indeed, but all the same worth noting.

To begin with, here is the normal day in the army. 4:45 A.M. pile out of my bunk, grope through the darkness for my shoes, pants, socks and shirt (I sleep in my underwear), and then make a dash for the lavatory downstairs, dodging spitoons on my way. By 5:00 A.M. I am washed, shaved, replete with uniform (fatigue clothes) and leggings. My bed is made without a wrinkle, and I'm standing out-of-doors, clapping my hands and swinging my arms to keep warm in the early morning Kansas chill. From 5 to 5:30 is "chow" ("chow" by the way is the official army designation for food). From 5:30 to 6 A.M. floors are swept and polished up. For one solid half hour the entire barracks is turned into a mad house of flying mops, streamy soapy water, and blue clad figures busily developing house maid's knees and dishwater hands.

Next comes calisthenics; luckily, these are directed by Lieutenants who no doubt have led as sedentary lives as most of the rookies, so that half hour is popularly considered a rest period. However, there is one Lieutenant who looks as though he'd spent the best years of his life running in and out of cold showers in a gymnasium, and we are all living in dread of the day he takes over.

The next half hour is spent drawing rifles from the supply room, and to the snappy rhythms of "hut, two, three, four," "Hut, two, three, four." This is the one part of the Army about which I feel complete confidence, for my R.O.T.C. (of beloved memory) gives me an edge over most of the other rookies. However, even I sometimes find myself lost in a maze of right faces, left faces, about faces, shoulder arms, and all the other hundred and seventy three conflicting commands that may be poured out by a leather lunged, acid-tongued top sergeant.

From 7 to 7:30 as likely as not our troop is double-timed from the drill field through the blocks of sand filled streets to the stables. Here our regular officers brush the good Kansas sand out of their eyes and teeth, turn us over to riding instructors, and dash back to the barracks for a short nap. (That's the rumor, anyway.)

Our riding instructors are in a class by themselves. They are all young, short, tough, and unanimously Southern. They know horses, live horses, breathe horses, smell horses (with a capital "S") and no doubt have the greatest contempt for us poor poltroons who don't know a horse's dock from his withers. They are good teachers, though. Our troop commander swears they're the best in the world. Probably they are.

The first day we learned to saddle, bridle, mount, dismount and ride on horses in a tight circle about the corral. Luckily I picked an old plug who knew all the commands better than I could ever hope to. The corporal would shout his command to start or stop, or move into line, or move out, and my old plug would automatically and placidly obey. I might just as well have been in Chicago reading a book for all the work I had to do.

My luck hasn't always been so good since then. Thursday I got a shaggy, wild-maned nag that had a "soft" or sore mouth. It reared and pitched and tossed its head and kept continually on the move. In case it has never happened to you, I assure you it is very embarrassing to call "whoa" to a horse, and have it plod on at its own self directed pace, especially when one is expected to mount, dismount, and saddle the "critter" while all this is going on. My horse and I were the "hit" of the show that day, and the sergeants and corporals worked their vocabularies overtime on the two of us.

The worst part of horsemanship, though, is the grooming. Naturally most of us rookies are afraid of horses, never having seen much of them except in movies or in the merry-go-round. And in grooming we give the horses their best cracks at us. Somebody is always getting a playful nip from some nag, when his back is turned. Either that or a good swift kick. Besides the danger involved, grooming is just one of those painfully unpleasant jobs that turn up from time to time. Luckily, it is an incidental rather than a major part of riding.

Finished with horsemanship, our troops spend the rest of the morning in various drills and lectures on first aid, military law and tactics. Friday, for instance, we had gas mask drill. We were each issued regulation gas masks, marched to a barrack that had just been completed but was not as yet occupied, and entered a room filled with a high concentration of tear gas. We had our gas masks on of course, but even then it was an eerie feeling, walking into the blue-green haze of the gas, and hearing commands that through the mask seemed to come from the ceiling or floor or any place but through the normal function of the vocal chords. Inside we lined up goggle eyed, blackfaced, elephant snout for a nose, and after about five minutes were given the command to unmask. We pulled off our masks, stared through the haze, and for thirty seconds that seemed like thirty years, we stood with eyes on fire and nostrils streaming, waiting for the command to rush out. It was half an hour before our eyes and noses were back to normal, but the officers seemed well pleased with the drill. If that drill was really characteristic, I hope they never try us out on mustard gas.

Lunch and realization from 12 to 1 and then 2-1/2 hours on the rifle range. As yet we have done no shooting, our time being taken up in endless drills in taking apart and putting together rifles, practice in sighting, trigger squeeze, and worst of all, trying to assume the contortionist positions considered necessary for shooting in the army.

Monday we will have actual target practice, and my knees are already quaking in anticipation. I'm not worried about being bawled out for blasting away the bull's eyes, but I am afraid of setting a record for consecutive misses. I shall go to bed tonight with my fingers and toes crossed for luck.

At 3:30 (the Gods being favorable), and the Major in good humor, we may count our day as ended.

More often than not, though, we rush to our barracks, pile out of our steamy sand filled clothes, shower, re-dress and rush out again for retreat.

Retreat is a military ceremony rendered at the end of the day—a parade in which all members of the post) kitchen help excepted) take part. Its real significance has so far escaped me, but I do know it comes at a darned inconvenient time and effectively destroys any plans for a pre-supper nap. Apparently it is universally dreaded, but equally apparently, it's a function that is here to stay.

Supper, reading, and numerous crap games round out the day. By 8:30 most of the barracks are in bed, and the remainder are giving the final touches to a pre-bed shave or shower. At 9 o'clock lights go out, but few would care to use them even if they did stay on. So ends our day in the army, which is probably a fitting place to end this letter.

Write soon, and write often, please. All's well with me.

[signed]

Bruce Carson never finished his cavalry training; he went to Officers' Candidate School and served two years in the Pacific theater. It was just as well, for within two years the cavalry had bid good-bye to its horses and become completely mechanized.

THE HOME FOLKS WORRY

When the teenage son or daughter went off to the service, mothers and fathers worried about virtually every aspect of their new lives, from the food to the sleeping conditions.

Letter from First Lieutenant Helen Perrell to Mrs. Helen Lovell[14]

A Marine officer writes to reassure an anxious mother.

11 June 1943

My Dear Mrs. Lovell:

I was very happy to hear from you and find that it was very fortunate on your part that you did write. You have asked what you should buy for your son Philip in the way of underwear, etc. This is the answer: Buy nothing.

You see, when your son goes to New River, he should take only those things he will need to wear to get there because as soon as he arrives, he will become completely equipped by the Government. He will receive everything that he should wear and will wear only those things issued by the Government. He will probably find, as I have found in the Service, that it is quite relaxing to get up in the morning and have no decisions to make as to what is to be worn that day.

Best wishes to you again, Mrs. Lovell, both to you and to your son, and should there be any questions that may come up that you would like to ask, don't hesitate to write to me.

> Yours very truly,
> *[signed]*
> HELEN PERRELL
> First Lieutenant
> U.S. Marine Corps Women's Reserve

Mrs. Helen Danforth Lovell
Windy Acres
South Pomfret, Vermont

American Legion Publication—"At Home: All Must Be Well"[15]

So novel was the situation of sending sons and daughters off to the service and so numerous its occasion that the American Legion produced a pamphlet of helpful hints about "home front" behavior. "Those at home who sit and wait, serve also."

A member of your family has been called into the service of our country.

It means a vast change in your and his life. It is not an easy change. But it is one caused by necessity.

We who have served under the flag of the United States, in time of war, know how the member of the armed forces felt when leaving home and because we are now fathers ourselves we know how you feel about the departure.

The service will be just what each makes it—the departure will be just what you make it. The type of service given will be greatly influenced by you.

The person who has gone is entering into the oldest fraternity known to man. No closer bond exists than that between men and women who have served in the common cause. While you cannot be a member of that fraternity, unless you yourself have served in the armed forces of your country, you can be of great assistance to those who are serving.

Those at home who sit and wait, serve also.

It's not always easy to be pleasant and carefree in your letters to him. Sometimes you may write with a heavy heart, but that must not be transmitted to him.

Mothers or fathers who continually write to their sons or daughters in service that they must not place themselves in places of danger, that they should not try for advancement as such advancement may put them into places of danger, that things are going very bad at home and that the money that the soldier or sailor brought in before he left is direly needed, that he or she could serve his or her country back home in a defense plant better than serving in the armed forces, are doing vast harm to those who are in the armed forces.

It's not easy to make the sacrifices called for by war, but those sacrifices must be made. If they can be good soldiers or sailors or nurses, you can be a good mother, father, wife or child. Your sacrifices are small compared to theirs.

We of The American Legion know these things for we have marched away, we have now seen our own sons and daughters march away. We have walked through the valley.

It is with a feeling of pride that we can offer to you our hands and hearts; to serve you in every way possible. We do this because we understand your need of service.

Be proud that you can be the close relation of one who is serving our country; one who is entering upon the Great Adventure.

So that you can know some of the things that just should not be done, we are offering you a few "don'ts" that may help you:

Do not expect a letter every day. There are days that are so filled with duty that it is impossible to write. If he or she does not write, don't feel hurt. Write them just the same.

Do not write and tell about all the troubles at home. Remember those in the armed forces have troubles of their own. Don't add yours to them. Above all, do not write and tell about the "best girl" going out with some other fellow. They are sore enough at the fellow or qualified girl that stayed at home.

Do not take too seriously the first few letters in which there is description of many things that are wrong in the service. It is like putting on a pair of new shoes, they hurt until they become broken in. And above all do not tell others the things that they are "crabbing" about. They are not nearly as hard as they think. Of course, they are going to become tired of the food. So did the man who had to eat quail every day.

Do not pass on rumors that they may write home. Only harm can come to do so. Keep what they say as something sacred to you and you alone.

Do not ask them to get leave every time you become homesick to see them or something happens at home. They can't get leave so often, and besides you have no right to ask that they request it.

Do not send unnecessary articles and most especially bulky articles. Remember they must carry anything that they have, and the load is already as heavy as can scientifically be carried.

Do not if they have been in battle, expect them to tell you of all the experiences, there are some experiences that just are not told. Do not ask that they talk about those things. They are theirs and theirs alone.

Do not fail to call upon the American Legion post, the American Legion Auxiliary Unit or the American Service Officer for any service, information or assistance that you may need. Such service, information or assistance will be given without charge and without obligation on your part.

But there are "do's" also.

Do write often and write newsy, encouraging letters. Maybe you do not think that it's important if the family dog is sick, but they think so. It may not be news to you. It is now a fond memory to them. Tell them about all the happenings at home.

Do offer up your prayers for their safety and tell them you are doing so.

Do send him or her packages of those things that they liked so well, just as long as they are in camp in this country. When they have gone overseas, you can no longer send them. No matter how good the food is in camp, the package from home is welcome.

Do send him, also, things like cigarettes, a new pipe, tobacco for that pipe, playing cards, letter paper and envelopes, air mail stamps that help the letters get home quicker, flints for his lighter, and needles for the phonograph (especially if he is overseas where neither matches nor needles can be had). A good pair of sun glasses is always appreciated, a good cigarette lighter, a fountain pen and automatic pencil, razor blades, waterproof tobacco pouch, a small flash light, a sewing kit with plenty of buttons and large eyed needles, extra socks and handkerchiefs, a good wrist watch and above all a real good can opener. If they ask for them send their radio, their record player, their camera, musical instruments, etc., but don't send them unless they ask for them.

Do keep your chin up. They are going to have the finest care that is possible for their government to give. Food will be good, not always cooked just as they will want it but it will be the best. Better in many instances than you will have at home, and more of it, too. In case of sickness or wound, he will have the finest medical and nursing service that anyone could ask for. With the new sulfa drugs and other medical discoveries, he has many more times the chance of recovery than his comrades of 1917–18 had with the same kind of injury. Everything will be done to keep him well and make him well if sickness comes.

Most American families had no choice but to try to follow this advice as they committed their sons and daughters to the care of the U.S. armed forces. It was all a new experience, but not for long.

■ SOURCES

1. "A Catechism on Universal Draft," prepared by National Publicity Division, The American Legion, n.d., "American Legion Publications (3)" File, World War II Participants and Contemporaries Collection, Dwight D. Eisenhower Library, Abilene, Kansas. Although undated, this pamphlet was prepared before the draft was enacted by Congress in 1941.

2. Petition to Franklin D. Roosevelt, n.d., "American Legion—National Headquarters, Petition to FDR, Sept. 1941 (1)" File, World War II Participants and Contemporaries Collection, Eisenhower Library.

3. Petition to the American Legion, n.d., "American Legion—National Headquarters, Petition to FDR, Sept. 1941 (1)" File, World War II Participants and Contemporaries Collection, Eisenhower Library.

4. "The Average Soldier," *Yoo Hoo,* Comic Corporation of America, March 1942, "Memorabilia (1)" File, Harry Cordell Papers, World War II Participants and Contemporaries Collection, Eisenhower Library, p. 38.

5. "The Recruit," by Lt. Lenhardt E. Bauer, n.d., "Jeanne E. Betcher—Memorabilia" File, Jeanne E. Betcher Papers, World War II Participants and Contemporaries Collection, Eisenhower Library.

6. The American Legion, "Fall-In," n.d., "American Legion Publications (1)" File, World War II Participants and Contemporaries Collection, Eisenhower Library, pp. 3–4, 6–9, 15.

7. "A Goldbrick in the USA," Diary of Nap Glass, "Diary—US Book I (1)" File, Nap Glass Papers, World War II Participants and Contemporaries Collection, Eisenhower Library, pp. 1–4.

8. The letters in this section are from William H. Herbert to Mother, December 3, 1942, "Dec. 1, 1942–Feb. 9, 1943, Camp Wallace, Texas (1)" File; and May 23, 1943, "May 25–July 10, 1943, Fort Bliss, Texas" File, 1943 and, "Camp Davis, NC (1)" File, Henrietta Cragon Papers, World War II Participants and Contemporaries Collection, Eisenhower Library.

9. Notebook, by Jeanne E. Betcher, 18th Company, 3rd Regiment, Army Post Branch, Des Moines, Iowa, "Jeanne Betcher—Notebook, Nov. 16, 1942–Dec. 31, 1942 (1)" File, World War II Participants and Contemporaries Collection, Eisenhower Library. This selection is a typed transcription, in notebook form, of handwritten letters to the author's parents.

10. The letters in this section are from Herbert Eugene Book, Jr., to Family, March 16, 17, 19, and 26, 1943, "Letters, 1942–March 1943" File; and April 16, 1943, "Letters, Apr.–Sept. 1943" File, Herbert E. Book Papers, World War II Participants and Contemporaries Collection, Eisenhower Library.

11. War Department Basic Field Manual 23-5, "U.S. Rifle, Caliber .30, M1" (Washington: U.S. Government Printing Office, 1940), "Printed Material (1)" File, George W. Dinning Papers, World War II Participants and Contemporaries Collection, Eisenhower Library, p. 1.

12. The letters in this section are from Richard Cipra to Eleanor Lewis, November 26, 1942, "Letters—Richard Cipra, 1941–42" File; and March 8 and May 12, 1943, and "Letters—Richard Cipra, 1943" File, Elmer Lewis Papers, World War II Participants and Contemporaries Collection, Eisenhower Library.

13. The letters in this section are from Bruce Carson to Family, March 30 and April 6, 1941, "Bruce Carson Letters, 1941 (1)" File, Richard Lowitt Papers, World War II Participants and Contemporaries Collection, Eisenhower Library.

14. First Lieutenant Helen Perrell to Mrs. Helen Lovell, June 11, 1943, "Scrapbook" File, Philip G. Lovell, Jr., Papers, World War II Participants and Contemporaries Collection, Eisenhower Library.

15. The American Legion, "At Home: All Must Be Well," n.d., "American Legion Publications (2)" File, World War II Participants and Contemporaries Collection, Eisenhower Library, pp. 7–10.

TWO

AT THE FRONT

F rontline service in World War II, as in any war, was a harrowing
and sobering experience. But, because this conflict was global,
the experience of combat varied widely, depending on the climate, branch of service, and particular enemy fought. Here is a
selection of letters and diary entries that reflect the great variety of
the American combat experience in World War II. They include the
accounts of infantrymen in the European and Mediterranean theaters, a frontline nurse in Italy, a sailor who took on the Japanese
and life-threatening storms at sea, and some who challenged the
Axis forces in the skies over Europe.

The selections document not only the variety of service affiliations and
geographic locations but also the range of combat exposure that
Americans faced in World War II. There are accounts here of great
battles and small skirmishes, from beaches and islands and open seas
to settled countryside and cloud-filled skies and Old World villages. If

nothing else, we can conclude that there simply was no common American combat experience.

Some of the confusion, fear, and danger of the fighting comes through in the selections of this chapter. So, too, though seldom mentioned directly, does some of the bravery and dedication. When we remember that those who risked, and sometimes sacrificed, their lives were carpenters and fruit vendors and university students, the words they left us about their harrowing venture into the greatest military exercise in world history take on a special meaning for Americans, with their long tradition of the citizen-soldier.

PEARL HARBOR DIARY

HAROLD CHUTES[1]

Pearl Harbor was bewildering for those who experienced it first-hand. Note the many widely held but inaccurate conceptions of what was happening contained in this account. It provides a vivid look at the confusion of war.

It was Sun. morning of Dec. 7, 1941, it was bright and clear and all Schofield Barracks lay sleeping.

I, Harold Chutes, was up early and on my way to the Hayside Baptist Church, Uahiawa.

It was about 7:30 that morning when I came within a short distance of Wheeler Field, our air base, when suddenly high overhead a plane came down in a power dive which attracted my attention.

After leveling off, a bomb left the plane at a 45° angle. It struck a nearby hanger, shooting flames at least 50 ft. into the air.

There was no doubt, war was on.

People began to look out of doors and windows and asking what was wrong. Soon all was discovered, and men, women and children ran out of their homes to the nearest shelter. Japanese with German planes soared over head with machine guns wide open.

A barracks was blown up in Wheeler Field, taking the lives of many soldiers. Ambulances and fire trucks worked fast to remove the dead and injured and take them to the Post Hospitals. Many planes were lost. U.S. planes were unable to leave the ground.

Pearl Harbor and Honolulu were struck with bombs, destroying a few ships.

The rest of the day remained quiet, but the night meant trouble.

On the morning of Dec. 8th about 2 o'clock, many Jap planes flew at a high altitude.

I was listening closely to some radio calls. Flash! planes headed for Wheeler Field, many! high! unidentified!

In a short time, Wheeler Field was firing huge anti-aircraft guns, machine guns, rifles and so on. Flash! planes driven off, headed for Pearl Harbor. Another flash said Planes are 18000 ft. above Honolulu. There are many unidentifieds. Planes dropping at 8000 ft. Pearl Harbor firing full force. Planes headed North west. One plane flying high over Schofield Barracks, be on look out. It was said that five enemy planes were shot down, and a few parachute troops were captured. Newspapers and radios announced saboteurs in Ft. Ruggles. Many spies are believed to be in Oahu.

Such was the confusion and lingering panic engendered by Japan's audacious strike at Pearl Harbor. For the record, no German planes or pilots participated in the Pearl Harbor raid, though some witnesses were positive they had seen both. No Japanese planes returned to attack Hawaii on December 8; they were all heading back to Japan by then, fully expecting an American retaliatory strike on their aircraft carriers at any moment. The rumors of downed Japanese planes were just that—rumors—as were the stories of Japanese parachutists (one such reported invader, fired on by a frightened citizen, turned out to be a Japanese-American employee of Western Union delivering a telegram), saboteurs causing traffic jams to prevent servicemen from returning to their units, and treacherous informants who had cut arrows in the cane fields to help the attacking pilots with their navigation. Before scoffing at how ridiculous many of these rumors were, we must call to mind the utter unreality and terror of history's first large-scale attack by carrier aircraft, undertaken on a calm and lazy Sunday morning, at a spot presumed to be thousands of miles from any potential danger, by a nation with whom Americans were still officially at peace. Veteran troops might well have been shaken by the onslaught, let alone green soldiers and sailors and untrained civilians.

A MESSAGE FROM THE PRESIDENT

FRANKLIN D. ROOSEVELT TO MEMBERS OF THE UNITED STATES ARMY EXPEDITIONARY FORCES[2]

It wasn't long after Pearl Harbor before American troops were heading overseas. Some fought in the Battle of the Atlantic or Guadalcanal or other operations in 1942, but many headed to Great Britain to take part in the two-year buildup of forces for the cross-channel invasion. All those departing U.S. shores received a message from their president.

You are a soldier of the United States Army.

You have embarked for distant places where the war is being fought.

Upon the outcome depends the freedom of your lives: the freedom of the lives of those you love—your fellow-citizens—your people.

Never were the enemies of freedom more tyrannical, more arrogant, more brutal.

Yours is a God-fearing, proud, courageous people, which, throughout its history, has put its freedom under God before all other purposes.

We who stay at home have our duties to perform—duties owed in many parts to you. You will be supported by the whole force and power of this Nation. The victory you will win will be a victory of all the people—common to them all.

You bear with you the hope, the confidence, the gratitude and the prayers of your family, your fellow-citizens, and your President—

Franklin D. Roosevelt

AN AIRMAN'S LETTERS

LETTERS HOME FROM ERVIN J. COOK[3]

Those who waged the bombing campaign against Germany fought their own kind of war. In relative safety and comfort when they were not actually on a mission, the airmen nevertheless faced stark terror in the skies and rather daunting odds against the safe completion of their tour of duty.

Feb. 26, 1944

Sat. Eve.

> *Shipping out for the frontlines was part of every combatant's experience. The emotions and questions it raised were many and varied, but here we get a good look at one soldier's response.*

Dear Folks:

Well, here I am in Ga., and I don't think much of it around here. It doesn't look like we are going to get a chance to get fed up with it, for we are supposed to leave next Monday or Tuesday. I really expected to be here longer, but I guess not. Lot of the boys have been getting leaves from here, but I guess it is just as well, for it would be hard to say goodbye. We want to get going, the sooner we get over there the sooner we'll be back. It's possible to be back by next Christmas if we get our Missions in. I figure on about a year though.

Well, there is some stuff that I want you to know just in case. You might be able to help Barbara out if she ever needed it.

She has my will and power of attorney, also an allotment voucher showing she is to receive $200 per month, and on the voucher it tells who to get in touch with in case of any discrepancy.

I just have the $10,000 gov. insurance on myself. In case of death, she does not get any lump sum but something about $55 per month for a period of years. Also in case of death she will get my pay for 6 months, and it won't include flying pay, which I am getting now. In case I am missing in action, she will get her allotment for 1 year, then they will start paying the insurance. Also I have a $1000 accident insurance policy on *her* in case something happens while I'm away. She has the policy with her. As far as money goes, we have some in bonds but no cash to speak of. She is opening a savings account in St. Joe, so we will have some in the near future. Another thing: if I send you any money, put it away for me, for I still haven't given up the idea of finishing school. That may be the only way I can do it—just to put it away separate. No use in telling Barbara or any one about it. Well, I thought it best to tell you just what's what so you will know just what's going on.

We have a pretty good time together as a crew, and they are a swell bunch. Don't worry about me, I'm coming back. I have to—I may be going to have a family! I probably won't be able to hear from Barbara for a long time, but I'm anxious to find out. Bye now and loads of love

Erv

*The conflicting emotions of the citizen-soldier are evident in these
next letters from the front. Proud to do his duty, fearful of not
coming back from a mission, and, eventually, numb to the horror
of suffering and death in the skies over Germany, the young man
endures his requisite number of missions.*

May 2, 1944

England

Dear Mom and Dad,

Well, it's another beautiful day today, no rain. Any day that it doesn't rain is
a beautiful day as far as I'm concerned.

I got my first letter day before yesterday from Barbara. After two months
with no mail, I felt like framing it when I got it. Then today I got four letters
from Barbara and also got a recent Graceland Tower.

I've been rather busy lately but like it here very much. Our laundry service and cleaning service is pretty good, which I have found is a very important item. I think the food is very good here and usually eat my share.

I get a candy bar every time I go on a mission. Remember that! They really taste good, since we don't have much candy. I always have my candy bar
eaten before I get off the ground.

I have been on some missions but cannot tell you how many. I've been
scared at times, and it's a lot of work at times, but to a certain extent you get
used to getting your fanny shot at. I haven't had to put on clean underwear
yet when I returned. There will always be times when I'll be sweating it out,
but there is a good deal of satisfaction connected with it.

Well, it's about time for me to hit the sack (bed to you). Lots of love to
you all.

Ervin

May 25, 1944

Dear Mom and Dad,

I received lots of mail today, six letters altogether. I got your letter, Mom, and
also the one Dad had written March 12. I enjoyed both the letters very much.
Dad certainly wrote a nice long letter, and I appreciated it very much. I think
I have learned to understand him much better the past two years. I certainly
admire him and think he has the right idea on how to live life. As the army
boys would put it, he is a "good Joe."

I have been very busy, and I am pretty well pooped out tonight. Usually
it's to the extreme, one way or the other. Either we worked like hell or don't

do hardly anything, depending upon the weather. When the weather is good, it is very necessary to get as much done as possible. I have other things to do beside going on missions, mainly school. Of course it is secondary, that is one thing that will continue until the war is over. There is an old saying in the air corps, "As long as you keep learning, you keep living." I have gotten thirteen candy bars so far, so haven't been very hungry for candy.* I guess I told you our ship is named "Slightly Dangerous" and Vessels is painting a beautiful gal on it. We also have the name of our ship on the back of our jackets. Looks pretty classy!

I have been going to save a piece of flak for a souvenir but always forget to hunt for a piece once the mission is over. Next time we catch some, I'll save a piece and try and send it to you. It's funny how your point of view changes. When I started to come over to here, I really thought it was going to be a one way ticket and I would never live through it. But now that I am actually in it, I have all the confidence in the world that I will get back O.K. Things get pretty rough at times, and I have been scared silly at times, but we always come back okay. A lot of times I am too busy to even think of getting scared. I am getting rather used to it now, though, and things have to get pretty bad before it bothers me much.

I am very happy here, and we have quite a bit of fun. I am happy that I am married but often wish that I was single so I wouldn't have to get back in the harness as soon as the war's over. I am glad we don't have any babies for one reason, I still cherish the thought of going back to school. I think I could get a lot out of it now. Looks like the government is going to help the boys who want to get back to school. Well, thanks again for your swell letters. I certainly enjoy them. Whenever I get mail, I always open your letters first to find out if you're all O.K. Take care of yourselves.

Much love
Erv.

June 15, 1944

England

Dear Folks,

The mail situation has been pretty slim lately, which is only natural in view of what is going on around here.** I finally hit the Jack-pot today and got four

---

*Refers to the practice of giving all air crew members a candy bar before every bombing run; thus, Cook has been on 13 missions to date.
**That is, the Normandy invasion.

Troops awaiting embarkation on docks at Newport News, Va. (Courtesy of the Dwight D. Eisenhower Library, Carl Hershfeld Collection.)

letters from Barbara and one from Dave. From what Barbara says, the mail has been getting back there very slowly, if at all. It'll probably take awhile to get back to normal.

Well, I am still working now and then but don't feel eager about it anymore. Although I had a good rest not long ago, I don't seem to be able to take much anymore. Using our favorite word, it doesn't take much to "horrify" me these days. I guess it is because it's all just routine now, with any of the newness worn off. If I ever had the spirit of adventure, it's gone now, all I want to do is get the hell home where I can grow fat and lazy. I am not griping, for it's just a natural letdown I have been expecting to come at this stage of the game. I am damn lucky to be where I am instead of on the ground, and I'm just the boy who knows it.

Dave told me what Warren was going into, and I was sure sorry to hear it. I know what they have to go through over here. Maybe he'll be sent somewhere else. I hope so. Don't say anything to his folks.

It's beautiful over here now, and I enjoy riding my bicycle through the woods. There are some beautiful estates over here which I would like to get closer to than just flying over them.

I have been feeling swell and quite happy although I hate to think how long this thing is going to last. Maybe things will move faster than we expect. Well, bye for now.

Lots of love,
Ervin

Ervin Cook completed his tour of duty in 1944 and returned home safely to his young wife.

FLYING FOR THE RAF

LETTERS HOME FROM ROBERT S. RAYMOND[4]

Robert Raymond left his native Kansas City and volunteered to serve in the French Army eighteen months before Pearl Harbor pulled the United States into the conflict. His training in France had barely begun when Paris fell to the Germans, and Raymond headed for England and a chance to carry on the struggle. He was discharged from the French Army and joined the Royal Air Force, where he was trained as a bomber pilot. His letters to a friend, who would one day be his wife, describe some of his missions. Although frequently physically demanding and mentally stressful, flying never lost its appeal for Raymond. He completed his thirty missions and was transferred to the U.S. Army Air Forces, in whose service he remained for the rest of the war. He thus enjoys the rare distinction of having served in the military forces of three different nations in the same war.

November 21, 1942

Dear Betty,

I am in London today, and after receiving your letter of October 24th several days ago I am still puzzled as to how best to tell you in the strongest possible terms that (1) I have written you at least eight letters during the past two months. (2) I shall continue to write regularly just as I have done in the past. (3) I have not acquired an English bride and an English home, etc., as your letters continue to suggest.

Have written you of so many things, of my meeting with Ted,* of the last few weeks of my training, of my new Crew members, of my posting to an Operational Squadron, of my experiences on Operations to Milan and Genoa, of speaking to the King, etc. I am sorry that you have not received any of them but am thankful that you have been loyal enough to continue what must from your point of view have appeared to be a very one-sided correspondence.

My Crew were due for leave yesterday, and I had arranged for them to be able to leave the Station at four oclock in the afternoon. Instead we were briefed for Turin, and they were very mad, partially at me, I think, because they suspected that my enthusiasm for Operations (which they do not share) might have caused the delay and hoped up to the very last minute that it might be cancelled due to the weather, as several previous ones had been. They didn't credit me with enough savvy to know that I considered their leave the best possible cure for their state of mind. After being on an Operational Station for six weeks, their families and friends will not consider their contribution of one raid to the war effort so very much. They were finally convinced of my strict neutrality and the validity of the orders, later.

We took off at six oclock, climbed up through a thick overcast, full of ice, to bright moonlight and sat up there breathing oxygen, with the temperature minus 25° Centrigade, feeling quite nakedly exposed to night fighters with so much light, for hours until we approached the Alps. Their rugged white peaks were weirdly wonderful, projecting above the low cloud that filled the valleys like a level milk-white sea lapping the sharply upthrust islands. Passed close to Mont Blanc, and soon far ahead down on the Italian plain—the fireworks, and it looked like they were throwing up everything they had, including kitchen stoves—red hot. A magnificent pyrotechnic display, but no one said anything on the Inter-com as they had over the beauty of the Alps.

I pointed the nose down, and the altimeter began to unwind. There was no cloud south of the Alps, but a ground mist made it difficult to pick up land-marks on the ground. A glance at the map will show you how necessary it was to lose height quickly, for Turin is quite close to the Alps. The streams of flak were flowing up far above us, and the flares hanging overhead made us plainly visible when I finally leveled out at 4000 feet. Carter said afterward that they must have been in their dugouts pulling strings attached to their trig-gers. A few of us had been ordered to go for the Fiat works to the south of the town with four-thousand-lb. bombs and to make sure of it at the lowest possible level. We were carrying one of them, among other things. Everyone was looking over the side trying to find our target while I obeyed the Rear

---

*Raymond's brother.

Gunner's instructions in dodging the light flak with which they were following our track around the sky. It was coming up on both sides of the fuselage at times. Went around the town three times before everyone yelled at once, "There it is." I saw it then myself, a big oblong building with a green roof, steered straight over it, and felt the blast of our cookie a few seconds after Watt said, "Bombs gone." Harmston said it was so light that he could follow our big one all the way down and saw it burst on the building with the incendiaries scattered like leaves around it.

I headed for the nearest exit and went up a deep narrow valley that turned out to be a hot spot—flak in it everywhere, but kept dodging and climbing until we scraped up over the twelve-thousand-foot ridge at the upper end and set course for Mont Blanc. My gyro instruments failed at this point, and I had to fly by means of the altimeter, airspeed indicator and compass all the way to Base (a rather sketchy combination). Return trip above cloud under a full moon was uneventful but very cold. Weather at Base was poor, and they sent us on north, and we landed at a strange aerodrome at 3:30 in the morning.

We ate there, slept three hours, and then flew back to Base soon after daylight. Interrogation after every raid is a dull business, just facts—times, heights, courses, numbers, etc.—nothing about the beauty of the Alps, nor the trouble or joys you had going to, over, or returning from the target. Shall see our photograph taken of our bomb burst when I return from leave. This is the second raid on which I have flown with my complete Crew alone.

Left the Station at noon and came to London by train. Shall not think of flying nor much of the war at least.

As ever,
Bob

P.S. I dived down on an unsuspecting Flying Fortress the other day, but he wouldn't play, so I came up alongside, stopped one propeller, and passed him. He was very mad.*

December 10, 1942

Dear Betty,

Since this will probably reach you after Christmas, I'll wish you a Happy New Year. I have little interest in holidays any more because there is no attempt to celebrate them on this side of the Atlantic, but more particularly because I have been accustomed to spending them at home with my family and friends,

---

*Raymond was flying the relatively new Lancaster bomber, a recent British design that was somewhat faster than the U.S. B-17 Flying Fortress.

among children, aunts, uncles, cousins, et al., and when they are missing, not to mention Mother's dinner table, the day is much the same as any other on the calendar.

I shall be interested to hear how you spent the school holidays and if you will continue to teach English at K.U.* for the remainder of the school year.

The following pages will contain an account of my own small part in the war effort, and since it is along the same lines as my past experiences, it will not sound very good if you've absorbed any of the "Peace on Earth, Goodwill toward Men" spirit of the Christmas season.

My crew and I in the Flying Jayhawk have delivered ten tons of "Hell from the Sky" to [censored] since I last wrote you. After we had been briefed every day for a week and had the Operation cancelled because of bad weather, we finally took off on December 6 for a city in southwest [censored]. The meteorologists promised us, among other things, that the cloud ceiling over the target would be at least [censored]. It was our first trip as a Crew to [censored], and since we hadn't faced any flak since November 20, due to our week's leave and bad weather, my boys were a little nervous. But soon after crossing the [censored] some antiaircraft gunner got us in his sights at the right second and cured them of nervousness. After that they were just plain scared. A heavy shell exploded beneath the plane with a big w-o-o-o-m-ph and added several hundred feet to the thousands on the altimeter, but fortunately the blast effect was all that hit us. No searchlights since we were above cloud but flak all the way. Over the target there was a cloud layer from [censored] down to [censored] thousand feet. I know, because we looked underneath in an effort to identify the target, but four searchlights pinned us immediately, and the natives appeared hostile or can you imagine Milton's Hell in "Paradise Lost?"; so we nipped smartly back upstairs again, estimated our ground position, and distributed our load over a wide area.

Watt said afterward to Elger's Bombardier that he didn't mind the flak so much, but with searchlights on us at that height, it was impossible to see the ground. That's an Irish witticism. Apart from flak, accurate night bombing is almost [censored] good, i.e., the air is clear over the target. Incidentally, we were the only crew to report the height of the cloud base.

Several hours later on the return journey Siddons told us we should cross the [censored] coast in thirteen minutes, also that his latest astro fix showed us sixty miles south of track, but he distrusted it, thinking he had erred in its calculation. A half hour later flak was still coming up ahead and around us. Then Griffiths reprted we had fuel for only two more hours' flying, Price

---

*The University of Kansas, in Lawrence, Kansas.

U.S. airmen informally posing at the bar in an English pub. (Courtesy of the Dwight D. Eisenhower Library, Wanda Mufic Collection.)

reported he had just received a message from Base that the weather was unfit for landing there, and the Gunners said they were cold. Siddons finally admitted that his navigation was up the creek, and I held an Inter-com conference with Price, decided on a change of course, and listened in on his Morse conversation with someone, somewhere in England, who hooked us on the end of a long tie line and never let go until we crossed our own coast and were circling an aerodrome an hour and a half later. We requested permission to land, and a string of six lights came on below us,—flew around the circuit again and lost sight of them—it was raining—round again and landed on what proved to be a long, smooth runway, where we rolled to a stop and sat enjoying the quiet, cold, darkness while our motors ticked over idly. In answer to our query over the radio telephone a voice with an American accent said, "Follow the Jeeps, park your plane, and they will bring you to the Tower." Two pairs of headlights led us down a side road. Imagine our amazement on climbing out to be surrounded by U.S. Army uniforms. We had landed at an American aerodrome. Took care of all the details and formalities at the Control Tower, then to the Mess in Jeeps, where we were fed so well that we have resolved hereafter to land only at U.S. Army Air Corps Stations. First white bread we had tasted for more than six months and plenty of everything.

None of the personnel there had been on Ops, done any night flying over England, or seen a British plane as large as ours. Got to bed at 4 A.M.—up at daybreak to get our plane refueled—breakfast—being driven everywhere in Jeeps—no one walks around on the ground as they do at our Stations, thanked them for their hospitality and so took off, anxious to get back to our razors, toothbrushes and pajamas again.

Elger landed at another Station the same night and saw MacFarlane spread his plane over the field in small pieces. All the crew severely injured but none killed.

Funniest incident of the trip—Price chucking leaflets down the flare chute while over Germany and yelling, "Get your papers here. Read all about it, you ———." Siddons's navigation error was due to an unpredicted wind of gale force which blew us south of trick. His astro fix was afterward proved correct. He'll trust the stars hereafter. Look at a map.

Carter has been hospitalized and did not fly with us. I enjoy my bicycle.

On December 8 our unit was detailed to attack Turin. Bad weather over England, flak and clouds over France, the Alps the same as usual and there was Turin brilliantly lit by flares on the plain far below. Red and blue streams of tracers coming up to 10,000 feet, heavy flak bursts above it, a few searchlights and our aircraft everywhere in the sky.

It was the shortest, most concentrated and accurate Blitz I have ever seen. The loads were incendiaries and four thousand pounders. We bombed among the first, then flew around for twenty minutes watching the fireworks. The incendiaries were laid down in mile-long strips that looked as though some one had flung down a bucketful of glittering jewelry. Their brilliant glow outlined the buildings sharply, and the patterns, from our height, made X's, N's, T's, etc., on the town. The four thousand pounders made terrific geysers and gaping black holes among the bands of incendiaries. A very pretty sight, scientifically, of course—we like to do things well. And so back to Base. Photos showed fires going merrily.

Since I do not believe in high altitude flying, our trips are always a compromise between myself and my Crew. My reasons are (1) it's uneconomical to haul the load up so high when you have to come down to identify the target; (2) since light flak (with tracers) is effective only up to about 8000 feet and heavy flak from 8000-40,000 feet, you're not really safe from ground defenses at any height; (3) high altitude flying means loss of maneuverability (it's like walking a tight rope) due to the loss of lift in the rarefied atmosphere; (4) night fighters are more likely to be encountered at higher altitudes; (5) searchlight range only goes up to 12,000 feet. So although those may sound like famous last words, there is an argumentative basis for them. My Crew reply only that they feel safer higher up.

Six hours' sleep, and they asked us to do it again. My Crew were dead on their feet, and Griffiths had to keep reminding me to weave over enemy territory. My arms ached. Turin still burning from previous night's attack, but visibility good, and we poured it on them again, laying our loads in an unburnt section around the railroad station and on it. More defenses than last night, but they gave up after the first 10 minutes, and we stoked up the fires again. They can start charging admission today like they do to see the ruins of Pompeii near Naples. It was ten times worse than Coventry and on such a scale that no Air Raid Protection Service or fire-fighting units could cope with it. We distributed Churchill's message to get out in the fields and watch their cities burn. We have a personal grievance against the Italians now. They hit the Flying Jayhawk, an accident, I assure you—they're not that good really—only a propeller.

And so back to Base, where the cloud ceiling was down to 1200, with a high wind, and all our kites roaming around and trying to get down on a muddy flarepath in the rain. Stan Price said every time he looked out of the astro-dome, there was another plane 10 feet from our wing-tip. Everyone short of fuel as usual, tired, cold, and hoping no one would smear the flarepath until he could have a try at it. My crew still like my landings (I just touched wood). Photos show little ground detail—mostly fire tracks and smoke.

The Canadian pilot with whom I roomed at O.T.U. for 4 months is missing from last night's raid.

Two funny incidents last night: A crew of officers landed at Base 2 hours after taking off. Reported the compass unserviceable. Everyone also experienced a big drift from an unusually strong beam wind but relocated themselves and went on—didn't blame it on the compass. With my Crew I had exactly the same response last August, remember? On an Operational Squadron you're either on top of the world or in the doghouse. The other incident was a pilot who flew a plane other than his own, taxied to his own dispersal from force of habit and damaged his plane there.

After eight hours' sleep, I feel like a human being again.

My crew are getting seasoned and steadier. They can talk in normal tones while over the target now. Siddons comes out of his warm, well-lighted office for a one-minute look while we're near the target, then goes back to his desk and tries to forget it. My faith in him has been amply rewarded. Air navigation must necessarily be done quickly and accurately under conditions of motion, noise and vibration. We know the route to Italy so well now that we steered courses we remembered from the night before until we saw Mont Blanc.

Weather continues cold with rain. Your latest letters are dated Nov. 1 and 16. The beer Ted sent me was for the Crew, because I do not drink beer. Period. Happy New Year!

Bob

January 27, 1943

Midnight

Dear Betty,

Have just returned from Düsseldorf, and sitting here in my quiet room, with Griffiths sleeping peacefully, it seems incredible that I was there only 4 hours ago. Griffith's curly blonde head is little troubled by the experience of another bombing raid, but I am not yet sleepy and shall tell you about it, for memory, particularly mine, is a transient thing and inevitably softens the clear-cut lines of any experience, however impressive.

Düsseldorf is a great industrial city situated in the Ruhr on the Rhine River, producing great quantities of vital war materials so urgently needed by the Wehrmacht on all fronts. It is vulnerable in that the great river is an outstanding landmark, enabling easy identification, and because it is less than 400 miles from England, making it possible for us to carry a much greater weight of bombs thee than, for instance, to Italy.

We took off under low cloud with the promise of better weather over the target and on our return. Climbed up through several cloud layers just as the sun was tinting them with the last golden red colours of the day, and so up over the North Sea with George flying. Some flak over the Dutch coast was sent up to our height through a solid layer of cloud, and from then on we were never entirely free from it until we had arrived within a few minutes of the target, when I remarked to Watt that, although we were quite sure of our position, it looked too quiet to be entirely healthy. But we were evidently the first to arrive, and the defenses were lying doggo in the hope that we would either pass over and not bother them or, being uncertain of our position, fail to locate the city. Neither happened; being quite sure of where we were even above the scattered cloud, we ran straight in and planted our cookie and incendiaries (more than 1000 of them) and, since the scattered cloud below made a good photo of the result improbable, I turned away immediately.

Watt said, "Bombs gone."

Immediately after the cookie blossomed into a great red mushroom glow and the string of incendiaries began to sprinkle on the ground, more than 50 searchlights concentrated on the place we should have been after dropping that load, and the flak was bursting right at the apex of the searchlight cone. The ground defenses had been quietly plotting our track all the while, and now that they knew they were to be the "Target for tonight," they threw up everything they had. I'm afraid we left our companions a hard row to hoe, but we have faced the same situation elsewhere.

Flak all the way to the coast, and finally the blessed emptiness of the lonely North Sea, where we found ice forming on our wings when we attempted to descend through the cloud, and so stayed upstairs at lower temperatures until we were over England and Price could get us the latest weather report from our Base.

An hour before we arrived the cloud ceiling was 4,000 feet and closing down rapidly. By the time we got there, it was down to 800 feet with rain falling and the air gusty and full of pockets (air currents) that tossed us around like peas in an empty sack between 300 and 1200 feet. Having [censored] just before setting course from Base earlier in the evening, we were even more cautious than usual. Discipline in the air is absolutely essential, for only the W.A.A.F. in the control tower knows where everyone is. Reviewing the situation now, I know that six months ago under such conditions I would most certainly have been listed as missing with my Crew from this night's Operations. But somewhere during my training I learned to fly confidently by instruments alone, and only that accuracy enabled me to maintain contact and land on the flarepath as smoothly and easily in darkness as it is possible to do during the day. All members of air-crew are trained, not born, for their jobs, and only hard work and practice enable any crew to live trough an Operational tour. I've known so many who trusted to instinct, luck and fortune to carry them through. Each serves in more or less marginal situations, but eventually there can be no substitute. For that reason an Operational Crew of proven ability is a premium product and a valuable unit. They can be developed from average material, but somehow the sum of their abilities must be so integrated that the whole is something greater than the sum of its parts. And that is one of the reasons why I still enjoy flying a bomber.

Primarily, I suppose, it's based on vanity. We live a life of comparative life and leisure, are fed, clothed, housed and paid more than others, but when the chips are down, it's up to small units of 7 men each, to do in a few hours what would otherwise cost the lives of as many thousands to accomplish. Our capacity for destruction is tremendous. God grant that in the days of peace to come we shall work as hard and be as zealous to rebuild and recreate the brave new world.

Several bursts of flak were so near tonight that the Gunners still think we were hit, since we could not examine the plane adequately in the dark when we had parked it at the dispersal point, but we shall see tomorrow.

Your last letter was dated Dec. 16, 1942, and I am glad that you had an opportunity to visit my parents. Have received letters from Ted, Roxie, and Nadine this week. All happy. Ted lives in a hotel, is working hard and trying to learn French from the chambermaid and Spanish from the civilians. Likes the climate and country.

My letters inevitably taper off to unconnected inconsequentials. Just remembered some sounds I would like to hear—the long, hollow whistle of a train—you, singing—birds on a spring morning—frogs at midnight—traffic on Main Street—the smooth patter of a salesman (with the goods)—wind in a pine forest—the K.C. Philharmonic—a church choir—the clatter of a mowing machine—the rustle of tall corn—the drowsy hum of bees around a hive—the crackle of a wood fire—carpenters sawing and hammering—and many others, but most of all your voice.

Two photos enclosed.

Bob

The London "Daily Mail" recently estimated the cost of a single night raid of 300 bombers over the Ruhr as follows: gasoline and oil, $13,280; losses, allowing three planes shot down, $240,000; bombs, $720,000; maintenance on planes, $270,000. Total: $1,183,280.

—Time

DIARY OF A SAILOR

RICHARD THOMAS MARINER[5]

The diary of a destroyerman, aptly named Richard Mariner, details some intense and hectic surface force action by the USS Thatcher in the Pacific. The Thatcher was in the thick of the several small actions with Japanese cruisers and destroyers in the Solomons/Rabaul area. This account, somewhat confused and riddled with baffling punctuation and grammar, conveys the great fear inflicted by combat—and also, occasionally, by storms. Yet it is also clear that men did their duty under these paralyzing conditions.

Oct. 31 [1943]

We left Tulagi with seven Cans* and Four Cruisers to bombard the shores of Buka Island, Japs' big air force operating place, we struck at midnight it lasted till about one-thirty then we bombarded Treasury Island, another important air base. We fired salvo after salvo into the island, we were dodging shore batteries greatly, we struck there at six A.M. and their batteries opened fire on us but with the

---

* Common sailor's term for destroyers.

grace of God they missed. That wasn't bad enough until four of our cans headed back to Purvis Bay to refuel so there were now four cans and four cruisers. We secured from G.Q. the day of Nov. 1, and I went on the six to eight watch. I hit the sack at 9:30 P.M. and G.Q. sounded at 1:30 A.M. Nov. 2, I had no idea what was up until they said prepare for a stiff battle with the Japanese task force trying to get our Marines at Bougainville Island, so by the time G.Q. sounded the Cruisers had been firing for two hours at the intercepting task force. I was at my battle station handling powder 5, all hatches secure and ventilation shut off. I was sweating during battle so much that after my pants felt five pounds heavier than they really were. I was sweating because I was scared. Either God must have given me courage. Now get this, this is our third major battle in twenty four hours. The one on Buka, Treasury, now the one on the Jap task force. Mother or Dad, whomever I am reading this to, I was scared to death, that means I could hardly get my breath twice. We were chasing two Jap cans, we fired torpedoes, and got them both, I was standing by with a powder in my hand I was knocked up against the bulkhead. We were hit by another can, it was ours, we were dodging a torpedo. The captain yelled, "Stand by for a ram." It was coming at us at thirty-two knots and we were doing thirty-five and that is doing some on the sea. It seems like eighty to ninety miles per hour. The captain yelled, "Stand by for a ram," the captain quick witted shot out on the port side, the left otherwise, to avoid a head on collision. God was with him. It side swiped us (Spence) and scared the livin' hell out of us. We tipped on the starboard side so much the fellows stationed at the twenties* were hanging on for life with water up to their stomachs. It damaged the starboard motor whale boat and the prop that held the forty millimeter guns and the after engine room, but I was over the scare in a hurry when I soon found out we sunk a P.T. boat and two cans, to the credit of the Thatcher, then daylight fell. I was scared to death at first of the Jap Torpedo planes over head. Soon, "Stand by!!" "Stand by!!" "Two planes coming in for us on the port bow." We were stranded out there in the middle of the battle with the foot** tied on behind us, the only casualty the fan tail was blown off. 36 men sacrificed, but as the planes were coming in we blacked them out like lights. Then more came overhead. I yelled "God Spare us please," and forty-eight P-38 fighter planes, ours of course, saved us and were knocking them down left and right. A tug came along and released us from the "foot"—we could only make seven knots with out her and with her three knots. Because of our after engine room. The casualties were little to us but very big to the yellow Japs. Out of their seven ships (four cans, three cruisers) were sunk six. The captain demanded to give the seventh a chase, my heart in my mouth, but the admiral in charge said, "No, captain, you have

---

*20mm antiaircraft guns.
**The USS Foote, another destroyer.

done your share and besides you only have a little fuel left and all our fish are fired and only ninety-two rounds of ammunition left." So here we are right at this moment with the foot damaged, a tug pulling her, and two destroyers—the other four that refueled in Purvis Bay had relieved us—and I went to the top side just to look at the damage and I saw the sea was black with oil for miles around, the Thatcher takes a victory. Me with hopes of getting my well proud earned stars for four major engagements in twenty-four hours' time. The longest sea battle of World War II in the South Pacific Area. The sad part is we are not back in port yet to refuel and it will be tomorrow sometime, expecting air attack on us two helpless ships any moment, the sad part is the *"Spence"* that rammed us lost all of her oil and laid out there in the midst of the battle just firing her best sitting still. The Captain is trying to find out what has become of her. *Now get this,* on Oct. 31 we started out to make our attack on Buka Island and we made it at midnight, starting Nov. 1st and at 6 A.M. we made another attack on Treasury, a Jap Air Base. We pumped salvo after salvo into the island. I'll admit the Japs have better star shells than we have, they flared up the night in sunlight brightness and they were firing on us but we got out five salvoes to their one. Dad, I am telling you I went through a nightmare. We outsmarted them by a long shot. They figured we would bombard the islands and beat it, but no, we stayed out, or up, and waited for them a full day and that night our plane spotter and gave us their course and said "now, go get 'em"; so here we were four cans and four cruisers. The cans including us (the "foot," *"Thatcher"*, Spence, and _____*) went ten miles ahead of the cruisers in to get these "rats." Finally the other four cans returned from refuelling at Purvis Bay, but before they got there we went into battle. We split up in twos and the *Thatcher* and *Spence* paired off together after four enemy cans and after firing and firing, we shot a full salvo of torpedoes, ours alone got two cans and a cruiser, then this moment of sure death came to me. When they said, "Stand by for a ram" the Spence was giving orders to turn right and so we did but they turned wrong and they were heading head on into us, we were dodging torpedoes all this time they went in front, and to the rear of us, and even under us; so, the Captain turned to avoid a head on. God was with him, we side swiped. I yelled, "Stein, we're hit!!" I grabbed my life jacket and was ready to abandon ship but the orders to commence firing were given, we fired for an hour and a half straight. We were sinking them left and right. Their salvoes were bursting over head and all around us. The ships that have been ours or with us in all kinds of duty were getting torpedoed. They blew the fantail off the front, what a feeling I had because I am below deck in the fantail. Their casualty count was 36 men, I saw them laid on the deck near sick bay and

---

*Though Mariner left this space blank in the original, the destroyer he left unnamed here was the *Converse*.

a sight that almost shocked me to death. When we left at 5:30 in the morning there was oil in the water for miles around and a couple of ships burning ready to sink. We got an air alarm following and the Foot was tied on to us and orders were to sit still in the water, and open fire on any intercepting planes; we knocked down a few, don't forget, we are damaged plenty too. With our starboard side smashed in. Now we are heading for "Kula Calf."

Nov. 3 [1943]

We just left Kula Calf, from refueling and an estimate of our damage. I am hoping, in fact all of us, including the captain are in hopes for Mare Island navy Yards. This great battle took place southwest of Bougainville and thirty minutes' flying time from Jap air base in Rabaul. Still we are in dangerous waters. May God continue being with us.

Nov. 4 [1943]

Thursday—We arrived safe and sound in Tulagi, Purvis Bay, and pulled up alongside the *Spence,* the ship we rammed in the terrible nightmare. She was damaged a bit on her port side. The barrels of her forties were knocked off and her depth charge casings were rammed also, her hull was in perfect condition. The Commodore claims it was our fault. Our Captain at this moment is in a conference with the big shots now. The Thatcher went between two Cruisers, one ours, and the other a Jap's, we had been ready to fire our torpedoes but the captain gave word "hold your fire," "we are not positive where *the Spence* is," and then came the terrible moment of the closing of our ship and the *Spence.*

The Admiral told our Captain Lapman to be ready for action as soon as possible. The ship will only turn over on one screw (Propeller) and the Captain said I want this ship taken in dry dock and repaired, but they said we are in terrible need of you in this Bougainville battle which is still going on. He said, "All right, if you want it that way we will go out tomorrow night on one screw," which means we can only make eighteen knots at the most. To me which is suicide. I am a scared rabbit right now because the can on the right was hit by two Jap torpedo bombs, one went right in the stack and the other right through the fan tail killing 39 men, and the "foot" on the left with her fan tail blown off, killing eighteen and one officer, our Doctor is over right now trying to help find the bodies of some of them. I just came down and had been only 70 feet away from those mangled bodies. Imagine this one fellow was thrown from the twenties right on the flag pole in front of number two stack. Well, I am praying to God something will have turned up that we will have to go to Boston Navy Yard.

Nov. 5 [1943]

Field day about the ship. I heard with my own ears that the Captain got his
answer from Washington. The Captain said give me Boston Navy Yards or I
go out on one screw, and the ammunition was cancelled, so no torpedoes and
projectiles and powder came aboard. We came in with only 83 rounds left.

Nov. 9 [1943]

We reached our destination safely with the convoy of ships, Espiritu Santo,
New Hebrides, we arrived at nine A.M. The gates were closed to us for there
are more ships in there, so we remained around for five more hours till one
o'clock and then went in for fuel and mail, we almost had to stand by for
another crash—we just missed the tanker by inches due to the waves, and only
one propeller screw. The Captain tore his hair out yelling "Where in hell is
that damn tug?" We managed to tie up while refueling we got our mail. The
tug came to take us away at four-thirty, we are now heading with a troop ship
for New Caledonia or Pearl Harbor, I am hoping to get home soon, "God
please keep us safe," After all our ship is seriously damaged.

Nov. 10 [1943]

We hit the biggest storm I have ever seen with my own eyes and have been in,
as you know the side of this ship is wrecked, the frames are cracked. Well, I
hit my sack at seven for I had the four to eight watch. I was awakened by a hell
of a noise. I got up, then coxswain Hargrave followed me up to the topside on
the fantail, the noise was that the powder canisters broke loose from their positions. I told Hargrave I can't sleep with these canisters rolling around, it's
enough listening to the side creaking loose all the time; so, I said I'm going
out and put them back in place. He said, "Dick, don't be a fool and go out
there." I got on my rain gear and went out in the storm, the rain was coming
down hard and cold against me. I got all the cans in place except the last two,
I just picked one up and the ship hit a swell and the wind blew me across the
deck, I had no control of myself. We did not have the inner life line up, the
outer line caught me, I hit it right square with my stomach. Hargrave yelled,
"Dick!! Dick!! where are you?" I could not answer because I hit the rail with
such force it knocked the wind out of me, but he finally found me hanging on
the line with my head and arms on the outside of the ship. I was so scared I
thought my time was up because we hit the next swell, the fantail shot up in
the air and the bow went down like a submarine. It threw me up against number 5 guns. I finally managed to get up with Hargrave's help, He took me in

the crew's head. I was not hurt except that I had the wind knocked out of me. I was so scared afterwards that I did not sleep below but stayed up thinking what could happen to the ship if it went through much more. The following day was the same storm of course, and we spotted a sub, which fifteen minutes before the Captain was notified was an enemy sub in this area. It was surfaced. Must have been charging its batteries. We opened fire on her, she crash dived, we could not stay round to see if we sank it because we were responsible for three thousand Marines who were the passengers on the troop ship and besides the condition we were in, the starboard side and the terrible storm.

Nov. 12 [1943]

We arrived in Noumea, New Caledonia, we are in dry dock. They have taken the starboard screw off and are going to set it on the fantail, we are supposed to pull out in the morning at eight o'clock, P.S. I haven't slept for two days and nights. I feel like I am eighty years old, a little nervous and probably look to be a hundred. I am praying to God that we go to the states.

ACTION IN NORTH AFRICA

LETTER HOME FROM ROBERT L. MASON[6]

American ground forces saw their first extended action against the European Axis in North Africa, where U.S. and British troops landed ("Operation Torch") in November 1942. Six months later the Allied forces captured the last German and Italian forces on the African continent. Here an American infantryman recounts his experiences in the campaign and includes his personal views on war after months of grueling operations.

May 20, 1943

Dearest Jerry:

Now it can be told, our experiences in N. Africa are no longer secret; Africa is ours. The Germans have been killed, have fled or are prisoners of war.

I can't remember all of the questions that you have previously asked me about various things or experiences in N. Africa, but I will, without doubt, answer some of them in this letter.

All of our time spent in Casablanca, bivouacked on the outskirts of the town, was devoted to the furthering of our training in preparation for what was to follow. We did get to visit the town a number of times on pass. I was there several times myself as color bearer on the guard of honor for such notables as President Roosevelt, P.M. Churchill, General Patton, General Giraud and the Sultan of Morocco. I have photographs of myself on these occasions in my possession but cannot send them!

From Casablanca we moved east to Rabat, a larger and more beautiful city; where we prepared for our long trek across N. Africa to Constantine and surrounding enemy territory. The long journey was made by train, some riding on flat cars and others in the 40 and 8 box cars (40 men or 8 horses). Upon arriving there, we unloaded our vehicles and journeyed up to Tebessa and from there to Sened, where we encountered our first real stiff opposition. We were supporting the advances of our troops with artillery while at the same time the enemy was bombing and strafing us at frequent intervals. In two days our forces took the town of Sened, and we moved into position near Maknassy; took the town after a short battle and moved into it. The enemy stood ground and held us there for quite a spell! The enemy held the string of mountains to our north, east and south-east and offered bitter resistance, blasting our positions with 88 millimeter artillery, mortars, tank fire, and from the air with bombs and at times strafed us. This was the real McCoy at last. We were no longer rookies, but men of experience. On the range to our North, the enemy had several gun emplacements in a large, abandoned phosphate mine that seemed almost impossible to knock out. They held every advantage in that they were dug in well on the opposite side of the mountains, whereas we were open to attack on all sides moving in across the open plains.

It was at Maknassy that the American boys learned the value of the fox hole (a modern version of the slit trench). When the going was toughest, it was necessary to seek protection offered by the fox hole. It offers greatest protection from bombings and artillery fire, unless scored upon by a direct hit! The path of the American soldier can be traced throughout Africa by the continuous line of fox holes and slit trenches.

After dislodging the Germans from the Maknassy area, we headed toward Sidi Bou Bid to support U.S. forces at Fiad pass; later on we moved northward a great distance and fought at Beja, La Calle and to south east of Beja, where we occupied the right flank on an attack on hill 609, which was one of the strongest of all enemy positions. From atop hill 609 it was possible for the enemy to see everything taking place in the surrounding territory for miles around. This was a bloody battle for the doughboys but cleared the path for the advance of our U.S troops to the town of Mateus, which we took very quickly and proceeded on to Bizerte, a large seaport on the Gulf of Tunis and a little to the N.W. of it. We offered support many times between then and the next town of Ferryville, where our final opposition was encountered and the stream of German prisoners began moving toward our lines. They were trapped by the British, French and American forces; even those trying to evacuate by water were caught and taken prisoner!

I suppose you have read from the newspapers the accurate report on the number of prisoners taken in N. Africa.

I have a German cap and a belt buckle, both bearing the swastika, also a beautiful German Luger (a pistol), all laid aside to bring home when that day comes.

Some were saying we would come home after the battle for Africa. I guess they were expecting too much, as we are probably needed elsewhere.

War is just as horrible as they tell you it is. Don't let anyone tell you it isn't. One either kills or gets killed—it doesn't possess all the glamour that the movies and story books give it—although it is exciting and is fun at times.

Into what strange land our next journey will take us, only God knows. He will be with us there too!

I will close this little note with a "hello" to everyone back home—just figured you and the others would like to know about a few of my past experiences! I will write you again soon.

> Love and kisses
> *Bob*

ACTION ON THE GERMAN FRONT
LETTER HOME FROM MARIO DAL CANTON[7]

Combat was sometimes so traumatic that men could not speak of it to their loved ones. Notice the nonchalance and emphasis on minor details in this letter, written by a GI fresh from a week in the frontlines.

April 8 [1945]

Somewhere in Germany

Dearest Sis,

Well, I guess I have been through what you might call one week of combat. I joined the last week while they were at rest, we were on the go for a week, now we are off again for a little while. I wrote to you last Sun. I have not received any mail as yet, but I should be getting some soon.

If you write home, Sis, let them know I wrote to you. I am not sure I will have time to today.

I have several souvenirs which I would like to send home. One is a German camera which I will send to you if I can, you can keep it for me.

I had a nice time a few days ago in a town we took, we were using a house in the far corner of town as an outpost, the place had everything a guy dreams about, feather beds, bath, hot water, I was there for only half a day but you can bet I enjoyed myself.

This is all for now, Sis.

Lots of Love
M.D.

ACTION ON THE ITALIAN FRONT

DIARY OF CASIMER PRUNCHUNAS[8]

An infantryman's diary relates the daily grind of combat. Covering less than three weeks of action that occurred months apart, these excerpts describe no great battles. Rather, they relate the seemingly endless process of patrols, limited advances, and relief from the line for rest and the inexorable return to combat. But death or maiming in a minor engagement was just as possible, and frightening to those in the lines, as it was in the battles that grabbed the newspaper headlines. And the rain was just as wet, the mud just as cold, a fox hole just as important.

May 19, 1944

Alerted this morning to be ready to move out at a moment's notice. Told to get rid of all old letters and anything that would identify our unit. Warm sunny day. Moved into Formia. Rain at night.

May 20, 1944

Moved into Gaeta and had road reconnaissance mission and to look for Jerry snipers. People are very grateful and threw bouquets of flowers (roses), cherries and bottles of wine. We also picked up all sorts of souvenirs in the blasted out houses.

May 21, 1944

Still in Gaeta. Went rummaging around and picked up some more junk. Also saw a woman with a leg blown off by a mine and a boy who lost both legs. Some of our men then cleaned out the mines. Pretty nasty work and extremely dangerous.

May 22, 1944

Today we received our first casualties when Lt. Hargrove, Pfc. Workman, T/5 Hearn and Pvt. M. Carter were wounded. Hearn and Workman accidentally by our men. The others by Jerry. Still in the town of Gaeta but moved out to Fondi in the evening.

May 23, 1944

Moved out in the morning and acted as a relay crew between the 337th and 338th infantry regiments. Stayed here all night. A battery of 105 howitzers firing about 50 yards away from our position.

May 24, 1944

Moved to guard a tunnel not far from Terraccina and saw my first Dead German soldier. Took a picture of him. There were also a lot of dead Italians in the tunnel, with many dead Krauts.

May 25, 1944

Another day still patrolling the mountains. Not much action, but we captured a few German prisoners.

May 26, 1944

Went on an uneventful patrol up a mountain, and the day was nice and warm. Getting back, we started for a mission at Sossieno. And passing through Terraccena, we saw the mess that our artillery had made of these Italian towns. We bivouacked for the night, and about 0200 in the morning, German artillery opened up on us and killed Pvt. Quinn and Pvt. McCarthy. Also wounding Holloway and Vance. These were the first casualties killed in the troop. Shortly afterward we pulled out to another spot. I slept through the whole barrage and heard nothing. Guess my number isn't up yet.

May 27, 1944

Today we were given a day of rest. It could be due to the fact of trying to get us to forget about last night. It is a shame that such nice kids should die. McCarthy had previously crossed a mine field six times and gotten help for Lt. Hargrove and others injured May 22. And he had a wife with a kid coming along in a couple of months. Quinn was single. Artillery is still battering the Jerry lines, and as of today, we are 17 miles from Rome.

September 21, 1944

Cool cloudy morning. Cleaned up all of our weapons and just laid around. Plenty of our vehicles are moving up to the front. Mostly artillery units. Had a PX and spent $1.45 for candy, soap, etc. There's a couple of women here that the boys are trying to make. They are wearing no under-pants, but as yet, no one has succeeded to crash their defenses. It rained on and off during the day. At night, while I was eating salami (which I had received from home) with French fried potatoes, we were told that we were moving up in the morning.

September 22, 1944

Got up at 0430 and moved out about dawn. Were to move to the town of Firenzuola. But as the bridges were blown out, the whole platoon wasn't able to go forward. So three jeeps and an armored car went out forward. And I was one of the ones on this patrol. We had to stop a couple of times to duck Jerry shells. But none of them came real close. Then we stayed in Firenzuola for the night, and the town was really plastered by mortars and artillery. But we were in a very deep, solid cellar, and it only tended to scare us some. During the day Cpl. Hagen and Pvt. Diorio were hit by 88mm Jerry shell fragments. Hagen got it in the back, and Diorio got hit on the wrist. This town is really battered up, and the Krauts just keep shelling it.

September 23, 1944

We moved out before dawn to take up positions on the left flank of the 338th. But nothing happened at our position the whole day. Only shelling of the town. We got some bad news when we were told that Lt. Scott had been killed by an 88mm shell at 1330. He had stepped out of the basement to do his duty (urinate) when the shell exploded and killed him. Also shocked T/5 Malkowsi and Pvt. Coppinger who were in the basement. In the evening, while on duty, I heard somebody walking down the road and went down to investigate. I came back with three German prisoners aged 16, 17 and 22. They were members of the 1060th regiment of the 363rd Division. Then in the night we moved up another half mile to take up another position. Pretty quiet and nothing happening. Artillery action during the night.

September 24, 1944

Boys are a bit jittery over the death of Lt. Scott. But they can't stop the war on account of a dead Lieutenant. Haven't been able to wash for three days and had very little water to drink also. Chow was late in getting here too. We are now in a building and sleeping just like rats. And the place actually smells. The fellows were ready to leave this house, when Jerry shells started to come in close by. But we only moved down to the cellar. The day was cloudy and drizzling in the morning and cool and a bit sunny in the afternoon. At night, we set up gun positions close by and again nothing happened. Drizzled during the night.

September 25, 1944

Sunny warm day, and we were told to pack up and get ready to move out at 1300. But just like the Army, we waited around till well after dark and moved out at 2300. Getting back to Firenzuola, we parked our vehicles at the cemetery. Then with Capt. Thompson leading us (2nd and 3rd platoons), we went to relieve part of the 338th. It was a fast march over a couple of high hills and believe me, we were all pretty tired when we got there a little after dawn.

September 26, 1944

We dug in, and just about all of the men went to sleep. Jerry was still shelling Firenzuola, and we could hear the shells going off. And a few shells landed around us—but did no damage. Bonomo, Sgt. Buck and myself have a beautiful hole dug and expect to stay very comfortable. At night Sgt. Buck took a six man patrol to make contact with the 91st Division. And it rained and got them all soaking wet. But I stayed dry. And during the night it was pretty quiet. Just the artillery dueling back and forth.

September 27, 1944

Still in the same positions, and it rained again during the night. Most of the fellows' holes are filled with water, and they all feel pretty miserable. But I'm still dry in our hole. As we have a telephone with us, we don't have to leave our hole. And so it's OK.

September 28, 1944

It's a rainy morning, and I had to go back to Paglio with two other fellows to bring the rations for the platoon. It was about two miles, and the road was very muddy, and the footing was very slippery. And the way back was uphill, and I did get a good workout. Then about 1000 we were told that we were to move back to Firenzuola. And we had a lot of fun sloshing through the mud and rain. And we crossed one swollen river by walking over trucks that were parked in the river. The current was swift, and it was almost impossible to cross just by fording. Getting back to Firenzuola, we made our bivouac in the cemetery and in a nearby house. I made my home in a crypt with about ten

Four soldiers of the 35th Div. in jeep with graffiti: "Heaven, Hell, or Home." (Courtesy of the Dwight D. Eisenhower Library, Mr. and Mrs. Frank J. Kozak Collection.)

other fellows. In another crypt we built a fire to dry ourselves and our clothing. We also had new OD's issued to us and also were issued winter underwear. It was really a treat. I got a very good night's sleep. And the artillery sounded far, far away.

'Tain't a fit night for man or Hitler.
—Fibber McGee

D-DAY RECOUNTED

LETTER HOME FROM ALFRED F. BIRRA[9]

The plethora of emotions the soldier felt in the anticipation of and then engagement in battle manifest themselves in this combat engineer's account of the early morning hours of the Allied invasion of the Normandy beaches, better known simply as "D-Day." The author's reversion to the present tense in relating the actual assault suggests how vivid those events still were five weeks after they occurred, and one can only wonder when D-Day slipped into the past tense for him.

July 12, 1944

France

Hello, Honey,

This makes the third time I've started this letter and always something comes up to interfere with its writing. We're on a new front, and I've just returned after a rather hectic night with Jerry. It seems we wanted to build a bridge at a certain spot, and Jerry, he didn't like the idea at all, at all. We built the bridge, all right, but it wasn't Jerry's fault that we did. I hardly know what to write about since I can't say anything about the present campaign. Perhaps a few highlights about the last one might prove interesting, altho you've read all about it by now.

You may recall a few months ago that I wrote you that the company had been detached from the battalion and was on some special work. At the time I couldn't say with whom, naturally enough, but now I can. For six weeks we attended special training in assault and amphibious work. Upon conclusion of this training, we were attached to the Fourth Infantry Division, which, as you probably know, was the first unit to land in France. We became part of what is known in the Army as a Combat Team. A Combat Team is composed roughly of a regiment of Infantry, Engineers, Artillery, and other attached technical units. Our particular team was chosen out of the Division to spear-head the Invasion. Thus we became the first American Troops to land on the coast of France. For months we practiced on ground which, altho we didn't know it at the time, was almost identical to what we found here. Every "dry run" or exercise was carried out to the smallest detail. We went through every phase of what we knew would one day be in store for us. The only difference was that on the "dry runs" we encountered no opposition. Thus, when early in May we began preparations, no one knew for certain whether it was the real thing or just another exercise. It was not until two days before we embarked and were issued our maps that we knew for certain it was the real thing.

We had been aboard ship for three days, living a life of ease and luxury and formulating our final plans, when the General came aboard. He made an address to the troops via the P.A. and left sealed orders with the commander of troops. These orders contained the information as to D-Day and H-Hour. At about five o'clock on the evening of June 5th, it was announced to us that at 0630 on the following morning we would land on the coast of France. The first platoon and the commanding officer of Co. C 237th Engineers would land with the first assault wave. The remainder would come ashore in suc-ceeding waves. We were breeching a concrete seawall and clearing passage-ways of obstacles and mines so that the tanks that were landing with us could get off the beach. A very vital point since without the support of the tanks with their armor and heavy guns, the Infantry would be too busy protecting its own skin to do any real good. Altho we knew most of this, it still came as somewhat of a shock, and we set about making last minute preparations.

There weren't many who got much sleep that night of June 5th. For the most part, we sat around, talked, played cards, drank coffee and did the usual things a man does when he is worried and a little scared and doesn't want to show it. At 0230 in the morning, breakfast was served, of which most of us partook heartily, since we knew it would be, if not our last meal, at least the last for quite a few hours or perhaps days. At 0330 we began the business of debarking. The weatherman had been, as is the wont with that particular breed, very wrong in his prediction. Instead of the smooth, glassy sea he pre-dicted, it was very rough and cold, and the night was inky black so that a man had to feel his way about the ship, stumbling and cursing softly. The small landing craft were loosened from the davits, and each absorbed its crew of men and equipment and was lowered into a black sea, which seemed to reach up with hungry arms to drag the frail craft down. How can I describe the feel-ing which grips you at this moment? Kent echoed my feeling exactly when he said that this precise moment, when the assault boat was being lowered from the mother ship, was the loneliest time in his life. No one says a word except the man at the cables. As the boat goes down the rail, the ship disappears, and with a slap that jars everyone aboard, the craft hits the water. The cables are cast off, and now you're entirely on your own and alone.

We chugged away, and in a few seconds the large mother ship became just a darker blob of darkness and then disappeared from view entirely. It was now time to start for the rendezvous area, where we would meet the rest of the craft that made up our wave. In just a few minutes the spray from the waves slapping the bow and sides of the boat had us all thoroughly drenched, and the men began to snap out of their lethargy only to find themselves miserably seasick. I can safely say that of the thirty men aboard, at least twenty were seasick. I myself didn't have time, nor could I display any form of weakness by getting sick. We were soon at the rendezvous area, and the boats comprising the wave got into their proper positions and began to circle. We were about six miles offshore at this point. Soon things began to happen that made even the most wretched sit up with interest. The show had started. And it started with the Navy. In the distance on all sides we could see the huge sleek forms of battleships and destroyers vomiting flames of fire as their fourteen and sixteen inch guns opened fire. The air was filled with deafening roars and the screams of shells. Then the coastal defense batteries opened up and added to the general hubbub. We had no sooner become accustomed to this when over the noise of the battleships we heard the roar of hundreds of motors, the air corps was coming in. And come in they did, literally in waves, and made for the shore and their targets. That their bombs were effective was evidenced by the fires that soon lit up the entire black night. That the enemy was striking back was also soon evidenced by that ack ack that started to crosshatch the sky. The entire picture defies description by my limited senses, and no matter how retentive, I could not possibly have absorbed the entire picture and all of the occurrences. But time to get busy now. Dawn has broken, and dimly in a haze of smoke we can see the beach. Now it's our turn. Men scrambled to their feet, equipment is adjusted, lifebelts made more secure, for all around us artillery shells are falling and already several boats have been hit. Rifles are loaded and the safety taken off. The shore is now right off the bow. The coxswain signals me that we're about to touch down, the ramp is lowered and the Sgt. and I stepped off into four feet of water. I look behind, and the men are already off the boat and scattered for protection against the bullets which are singing around us but for the most part hitting the water. It was a hell of a feeling. We had about 500 yards of water to cross, we couldn't run cause the water was too deep, we couldn't crouch, we couldn't do anything except just what we did. Wade on into shore. Finally we made it, we were on the beach and could begin to fight back and to do our work. How well we did it you have read about in the papers told to you by men more gifted than myself. How well we did is also evidenced by the citations we've won. One for the entire battalion, and a separate one for C Company and for A Company. Sometime when I can I'll write, or better yet, tell you about more that happened, both humorous and tragic. Like the Colonel who came over to me in the midst of heavy fire and said, "Captain, how in the hell do you load this rifle?", or like the time that Kent and I were lying in a ditch. I was getting a light from Kent's cigarette when a shell landed so close the concussion blew us about a foot apart but both of us got up unhurt.

I really must go now, darling, . . .

Al.

A GUNNER IN GERMANY

POEM BY CHAS RIORDAN— "THE ARTILLERY IN GERMANY"[10]

A crew member of an artillery battery wrote this piece in odd moments between fire missions. While perhaps not a literary masterpiece, this doggerel captures the flavor of the tiring but strangely impersonal war of a gunner.

THE ARTILLERY IN GERMANY 11-20-44
PART OF 135 GUN SECTION IN A SHACK

Outside it rains, it's almost sleet
So we come inside to absorb some heat
I sit down and prepare to write
By Salerno's M-1, smoke pot light
My back against the wall, my blanket's underneath
This life is not so bad, it's really quite a treat.
Let it rain outside, let it beat against the wall,
It can blow for all it's worth but it can't hurt me at all.
I reach for my box and I begin to write
It's the twentieth of November, in Germany, at nite
I finish the heading, then a tinkle ripples the air,
The telephone is ringing, the guard will soon be there.
I listen very closely, hoping not to hear
That voice that takes me every nite
Away from you, my dear.

But as I expected, it soon split the air
"Fire mission, you guys, let's get out there!"
Sgt. Forte who was almost dressed
Is the first to hit the floor
But Novak wasn't far behind as he reached the door
I'm very busy as I'm struggling with my cap, my coat, my shoes,
And last, but not the least by far, my overshoes.
Soon, I'm out there pitching, there's a job to be done
It takes the best from all of us, for this war to be won.
The net is pulled back, and the breech is open,
The tray slid in place to receive that token.
That three hundred and sixty-five pound token of death
That Hitler has asked for along with the rest
The rest of those "supermen" who have followed his rule,
Those guys who since the age of ten, have gone to his school.
For the commands we waited, in silence, in the rain
Battery adjust! Shell H. E.! Fuse, Quick! they came
Base Deflection, Left 2–4 ! one round!
Quadrant 6–2–3!, and then came the sound.
The sound of the shell, being slid up the tray
Ready home! Ready Ram! I hope this will pay
For Batson, Boldue, and Allen, who aren't with us anymore
And my skinned nose, bumped chin, and head that was sore.
The powder charge followed and now the breech will close
Rebe calls, "Loaded!!" and the tube arose
I level the bubbles and then holler "Set!"
But Cormier can't see the stakes, he's not ready yet.
Someone in the darkness holds the net steady
Now Cormier sees them and yells "Ready"
"Charley, one is ready" as it goes through the wire
We wait quiet and tensely, for the command "Fire"
Six minutes delay, again we're at ease
Six minutes to wait, time to bat the breeze,
We talk about the mud, or the weather to kill time
Mike fell in a foxhole, he's covered in grime
The time is getting closer, we get the command "stand by"
Up on our toes, hands on our ears, soon the shell will fly
"Fire!" it finally comes, the lanyard is pulled tight
Our big gun flashes, thunders and the shell is out of sight.
Now I'm back again, to finish the letter I started
Probably in another hour, once more we'll be parted

But I'd rather be parted in letters, while here
Than be separated once again, at a later year.

By PFC. Chas Riordan
West Springfield, Mass.

A COMBAT NURSE IN ITALY

DIARY OF 2ND LIEUTENANT MARY FISCHER, A.N.C.[11]

*Mary Fischer was a combat nurse who saw action at Anzio.
Cursed by some as pampered and frivolous, revered by many as
models of American womanhood, the U.S Army's female nurses
were frequently the center of attention in the combat theaters. Six
weeks of Fischer's diary entries demonstrate that, above all, the
nurses in forward areas were true combat veterans.*

Sat. Jan. 1, 1944

Capua, Italy

Terrific hurricane all day. To top it all, we had hangovers—cold—had to struggle to keep the tents up. Several times today the tents caught on fire. Was glad
to go to my tent at 7 P.M. The storm subsided at 7 P.M. We had Mass today at
4:30 in the O.R.

Sunday. Jan. 2 [1944]

Tonite went to an R.A.F. dinner and had a typical circus. The "powder room"
was outdoors and was fixed up real cute. Had palm trees in the entry. Wood
floor—lantern—back rest—great big canvas Red Cross back for the stool, etc.
Dinner was toast and sardines, potatoes, beans, peas and pork roast—apple
tart c̄* sauce, figs, oranges, apples, candy, choc., cofee. Drinks: whiskey, vermouth and cherry brandy. My partner was Terry—the C.O. Danced.

Monday, Jan. 3 [1944]

Al Chekanski paid me a surprise visit today. Was delighted to see him—so he
and 2 other officers came back tonite. Andy and I entertained them in our
tent. We went to a Ward and got Tom Donovan, who was a pt. there. Had
pop-corn, fudge that Cele sent me, coffee and cookies. Drank vermouth,

---

*Abbreviation for "with," often used by those in the medical profession.

cognac and cherry brandy but very little of each. Closed up today!

Jan. 4 [1944]

All thru c̄ work here at Capua. Orders not here yet—in meantime we'll "rest." Packing, etc.

Jan. 7 [1944]

 Orders to leave tomorrow. My watch is with the British officers. Andy and I got transportation at the motor pool (driver O'Hara) to go to their camp after my watch. What a time we had—knew only that it was a British camp and the C.O. was Maj. Terry. Got lost—inquired all over—finally stopped a Brigadier Gen. who directed us—found the place (Maj. Terry Willett). I spent the evening packing.

Jan. 8 [1944]

Left camp (Capua) and went to Staging Area at Naples. Staying in a sulfur bath bldg, called "Terme"—21st Gen. Hosp. Place reeks of sulfur. Funny Italian writing on walls in rooms—also what we call tomb stones.

Jan. 10 [1944]

Andy and I went to 21st Gen. Hosp to get a pass for Naples—as N. is off limits to G.I.'s due to V.D. and Typhus.

Jan. 11 [1944]

Set out to find Willie today—Andy and I. At the P.B.S. inquired—no luck. Went to 3rd A.S.A.C. where they said Willie is at Pamigliano. At the Dispatch Office, they gave us transportation, and we took off. Arrived at the 10th Sq. at noon. Willie and his pals took us to their tent and brought us a tray of food. Visited all afternoon—had supper—then started drinking "Vesuvius"—mixture of Rum, cherry brandy, cognac and lemon juice—also had champagne. Got a "wee bit" high—then set out for our abode at Naples. First Sgt. and Willie took us in a jeep. Left at 2:30 A.M. and what a terrible time we had finding the darn place. Inquired all over—got to it at 6:30 A.M. We were about frozen by then.

Jan. 12 [1944]

Had meeting at 8 A.M. Got up for that then back to bed until dinner time. Meeting at 1:00 got new sleeping bags. Slept all afternoon until supper time. Bath tonite fixed hair. Manicure and bed early. Had 13 letters today.

Jan. 13 [1944]

Feeling much improved. Wrote letters all day. Got 10 letters. Cute one from
Sr. Edith. This evening Willie came after us and we went out to his Camp.
Scads of fun. Italian prisoner waited table on us. He had cooked delicious
spaghetti and served champagne.

Jan. 15 [1944]

Andy and I washed our hair today at the Sulphur Spring. The water was boiling hot. Some Italian kids poured oceans of water on our heads. Slight earth-
quake today.

Jan. 16 [1944]

Sunday. Went to Mass in an old bldg. Painted walls of shepherd playing bag-
pipe to his sheep.

Jan. 19 [1944]

Andy and I went on detached service at 21st Gen. Hosp. Hate it. 3 days of it.
Lots of "goons".

Jan. 22 [1944]

Willie came in this evening. Visited about an hr. or so. Promised to come after
us tomorrow. Packed tonite.

Jan. 23 [1944]

Sunday. Plaster keeps falling on us. Great big chunks of it fell on beds.
Ventilation is atrocious and many girls are ill. Willie did not show up today.

Jan. 24 [1944]

Nine mo. overseas—4 mo. in Italy. Andy, Gallagher, Cornellson and I went for
a walk to take pictures. On our way to "Aqua Apollo" the ack-ack suddenly
started flying fast and furious whizzed right past us. We got panicky and dashed
back. Then wandered on and finally saw a Vino Shop- after entering we saw a
couple of G.I.'s eating fresh eggs—so we also ordered fresh eggs (2 each) and
fried potatoes. Cost us 75¢ each but it was worth it. Clean place—even had
white tablecloth on table. We were worried the kids mite be leaving so we
dashed back to the "Terme." We're on a 2 hr. alert. Came back at 11 A.M. and
loafed until dinner time. Put a sign on door "Please Be Quiet—rest hour" and
went to bed till 3:30 then put sign on door "Please close door easy and preserve

heads of your fellow-workers as well as the plaster, signed the Sulfur Plaster Kids." After supper had an air raid. They were trying to bomb Caserta.

Jan. 25 [1944]

Awakened at 2 A.M. by air raid. Dressed hurriedly but stayed in bed till it was over. This A.M. the Italians knocked the plaster down in our room. Went to 23rd Gen. Hosp. for show, but there wasn't one. Tonite made fudge—no good. Another air raid at 9:30 P.M.

Jan. 26 [1944]

Mary Jane Shilven's birthday, so we celebrated in our room, with white wine and champagne. The Sulfur-Plaster girls did it up right—drank to everybody. Had an air raid around 1 A.M.—no one even bothered to dress.

Jan. 27 [1944]

At 11 A.M., eleven of us went up the road and had fried eggs and potatoes. Took up 2 loaves of G.I. bread and coffee. Lane (who had taken C.Q. for me) came up at 11:30 c̄ news we must be packed by 2 P.M. Enjoyed the meal lots. An Italian girl played piano and we all sang. Packed—and waited, as usual. At 3:30 they served us cocoa, sandwiches and pie. At 4:30 we said good bye to the sulfur fumes and went via truck to the docks. At 5:15 we started sailing in an L.C.I. in a convoy of L.S.T. We had several air raids at Sea. Tried sleeping on deck but it was too terribly cold, so went below and finally slept—but still cold.

Jan. 28 [1944]

Travelled all night, air raid again at 7:30 A.M.—saw one plane shot down. No breakfast but they gave us a cup of coffee. Latrine facilities were abominable. Landed at 10:30 at Anzio, Italy—greeted c̄ air raid as we got off the boat. Dashed to a wall, some laid down on ground. Loaded in trucks and off to a staging area. Some 23 of us were dumped off in a God forsaken field c̄ only a small bldg. for shelter. There were 2 very heavy air raids while we waited for transportation. During raids we dashed to the phone and called the 95th. Got to our unit at Nettuno at 1:30 P.M. Glad to see the outfit. Nettuno (Paradise of the Sea) is really a paradise indeed—beautiful place. In peace time was resort for Romans. But the place is right on the Beach. We helped dig our fox holes, right under the beds. Had our pictures taken today by A.P. fellows. Gallagher and I digging fox holes, carrying bags, etc. Went to bed at 8 P.M.— utterly exhausted. Our night clothes are a pair of fatigues. An uneventful night, except for screaming meemies and artillery.

Jan. 29, Sat. [1944]

On duty at 7 A.M. Ward 6. Surgical. Loads of patients—all battle casualties. At 7:30 A.M. had a very heavy air raid. Ship in harbor was bombed. One German plane shot down. We carry our helmets continually. Boys have gone thru hell, they look haggard. Off duty at 7 P.M. Got the news that tonite 4000 German paratroopers were to jump in our area. We were plenty scared—didn't know what to do. Went to bed, exhausted both physically and mentally. At 10 P.M. came *the* air raid and it was the worst one I was ever in. Directly over us and scads of enemy planes. Tremendous am't of firing going on. It was horrible. Andy got in my fox hole c̄ me and we were both shaking for all we were worth. Twice the planes came. Zooming so low and directly over our tents. I was breathless c̄ fear. I shall never forget it. The foxholes were icy cold and damp. Our clothes got muddy. We were just out of it when another raid started and back into the foxholes we went. At 11:30 it was over and we were so terribly tired and scared. Then came the darn "screaming meemies" and they scared us nigh unto death. Zoomed over us and hit their target c̄ a tremendous thud.

Jan. 30 Sunday [1944]

Such weird sounds all nite. One noise sounded almost like owls, we couldn't make out what it was but heard later it was our own anti-aircraft boys signaling to each other. Screaming meemies came at 1:00 and 4:00 and 6:00. At 4 we were awakened by a number of explosions and all of a sudden there was one terrible explosion that shook the ground. Found out later it was an ammunition ship which was hit at the 10 o'clock raid last evening, and our Navy was trying to sink the bombed ship. What a day this is, everyone is weary, looking haggard and spent. But this is no place for a hospital so we evacuated all patients today and packed the wards. All is quiet and peaceful and we went to bed at 7:30—slept all nite. Mass today in a beautiful chapel. We went to Communion.

Jan. 31 [1944]

Got up and packed our things. Rolled our bed rolls again, everything ready by 10 A.M. At 11 we went to some of those gorgeous homes by the Beach and looted the place. Several kids got furniture, etc. I found a beautiful plaque that I took, and a candle holder. The waves of the Sea were dashing up against the house, and our hosp. is across the street—about time we're leaving. Helped the boys c̄ the dinner dishes, took snap shots and left at 1 P.M. for our new home—Hospital Row. The 33rd Field, 56 and 93rd Evac here too. Tents up by 4 P.M. To bed early. Screaming meemies came over all nite—heavy artillery firing all nite.

Feb. 1 Tues [1944]

Working in Wd. 6. Many pts. admitted. Air raid at 4:30 P.M. Screaming meemies all nite—bombs falling all around us—hope they keep missing us.

Feb. 2 [1944]

Started nite duty.

Feb. 4 [1944]

Nite duty—very cold—lots of casualties. Raining heavily today and nite, wind howling, meemies are screeching, sometimes sound as tho' they're coming rite into the tents—pts. get nervous and excited, so do I. I'm scared stiff of them. Artillery firing is very heavy, near, and lights up the sky like a ball of fire, besides that everything is pitch black outdoors, unable to walk.

Feb. 5 [1944]

The artillery firing is fierce tonite—very loud, tent shaking from it. Whistling Susie comes oftener than ever. Scares me pink! Went to bed at 9 A.M. At 9:30 we had an air raid. Gallagher called me: "Mary, put your helmet on"—I had taken nembutal and was rather groggy so I mechanically put on my helmet and pulled covers over me. She said "Get up"—I did. "Get under the bed." I did—and the ice-cold ground made me come to. I dashed back into bed. Had another raid at 2 P.M. I did not even hear it, neither did I hear the heavy firing all day. Got up at 3:45 went to supper—Mass at 5:15 and Comm. To work at 8 P.M. Fried potatoes in Post-Op.

Feb. 6 [1944]

It's so blamed cold, my feet are freezing. Got in "Anzio Express" "Screaming Meemie" casualties. Heavy firing again tonite and the whistling is terrific. At about 4 A.M. we had a bad air raid. But at 5 to 5:30 we had the worst one yet. Planes zoomed above us and one time I thought sure he was coming into the tent, or the bomb was coming in. We all crouched on the ground. The bombs (8 of them) landed in the Eng. bivouac area about 1/4 mile back of the nurses' tents. There are many cuts, etc., in the tent from flak. I picked up a large piece of a 90 m.* gun (shell) which fell in front of me. Off duty at 8 A.M. Mass at 10—and at 11:30 A.M. had another raid. Slept from 12–6 P.M.

---

*Fischer must mean a 90-millimeter shell.

Feb. 7 [1944]

So many air raids last nite—I can no longer keep track of them all. Margaret G.
was sick during nite. I went and woke Sigman to report to her. Little did I dream
it was the last time I'd talk to her. At 8 we went to our tent to sleep—first had
several air raids to keep us awake. Finally at noon the planes came very low and
zoomed over our tent—they were strafing. I woke up and screamed at Mugs
to get up and under the bed we went. Later we discovered bullet holes in our
tent. We went back to sleep and at 3:30 P.M. were again awakened by a terrific
noise, we ducked under our beds and after we heard the planes going by we
looked towards the hosp. area and saw people running, the wash tent down,
etc. but still too dazed to realize. Saw a bunch of mail for us and started reading it when Cornelson came in crying and said the hosp. was bombed. Eight
anti-personnel bombs hit the far end of the area near the place where the large
cloth Red Cross was located. It hit Administration tent, Receiving tent, X-Ray,
Laboratory, Evacuation, Pre-Op, Post-Op, Wards I, II and III. All other tents
received plenty of shell fragments. We found dead and wounded all over.
Everyone got started and first aid was given to those that needed it, pulses were
felt of others and then covered c̄ blankets. It all happened so fast and the patients
from the bombing were evacuated as quickly as possible to the near by hospitals. Miss Blanche Sigman, Chief Nurse, and Carrie Sheetz, Assist., were working side by side in Pre-Op giving blood plasma—they were killed instantly. My
Wardmaster Sgt. Elmer Fry had taken a pt. to X-RAY—he too was killed instantly, as well as almost every one of the X-Ray boys except Shikel and Cravack.
Maj. Truman Chief of XRay has a fract. knee and will return to the States. Miss
Gertrude Morrow, Esther Richards, Burkley, Wingred all hurt. MacDonald badly
hurt—Capt. Stroder killed instantly—also Pvt. Allen. What a terrible day. Took
the starch out of all of us. Mass at 5:30 and Comm. Packed house. Miss Talboy
is acting Chief Nurse. But work must go on and so I went on night duty at 8
P.M. Gallagher went with me. Scared stiff all night. We counted 6 Screaming
Meemies duds going over us, never knowing when and where they would land
and explode. Two nites ago one landed in the enlisted men's area—thank God
it was a dud, another landed back of our tents. All night long we had air raids.
I get so scared of them I shake all over and can't control it a bit. Pfc. Peterson
is on night duty c̄ me and he is grand.

Feb. 8 [1944]

During the night Miss Morrow died—on the O.R. table. She would have been
a life-time invalid. Miss Esther Richards, Red Cross Worker, also died. Lt.
Claywood and Sgt. Smith died. All the tents have thousands of holes, look like
mosquito netting. Many patients were killed. After breakfast we went next
door to the 33rd Field Hosp. to visit Mac and Beavers, Buckley and Wingred.

Had scads of air raids during nite, also "screaming meemies" as well as heavy artillery fighting. Everyone busy digging foxholes, have one, again under my bed. Patients have foxholes in their ward tents also outdoors. The hospital is now acting as a Medical Hosp. since we are handicapped without our boys, X-Ray equipment, all electricians gone. Burns died today. So far out of our unit, 24 deaths and 50 wounded. Went to Saari's tent today to sleep—slept about 1 hr. Had several bad air raids. Tonite Andy went to my Ward c̄ me to sleep there. Several times I had to wake her and tell her to put her helmet on as there was an air raid going on. We had more mail today—not interested. Didn't think the day would come when we wouldn't be interested in mail.

Feb. 9 [1944]

After breakfast we went over to the 33rd Field Hosp. to see Mac, he is so terribly depressed and wants to get out. Beavers is not so good. Everyone is fearfully unhappy and very frightened and apprehensive. Slept about 2 hrs. today as air raids bothered us again. On duty tonite—had 5 air raids during the nite. Andy c̄ me again.

Feb. 10 [1944]

Air raids again today, very little sleep today, about 1 1/2 hr. So tired. Watched bombers go over today and one was shot down, flames. We packed our things today hoping we can get out of this hell hole soon, but must wait for another outfit to take over. About 4 P.M. the 15th Evac. moved in. After supper Andy and I were in our tents sitting on the bed talking, when we all at once heard the most terrific noise which shook the beds and the ground. (Later we discovered it was a German tank which got thru the lines and fired at random.) The shell had landed back of our tent. Andy and I grabbed our helmets and just then another terrific noise (in front of headquarters) or so we thought at the time but I ran to the door and saw black smoke coming from the hospital area. I yelled at Andy "they hit the hospital again" and we ran towards the hosp. A heavy rain and strong wind was in full force, and while we were on our way to the hosp. more shells dropped and we got down on the wet ground, praying and that's all we could do. We ran to the sterilizing room and got down into the foxhole with 2 fellows. The sterilizing room was full of fellows all on the ground. After no more shells came we went to the 33rd Field Hosp. where the shell had fallen—it killed 2 nurses (the Chief Nurse and one girl from the 2nd Aux.). They were evacuating patients to the 56th. We went over there and offered our services, several officers and men and patients were hurt—hit the generator which caused the fire. We went back and to my Ward, told the boys I wasn't coming to the Ward tonite to work as I was too scared, tired and sick both physically and mentally. Back to my tent but was too uneasy and felt guilty, so Andy went c̄ me and

I went on duty again. Boys were so very glad to see me as we had a Ward full of sick patients which were transferred in from the 33rd.

Feb. 11 [1944]

Mess tent is down this A.M. At 10 A.M. we had everything packed - "Hurry and wait." To top it all off it hailed today. We're praying that the wind will calm down so the boats can leave. Andy and I went to the 56th Evac. to say good-bye to Mac and Beaver. Mac is so darned scared. Beaver is bad. Doubt if he's conscious. About 3:30 we had roll call—the entire unit and soon were on trucks and on our way out. We had no regrets leaving this hell hole where we had nothing but sorrow and grief. Little did we dream we would have to leave so many of our people behind. We waited at the docks for hours scared to death, so very tired, so cold, so hungry and so very anxious to get out of the hot spot. We finally embarked on an L.S.T. and set out at 8 P.M. No food, but found some hot water and made hot coffee. Got our life belts, took off our shoes and went to bed. Andy and I slept together in one bunk. Tired unto death—scared—but I was exhausted and slept. During the nite I was awakened several times by loud noises, waited for the "alarm" but none came so went back to sleep. Heard later we were being shot at.

Feb. 12 [1944]

The docks of Naples never looked so good to me before. We are so hungry but so very glad to be back. Italians rowed out to the boat selling their stuff such as potatoes, oranges and nuts. We ate raw potatoes and liked them. Around 9 A.M. we landed, safe and sound, much to our surprise and extreme joy. A long trip c̄ no food. We were on trucks. Stopped at 17th General for 10 min. Old Mt. Vesuvius is very majestic this A.M., beautiful and snow covered. We arrived finally at our destination near Reardo where the 15th Evac. left their hosp. for us. Andy, Margaret, Mugs and I tenting together. We are in a beautiful valley here, surrounded by mts.—village set up on a peak—very pretty. It's so quiet and peaceful here—*almost* think we had a bad dream at Anzio. At 5 P.M. we had chow—real food at last of pork chops, potatoes, real bread and butter. Marvelous. Like the 1st Thanksgiving. To bed early tonite and really wore pajamas again. No air raids, no shelling.

Feb. 13 [1944]

What a wonderful sleep I had—aided c̄ Nembutal. Setting up the equipment to suit us. Washed our filthy hair tonite and got some of the foxhole dirt out of it. Bed early.

Feb. 14 [1944]

Meals grand. We can hear the shooting—but at a distance. Went to Confession today. Started Novena.

A̲t the Enid, Oklahoma, Army airfield, a very young combat returnee was asked where he was from. "I was born in Brooklyn," he replied, "and raised in New Guinea."

■ SOURCES

1. Harold Chutes Diary, "Harold Chutes Diary" File, Gene LaPosta Papers, World War II Participants and Contemporaries Collection, Dwight D. Eisenhower Library, Abilene, Kansas. The selection presented is the entire text of the diary.
2. Franklin D. Roosevelt to Members of the United States Army Expeditionary Forces, n.d., "Avery, Thelma—Miscellaneous Papers (2)" File, World War II Participants and Contemporaries Collection, Eisenhower Library.
3. The letters in this section are from Ervin J. Cook to Parents, February 26, March 6, May 2 and 25, and June 15, 1944, "Letters to Parents, Feb.–Dec. 1944" File, Ervin J. Cook Papers, World War II Participants and Contemporaries Collection, Eisenhower Library.
4. The lettes in this section are from Robert S. Raymond to Wife, November 21 and December 10, 1942, and January 27, 1943, "Diary (4)" File, Robert S. Raymond Papers, World War II Participants and Contemporaries Collection, Eisenhower Library.
5. Diary of Richard Thomas Mariner, 1943, Jeanann Olds Papers, World War II Participants and Contemporaries Collection, Eisenhower Library.
6. Robert L. Mason to Relative, May 20, 1943, Agnes M. Mason Papers, World War II Participants and Contemporaries Collection, Eisenhower Library.
7. Mario Dal Canton to Sister, April 8, 1945, "Letters, 1945–47" File, Rena Dal Canton Papers, World War II Participants and Contemporaries Collection, Eisenhower Library.
8. Casimer Prunchunas, Diary, "Diary (1)" and "Diary (2)" Files, Casimer Prunchunas Papers, World War II Participants and Contemporaries Collection, Eisenhower Library.
9. Alfred F. Birra to Wife, July 12, 1944, Alfred F. Birra Papers, World War II Participants and Contemporaries Collection, Eisenhower Library.
10. Charles Riordan, "The Artillery in Germany," November 1944, Stephanie Salada Papers, Private Collection, Pittsburgh, Pennsylvania.
11. Diary, 2nd Lieutenant Mary Fischer, A.N.C., "Diary, Jan.–Dec. 1944" File, Jolenta Fischer Masterson Papers, World War II Participants and Contemporaries Collection Eisenhower Library.

THREE

HEALING

D isease, injuries, and wounds were often the soldier's lot, even if he never made it into combat or overseas at all. Medical care in the U.S. armed forces was the best in military history to that point and included treatment of the psychological side effects of military duty as well as physical ailments. The wounds and trauma inflicted by combat in World War II were many and varied, and most who suffered from the travails of the industrialized slaughter faced weeks or months of treatment in a whole series of facilities. A soldier wounded in battle might well receive emergency treatment by a corpsman while still near enemy lines. He would be sent back to a field hospital as soon as possible, where his injuries would be attended by physicians with a modicum of equipment and pharmaceuticals. From there the more seriously wounded would be sent back to well-staffed and well-supplied semipermanent facilities in the theater's rear areas, where his stay for treatment could easily last weeks or months. Those requiring extensive or long-term therapy would be shipped back to the United States, where a system of hospitals and other facilities provided first-rate care. Here the stricken citizen-soldier, perhaps permanently disfigured or disabled, was prepared for rejoining society.

The care of those traumatized in battle is one measure of the effectiveness of a nation's military medical services, but we should never forget that the majority of Americans who served in the armed forces never saw frontline action. Yet these millions sustained injuries during training, had to be inoculated for overseas duty, came down with colds, influenza, and other common diseases, sometimes contracted venereal diseases, and in general required regular medical and dental care. The treatment of the mundane illnesses, aches, and pains of these millions, however, escaped the headlines. An unmistakable sign of the success of the health care offered to the many millions of men and women in uniform who never saw combat is how little public attention it garnered during four years of war.

And make no mistake about it: treatment of casualties involved not only care of the physical consequences of battle but also assuring the family of the wounded soldier that their son, husband, or brother was receiving the best care possible in return for his sacrifice. The confusion and frenzy of combat and the tremendous scale of the confrontations between military forces in the industrial age made keeping track of all those servicemen entrusted to the medical system a formidable task. As some of the selections below demonstrate, there was much opportunity for error in keeping the families of the wounded informed, yet one cannot but marvel that errors were not more frequent. The American experience in World War II contrasts sharply with that of most of the war's other belligerents, to say nothing of soldiers in bygone years, whose parents and spouses often never learned for certain what became of their family members until the disabled soldier came home, if indeed he returned at all.

The documents in this chapter acquaint us with a variety of experiences, from the point of view of patient and caregiver alike. Considering the numbers of Americans in uniform and the range of infirmities, maimings, and maladies that afflicted them, we must recognize the U.S. military medical services in World War II as one of the most remarkable organizations behind the victory.

In Honolulu, Judge Franklin devised a special fine for blackout violators: $25 and a pint of blood. The physically unfit pay an extra $25, to buy blood.

—This Week

IN AN OVERSEAS MILITARY HOSPITAL

LETTERS HOME FROM WILLARD H. FLUCK[1]

A series of letters to parents from a convalescing soldier testify to the quality of American medical care in the combat theaters. One of the letters also describes some details of the soldier's service previously deemed too confidential to survive excision by the censors. The last letter of the series, written barely two weeks after the first, shows that the care was good enough to make everyday life distinctly boring after awhile.

May 8, 1945

Somewhere in France

Dear Folks,

Well, it looks as though the war in Europe is over. We had a little ceremony here at the hospital this morning, including church services. It was all very nice. I imagine there was a lot of celebrating done at home. Everybody I've seen has taken it calmly–even the German prisoners. The hospital has been using the Heinies to keep the buildings clean and to do odd jobs around the place.

We saw a movie tonight. This sure is the life. I laid out in the sun a few hours just absorbing the sunshine and getting a tan and remembered all those rainy days last fall and all the snow and cold last winter. It sure will take a lot of that warm sunshine to make up for *that*.

How's little Diane? Try to send me a picture now and then. I've got to see how all my nephews and nieces are progressing.

Well, I guess that's all for now. Tell Ross he should see all the pretty American nurses we have here. Oh boy!

Must close. Stay well.

Love
Bud

May 12, 1945

Evreux, France

Dear Folks,

Here's your dearly beloved son again. Since some of the censorship restrictions have been lifted and since there's nothing else interesting to write about, I think I'll tell you a little about my trip since we left Camp Claiborne, La. I just figured you might find it a little interesting anyway. It's a pretty long story, so sit your fanny down and get yourself comfortable.

Leaving Claiborne, we came up along the Miss. River on up through Chicago and across the border into Canada. Turning southeast, we passed through our beloved Pa* and came as close to home as Bethlehem and Easton and wound up in Camp Kilmer in N.J.

That's where I was when I got my last pass home. Although I didn't tell you where I was, you probably guessed it. By Sept. 20, we were on the boat headed out of New York harbor to Europe by the southern route, which took us as far south as the Azores, then up the coast of France and right on up to Glasgow, Scotland. Scotland is a very beautiful country. From there another train ride took us down southwest of London to Barton Stacey. It was from there that we got our passes to London. What a place. Incidentally, the boat trip lasted thirteen days. We had one submarine scare, but we dodged them. We spent almost a month in England and then crossed the channel from Southampton to Omaha beachhead, where one of the landings was made on D-Day. There were still a lot of ships sunk off shore when we got there. That was around the 1st of November. A few days there, and we were off again, this time by truck convoy through Paris (I still haven't been there on pass) and on up through Belgium into the very southern tip of Holland. It was in Geleen, a little town west of Sittard, that I met the Spronken family. We became quite good friends. We sat by the hour while he told me stories of what the Germans had done to them and their country. I developed a pretty good ear for their language from him. They were very poor people, and the children had sores on their bodies from the poor food they had—mostly apples, applebutter, and bread. But even with what little they had, they always offered me some.

Well, we were there a little over a week, I guess, and then moved across the border into Germany right smack in the middle of the Siegfried Line. A lot can be told about that, but I won't here. Then we began to hear about

---

*Pennsylvania.

the breakthrough south of us, and next thing we know we were down there helping to stop the Bulge from bulging. We moved into Manche just one step ahead of the Germans. Christmas day was spent in the woods near there. That's when our canteens froze solid and broke open. The following five or six weeks were spent cutting the Bulge to pieces. A lot more can be said about that, too. That "Somewhere in Belgium" on my letters around the end of January came from Borlon while we were on rest there. We spent several weeks resting, and then found ourselves back up there in the Siegfried line. We sat on the West bank of the Roer River for a while. From there to the Rhine. And from the Rhine to the Elbe. From there I flew most of the way back to where I am now, at Evreux somewhere northwest of Paris.

Life sure is calm and peaceful here in the hospital. Eat and sleep is about all we do. They're working on my eye, and I think it should be altogether cured shortly.

Well, I guess I'd better close. I hope you're all fine and not working too hard. Stay well . . .

Love
Bud

May 17, 1945

Evreux, France

Dear Folks,

Hello again! I'm still here in the hospital and am getting treatments for my eye. They X-rayed several of my teeth last week, and last Saturday they gave me a shot of Typhus serum (or something) to give me a fever. The fever is supposed to help clean my eyes out. It made me feel pretty bad for a few days, but I sort of doubt the results.

The weather has been swell for the last two weeks. It's like June back home. I've already got a good start on a sun-tan. We have movies, ball games, show, parties and all kinds of stuff like that here. It's really a swell life. I've had so many oranges since I''ve been here I can't look at them anymore.

Do you ever hear from Ken? He has owed me a letter for months.

Well, I guess that's all for now. I've about quit writing letters until my mail gets to me. There's just nothing to write about.

Stay well and write.

Love
Bud

May 24, 1945

Evreux, France

Dear Folks,

Time seems to go fast lately. I've been in this hospital almost three weeks already. I believe I'll be leaving here soon, though—probably for another hospital.

I'm getting a little tired of this life—not that I crave excitement. I've had my fill of that. I'm doing a lot of reading using my left eye. The other one is getting a "rest cure."

Saw a movie tonight, and last night a French orchestra came out and played for us. Their version of American swing is pretty lousy. It's even worse than the English version. They just can't play our music.

My mail hasn't come through yet, but I'm sure it will get to me one of these days. I hope you're still writing. As long as you use my same address, I'll get the letters.

Don't worry about me. I'm doing swell. I couldn't ask for more.

Must close. Stay well.

> Love
> *Bud*

When an officer of a naval officer in California found many beds empty in a ward supposed to house marines and sailors back from the Pacific war zone, an orderly explained: "The men are accustomed to sleeping on the ground and they didn't rest well on mattresses. They're under the beds, sir."

—Rennie Taylor, Minneapolis Tribune

A MEDICO'S POINT OF VIEW

LETTERS HOME FROM HAROLD PORTER[2]

A medical technician writes to his parents about many of his experiences at work in a forward hospital.

Souvenir hunting and cemetery tours are just two of the activities described in this letter.

14 January 1945

With the Seventh Army
Somewhere in France

Dear Mother and Father,

It's 1:15 A.M. and the ward has quieted down enough so that I'm going to try to catch up on my letter-writing. Besides it will help me to stay awake. I'm having the same trouble re-adjusting my habits with the shift to night duty that I used to have when the shifts changed at Willow Run.*

A new decree has been issued forbidding us to let the Germans think they have anything that could possibly interest us. This has affected our popular past-time of souvenir collecting. The situation had reached the extreme though, because some fellows used to meet the incoming ambulances and strip the prisoners of buttons, collar and shoulder insignia, medals, badges, hat insignia, wrist watches and even wallets. Now this has all been stopped. The only way now to complete insignia collections is to salvage them from the bloody clothing just before it reaches the incinerator.

The outstanding souvenir collected so far is a complete suit of medieval armor which one of the boys found—and it fits him! Of course it will be a head-ache lugging it around when we move, but he plans on sending it home piece by piece.

Now that I'm on nights again and have my days free, one of my ambitions is to ride up to the front. I've been trying to make arrangements with the ambulance drivers, but can't get any assurance that I'll be back here the same day. After talking with the patients, I've decided that no one can really say he participated in the war unless he's been on the front. Besides, one of the threats they hold over our heads here for punishment for inefficiency or too much complaining is that we will be sent to a battalion aid station at the front. The time may come when I get so bored with this work that I may want a change at any cost. So I'd thought I'd like to see if things at the front are really as rough as everyone says.

One of the laboratory technicians had a peace time hobby of collecting odd and humorous epitaphs from New England cemeteries. This part of

---

*The largest aircraft assembly plant in the world, constructed in Michigan during World War II for the production of B-24 bombers.

France, having been a battleground so often, is cluttered up with cemeteries so I went out walking with Laylor one morning to see if we could add to his collection. We didn't find any particularly interesting ones, but the cemeteries and stones themselves are rather unconventional by American standards. There's a big military cemetery right behind our hospital which has a lot of mass graves. All the French graves have the standard white Christian cross. The Germans use a Maltese cross with a swastika in the center—and the color depends upon the soldier's grade—commissioned officers and N.C.O.'s being distinguished from the privates. The colonial troops, being Moslems, are all lined up facing Eastward despite the fact the fact that this ruins the symmetry of the rows. Visiting graveyards is really not as morbid a pastime as you may think. In fact, it's very satisfying to see so many German graves.

So you are having real winter weather in Michigan this year. Certainly wish I could go on some of those toboggan parties at Huron Hills with Claire.* The weather here is about like a typical Michigan winter—particularly with regard to sunshine. It's cloudy 80% of the time—and until recently we had lots of rain. There is snow on the ground now though and the local kids are skiing and sleighing on the hills despite the fact that there are signs all over stating that the mines have been cleared only as far as the ditches. The Saar is frozen over now, and from the top floor of our "barracks" we can see skaters on some of the wider parts. How has skating been this year in Ypsi?** Does Claire ever go to the University rink at all?

Love,
Harold

At the time of the German surrender, the medico's unit was approaching the Nazi concentration camp at Dachau. Besides relating some rather gruesome details about conditions at the camp, he expresses a very low opinion of American female nurses. It is interesting to compare this perspective with that of the diary of a combat nurse included in Chapter 2 and the views expressed in later selections in this chapter.

---

*Porter's sister.
**Porter's hometown was Ypsilanti, Michigan.

26 May 1945

Dachau Concentration Camp
Dachau, Germany

Dear Mother and Father,

Father's letter describing Alamasa came yesterday along with letter 37 from mother. When mother said the town* was in the same Presbytery as Pueblo, I had visions of the desert country around that part of Colorado. I certainly am glad it is located in the mountains and that it has decent winter weather. Like mother, I must have a distinct change of seasons including lots of snow in the winter time. I'm all excited about going home now even though I know it will be a long time yet.

Mother wanted to know if there would be any chance of my getting home before going to the Pacific. That is exactly the same question four million others are asking. It's highly unlikely—preference will probably be given to combat troops.

When we do move, let me know our new address so I can have my war bonds, insurance, etc. sent to the right place. You might as well transfer my A.A. bank account to Alamasa too, as I'd rather have you do my banking for me than deal with the bank by mail.

We have at least one German nurse on each ward now, and German medic P.O.W.s are being briefed concerning our techniques and systems. It rather looks as if we're going to leave. The patients have all been switched from American to German army rations.

The German nurses are infinitely more competent and capable than our American nurses. I am anxious to learn if their medics are, too. Comments concerning female army personnel have been strictly forbidden during the censorship era, so you never have known my opinion of our nurses. No matter what the official army policy is about needing more nurses, you will never find any medic personnel that agrees with the army. Certainly they're not needed any further forward than a general hospital.

Frankly, most nurses seemed to have joined the army for the same reason that so many girls go to college. Overseas, women are at a premium, and no matter what a girl is like she is always the center of attention and highly in demand—particularly among combat men, who see far fewer girls than the rear echelon troops. This explains the occasional praise an infantryman has for the nurses. It's just that she's an American woman, and not that she's a good nurse, that she is praised. Social life is their whole life—nursing here is

---

*Porter's family was in the process of moving from Michigan to Pueblo, Colorado.

just a means to an end. One of the doctors was heard to remark that "Although the German army certainly had a lot of 'camp followers,' as far as he knew the American army was the only one to give the whores a commission." This is rather a blunt statement that too accurately describes conditions in most field and evac. hospitals.

Professionally the older nurses have some ability but little interest. The younger nurses—graduates through the army cadet system, are utterly incompetent and helpless—besides having a lot of false modesty for which there is no place in the army and which a German or French nurse does not have. I've seen American nurses who would refuse to look at or help you change a dressing on a genital wound where no French nurse would mind this at all. Perhaps I've been too inclusive in my condemnation. Of our 40 nurses, there are about three who are really capable, but even they would be doing more good back in a general hospital.

I see by Time magazine that the American public has already been informed of conditions at Buchenwald and other camps, but so far I've heard or seen nothing of your knowledge of Dachau. I don't know whether I mentioned it, but cannibalism as described at Buchenwald was also common among the Poles here. When a body died, it would be hidden until it nearly disintegrated so that its rations could be drawn. Also, the heart, liver and kidneys (the only part where any meat was left) would be torn out and eaten. However, we have no evidence that the Germans actually slaughtered some to use as food for the others.

Tomorrow I'm off—my first full day since we landed in Europe—although the last week has been very light.

Love,
Harold

WOUNDED IN BATTLE

DIARY OF CASIMER PRUNCHUNAS[3]

These diary excerpts chronicle the wounding and treatment of an American GI, just one of the hundreds of thousands mangled by battle. After four months in overseas hospitals, he finally made it back to the United States for further rehabilitation.

October 3 to 8, 1944

Stayed in Giugnola and sent patrols from here. Most of the time there was a drizzling rain. But it wasn't too bad, as we were staying in a house with a fireplace and could get dry and sleep warm. I was on one patrol and had a mortar shell burst about 40 feet away. But luckily, it didn't get me or anybody else. Then on the night of October 8th, we moved out on a mission. And it was raining cats and dogs. While here, we were issued new bed-rolls, sweaters, jackets, socks, and new type shoes.

October 9, 1944

We reached our destination about 0100, we parked our vehicles and then with ten men each from the 2nd and 3rd platoons and two machineguns, we started out for our forward positions. I was on this patrol. We crossed a couple of deep streams, and it was raining very hard, and it was slippery going. We had nearly reached our destination and were near a blown out bridge, when all of a sudden about a dozen rounds of mortar shells fell all around us. Then as we thought it was over and started to move out and as I started to get up, I heard a whistling, screaming noise, and I flattened out on the ground. THAT WAS THE ONE THAT HIT ME.

It felt as if it landed on my back, and I could feel the blood drip out. I hollered that I had been hit, and then Medic Bill Meredith gave me first aid and a morphine shot. Then they made a makeshift stretcher. From then St.* Buck, Rubeck, Rockenbach, Coppinger, Hegstad and Lt. Cavett carried me back to our vehicles. They were constantly complaining on how heavy I was. (165 pounds) And they also had to cross a couple of streams, and I was afraid that they might drop me. And I believe that I was conscious most of the time with hardly any pain. Then Hegstad and Coppinger took me over some very bumpy roads back to a Field Hospital. I did feel a little bit of pain on the ride. At the field hospital, I was taken into the operating room for examination, and when they found out I had been hit in the side, they didn't let me drink any more water. Only wet gauze between my lips. Then I was put to sleep, and when I came-to later on in the day, I was wrapped up like a mummy.

October 9 to 31, 1944

I was in the 32nd Field Hospital and was being given glucose, plasma, morphine and penicillin for my wounds. I had over 200 shots of penicillin, many shots of morphine and a lot of bottles of glucose and plasma. Didn't feel much pain at anytime. Don't know if I was immune to pain or they kept me doped up. My left leg swoll up to nearly three times its size (phlebitis). It was elevated, and it took about ten days for the swelling to go down. The care was very excellent, and the nurses treated me fine. I got scared a lot of times when

---

*Sergeant, more commonly abbreviated Sgt.

the Germans were shelling a crossroads nearby and I could hear the shells going over the hospital tents and exploding. It's a scary feeling when you can't get out of bed. Was sent out October 31st.

October 31 to November 3, 1944

At 8th Evacuation Hospital about 25 miles north of Florence. Here the care and the nurses were swell. Left here about 0700 on November 3rd. After an ambulance ride to Florence, was put on a plane and flown to Pisa. Saw the Leaning Tower of Pisa on my back through a port hole of the plane. Then another ambulance ride from Pisa to Leghorn.

November 3 to 18, 1944

I am now in the 33rd General Hospital in Leghorn, Italy. Here I have a nice hospital bed for the first time since getting wounded. Just resting and having my bandages changed daily. Also medication. Food is very good. Nothing is being done to me here, only letting my wounds heal. Nurses treat me OK.

November 18, 1944

Boarded the U.S.S. Hinds, which was a hospital ship, and after an all-night trip along the coast, pulled into Naples harbor about 1800. This was a nice trip. Nice clean looking compartment I was in. Music and very good food on the whole trip. Even fresh milk. My leg pained me a bit during the trip.

November 20, 1944

Today is my BIRTHDAY. Left the boat, and as I left the gangplank, a Red Cross worker handed me a copy of Stars and Stripes, two cakes and a Hershey candy bar. Then I was put in an ambulance and taken to the 300th General Hospital in Naples. Here I was assigned to Ward F4A-Room7 and bed #1.

November 21 to ?, 1944

I'm in a ward with some pretty nice fellows, and we have a good time exchanging experiences, etc. Plenty to eat and a lot of rest. Christmas packages are arriving for us, and mine are also. I got some of my operations done here, although they can not do anything to my leg. Doing a lot of reading and waiting to be sent home.

January 1, 1945

New Years was ushered by a lot of whistles, horns, rifle shots and flares here in Naples. It sure seemed funny to me.

January 3, 1945

Today I found out that the last skin graft didn't take. So I'll probably have another skin graft operation.

January 5, 1945

Had a cast put on my leg from my hip to my toes. And told to walk around as much as possible. Things are looking up.

January 6, 1945

Got out of bed and walked around some for the first time in three months. It sure felt swell to be up. Also went down to see the movie "Hollywood Canteen."

January 9, 1945

My friend from the bed next to me (T/5 Dahlstram) was transferred out of this Ward into X2. When he came in at night, he told us, as they were walking through a small village close by, an Italian kid peeked around the corner of the house and hollered, "Hey Joe! How about a piece of ass?" Only $2.00. Then at night, he and a couple of other fellows went over the wall and bought some cognac at $2.00 a bottle. And a girl at the same price.

January 10, 1945

Today Dahlstram brought me a bottle of cognac which I'm bringing for Pa. It also snowed here in Naples.

January 12, 1945

Funny way of snowing here in Naples with lightning and thunder. Went down to see a USO show this afternoon and had to walk up three flights of stairs to get back after the elevators failed. It was a good show. Also took some pictures.

January 21, 1945

Sunday, and before dinner the Red Cross worker came in and handed me a blue bag. And in this hospital, it signifies that one is to catch the next boat. It really came as a surprise to me. And I'm very happy about the whole matter. In fact, a little excited. Was told this evening that I'm supposed to leave at 6:30 AM tomorrow.

January 22, 1945

There was a nice layer of snow this morning. Didn't get loaded on the ambulance until 9 o'clock. And then loaded on the boat about 11:20 AM. The boat was the U.S.A.H.S. ACADIA. It was a hospital ship. In between there was a lot of delay and waiting. Left Naples at 4 o'clock in the afternoon. First night out was a bit rough, and for a change I didn't even get seasick. Just a bit light-headed. Looks like I'm getting to be a sailor. Watch out Navy—here I come.

January 23 to February 3, 1945

On board ship, we had a movie every day. And ice cream daily. Good food and a big variety of it. Most of the pictures I've seen before. Only "Holy Matrimony" and "Dough Girls" were the two that I haven't seen. But as most of them were musicals, I enjoyed them very much. My bed was situated about 10 feet from the washroom, and the projector was put in front of my bed. The nurses are exceptionally friendly and very efficient. I liked the way they fussed over us. Plenty of milk to drink and fresh fruit to eat whenever we wanted to. The weather was mild, and only the last three days were a bit rough. But it was a pleasant 5000 mile trip.

February 4, 1945

Landed at Charleston harbor and were taken to Stark General Hospital. Here the chow was the best that I had ever tasted in the Army. Also plenty of milk. On my stay here I averaged two quarts of milk per day. And I'm putting on a bit of weight around the belly. Wac's here are used as Ward help, and we had a pretty good one. Lots of fun and laughs. And now that I'm leaving for Illinois tomorrow, I feel a lot better already.

February 12, 1945

Was woken up about 0530 and left Stark General Hospital about 0645 and was taken aboard a hospital train. It was a very nice comfortable trip across the United States. Beautiful scenery for me, as I was glad to be back. And after a trip of about 42 hours, we arrived in Galesburg, Illinois and were taken by ambulance to Mayo general Hospital. Plenty of good food and milk is plentiful. At the hospital the Wac's do the work around here instead of men.

February 14, 1945

Entered Mayo General Hospital to Ward C-8. Had operation performed on my leg, during my stay here.

INFORMING THE FAMILY

THE MCKINNEY FAMILY SAGA

A combat casualty's family was notified of the misfortune as soon as possible by government agencies. However, the natural chaos

*of battle and the size of the forces engaged meant that govern-
ment agencies were not always able to notify a combat casualty's
family with swift and accurate information. Sometimes the family
learned of the misfortune before receiving official word.*

Letter Home from Walter McKinney[4]

*A son, assuming his parents have received government notice of
his wounding, writes an exasperatingly vague note to reassure
his family. One can only imagine the unintended distress this letter caused. This letter was received by Mr. and Mrs. McKinney on
March 30, 1945.*

March 19, 1945[4]

Dear Mother and Dad,

By the time you receive this V-mail you will probably know that I have been
wounded. Don't worry, as my wounds aren't very bad. However, before very
long I hope to be back in the States again where they will probably send me
to recuperate. I'll probably go to Walter Reed Hospital, so I hope that by the
time I get there you will not have transferred out of Washington to Winnipeg,
Canada. Right now I am feeling fine and hope to be soon on the complete
way to recovery. Again I ask you not to be too concerned or worried over my
health as you will only make me feel worse by doing so.

Your loving son,
Walter

Telegram from Adjutant General to Mrs. Julia W. McKinney[5]

*We can be sure that receiving the official notice was never easy,
but Sergeant McKinney's family must have been more confused
when they read this telegram, which arrived three days after their
son's letter but still did not specify the nature of his wounds. The
fact that the telegram's spelling errors included their son's name
could only have added to their frustration.*

WP273 63 GOVT=VIA RT MSRTE=WUX WASHINGTON DC 2 742P
MRS JULIA W MCKINNEY=
11 RIGGS RD APT 326 WASHDC=

THE SECRETARY OF WAR DESIRES ME TO EXVRESS HIS DEEP
REGRET THAT YOUR SON S/SGT MCKINNEY WALTHER H JR WAS

SERIOUSLY WOUNDED IN ITALY 18 MAR 45 UNTIL NEW ADDRESS IS
RECEIVED ADDRESS MAIL FOR HIM QUOTE RANK NAME SERIAL
NUMBER (HOSPITALIZED) 2628 HOSPITAL SECTION APO 698 CARE
POSTMASTER NEW YORK NEW YORK UNQUOTE NEW ADDRESS
AND FURTHER INFORMATION FOLOW DIRECT FROM HOSPITAL=

J A ULIO THE ADJUTANT GENERAL.

Letter from Percy Jones Hospital to Walter H. McKinney[6]

*Months after their son's return to the United States for long-term
treatment, the McKinneys still did not have an accurate idea of
the nature of and prognosis for their son's injuries. At long last,
seven months after Sgt. McKinney was wounded, their inquiries
produced some answers.*

22 October 1945

ARMY SERVICE FORCES
SIXTH SERVICE COMMAND
PERCY JONES HOSPITAL CENTER
FORT CUSTER, MICHIGAN

Reply Address:
Register, Percy Jones Hospital Center,
Fort Custer, Michigan

Walter H. McKinney
American Consul General
American Consulate General
Winnipeg, Manitoba

Dear Sir:

I am in receipt of your letter dated 17 October 1945, and I can readily understand your concern regarding your son's physical condition. I also can appreciate the fact that if you knew the type and character of the injuries he has
sustained and their present condition, along with the contemplated treatment
of the injuries, you would be very much re-assured.

Your son had an amputation of the right leg in the lower third, at the 8th
Evacuation Hospital overseas on 18 March 1945. On 12 June 1945 at Percy Jones
General Hospital, re-amputation through the middle third was performed. No
further surgery will be required on this stump and he will be fitted with a pros-
thesis as soon as his left leg is sufficiently strong for weight bearing. He had
fractures, simple, comminuted, of the left tibia and fibula, through the middle
third. The fractures of the tibia and fibula were reduced under direct vision,

and the tibia fixed in place with bone screws on 12 April 1945 at 12th General Hospital overseas. On 7 August 1945, at Percy Jones General Hospital, sequestrectomy and removal of screws from the left tibia was performed. On 11 September 1945, incision and drainage of abscess, and exploration of sinus of the left leg, was performed. At the present time this surgical wound continues to drain purulent material. The cause of this drainage is undoubtedly a sequestrum, or in non-medical language, a piece of devitalized bone. This would necessitate another operation for removal of same in the near future. The fracture of the tibia and fibula is firmly united, and the possibility of his presence at home this Christmas depends entirely on the cessation of drainage from the left leg. Every effort will be made to accomplish this.

Your son also sustained fractures, compound, comminuted, complete, of the 3rd, 4th, and 5th metacarpals, and the 2nd, 3rd, and 4th proximal phalanges of the left hand. Also, the left index finger was amputated through the proximal end of the proximal phalanx. It is contemplated that following the complete recovery of his left leg, reconstructive surgery of his left hand will be performed. This will require several operations; first, a pedicle skin graft from the abdomen to the dorsal surface of the hand, and second, bone surgery.

If it is at all possible, and there is a fair possibility, your son, S/Sgt. Walter H. McKinney, Jr., will be given a convalescent furlough in order to spend the Christmas holidays with you.

Very truly yours,
W. R. McDonnell
W. R. MC DONNELL,
Capt., M.C.
Ward Officer, Ward 20

Citation for Bronze Star Medal Awarded to Sgt. Walter H. McKinney, Jr.[7]

Sgt. McKinney was awarded the bronze star for the action in which he was so severely wounded. Here is the text of the citation.

CITATION FOR BRONZE STAR MEDAL

Staff Sergeant Walter H. McKinney, Jr., Company A, 168th Infantry Regiment, volunteered on 17 March 1945 for a daylight rescue mission beyond the Allied lines near Bologna, Italy. Despite the dangers of enemy observation and a thickly-sown minefield, he heroically pressed forward until seriously wounded in his attempt to reach an officer whose airplane had crashed.

The simple phrase "seriously wounded" in this citation is a classic understatement of the years of medical procedures and rehabilitation Sgt. McKinney had to undergo as a consequence of his heroic actions. It also conveys nothing of the great anxiety his parents endured for weeks and months while they struggled to learn the full story of their son's injuries and status. Amid the sufferings of so many in a nation at war, such family tragedies became commonplace.

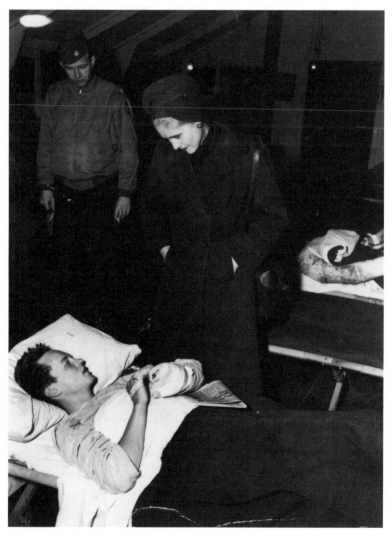

Clare Booth Luce visiting McKinney in the hospital. (Courtesy of the Dwight D. Eisenhower Library, Walter H. McKinney Collection.)

■ **SOURCES**

1. The letters in this section are from Willard H. Fluck to Parents, May 8, 12, 17, and 24, 1945, "Letters 1945 (1)" File, Willard H. Fluck Papers, World War II Participants and Contemporaries Collection, Dwight D. Eisenhower Library, Abilene, Kansas.
2. Harold Porter to Parents, January 14, 1945, "Letters Jan. 1945" File; and May 26, 1945, "Letters May 1945" File, Harold Porter Papers, World War II Participants and Contemporaries Collection, Eisenhower Library.
3. Casimer Prunchunas, Diary, "Diary (2)" File, Casimer Prunchunas Papers, World War II Participants and Contemporaries Collection, Eisenhower Library.
4. Walter McKinney to Parents, March 19, 1945, Walter H. McKinney Papers, World War II Participants and Contemporaries Collection, Eisenhower Library.
5. Western Union Telegram, Adjutant General to Mrs. Julia W. McKinney, April 2, 1945, Walter H. McKinney Papers, World War II Participants and Contemporaries Collection, Eisenhower Library.
6. Captain W. R. McDonnell to Walter McKinney, October 22, 1945, Walter H. McKinney Papers, World War II Participants and Contemporaries Collection, Eisenhower Library.
7. Citation for Bronze Star Medal, n.d., Walter H. McKinney Papers, World War II Participants and Contemporaries Collection, Eisenhower Library.

FOUR

SO THAT OTHERS MAY FIGHT

The U.S. military proved to be a formidable creature, but the beast required a lengthy and abundant logistical tail to sustain its fangs. Because the war was waged oceans away from the locus of American power, huge resources had to be diverted to the construction, operation, and maintenance of what eventually became a worldwide transportation network to move and supply American fighting strength at the fronts. Remembering that the GI was better fed and equipped than his counterparts in the rest of the world's armies, we can envision the staggering quantities of items, from five-hundred-pound bombs and Sherman tanks to coffee and mail, that traveled by truck, ship, and train to the troops in the field. Specialists in transportation, from railroad firemen to motor mechanics, were drafted to meet these needs. Many more average Joes, just out of high school or the unemployment line, learned such skills as part of their service experience.

As we follow the supplies that feed the fighting beast through the military distribution network, we note that every article has to be packaged, loaded, unloaded, counted, organized, checked, and accounted for at every stage in the process. Hordes of managers and clerks armed with typewriters, clipboards, and lots and lots of standardized forms were necessary to see that what was needed got to where it would do the most good in the shortest possible time. That fact that so many American soldiers, sailors, and airmen were more businessmen than warriors says something profound not only about the nature of World War II but also about why the United States was part of the winning alliance.

The mushrooming military forces and expanding industry placed such demands on the available manpower that shortages soon developed, even in a nation of 150 million souls. Increasing mechanization of armies in the field and the workplace at home helped ease the strain, but it was not enough, and the country dipped into other reserves of personnel that were traditionally underutilized. These included racial and ethnic minorities, the economically underprivileged, and women. So it was that Latinos and African Americans gained unprecedented opportunities for factory jobs at decent wages, "okies" learned to march and fire artillery, and "Rosie the Riveter" was born. As some of the selections in this chapter illustrate, the all-American girl showed up in uniform, too, very often tangling with the enormous task of feeding the voracious war animal.

When we consider the dimensions of the logistical task faced by Americans, made more challenging than that confronting any other nation because of North America's distance from the battlefronts and the U.S. function as "arsenal of democracy," we should not be surprised that far more American men and women served in support rather than combat roles. The diversity of tasks undertaken by the logistics laborers, from the mundane to the highly specialized, is well illustrated in the passages below, but a hundred more jobs had to be done for every chore mentioned here. Bakers, truck drivers, typists, signalmen, stevedores, and airplane mechanics kept 'em sailing, marching, and flying to victory. From the supporting personnel near enough to the front lines to risk their lives to those who never left the United States, theirs was a far less celebrated but much more common experience. Receiving little attention and no glory, they nevertheless provided the building blocks of victory. Such is war for those who toil so that others may fight.

CLOSE SUPPORT: IWO JIMA

Iwo Jima was a gruesome slugfest, the only battle of the Pacific War in which American casualties outnumbered those of the Japanese. But for every Marine risking his life on the black lava sands of the island, there were several support personnel toiling to maintain his combat efficiency. To the sailors of the supply vessels offshore, Iwo Jima presented its own perils and challenges.

Letter Home from Eugene G. Barber[1]

An ensign aboard a navy transport relates his experiences at Iwo Jima.

April 20th [1945]

Friday morning

Dear Family, All of You—

I may have time to write you some news today, and I may not. Anyway I will start, and we shall see how long I go before being interrupted. This will be the story of Iwo Jima, as I know it. I'm sure that my side of it is very mild compared to that of many fellows. However, it will undoubtedly be of interest to you.

I wasn't there on D-day—nor for several days thereafter. We were in Pearl Harbor, freshly arrived from the States when the "Rock" was first hit. That was on Feb. 19. I read about the invasion in the Honolulu Advertiser. The very first dispatches carried the reports of very fierce fighting, as you will know. Iwo Jima sounded very remote—and I promptly dismissed it as a possibility for us when I found that our "passengers" we had brought from the States weren't getting off at Pearl. We were taking them on to Majuro in the Marshall Islands. This I have already told you.

As you know, our stop in Pearl was a short one. We pulled out two days later—early—for the Marshalls. After four uneventful days at sea—except for challenging a ship one night which didn't reply, but which the Captain correctly decided was a merchantman too scared or too sketchy on naval challenges to risk a reply—we arrived in Majuro. A barge came along side us as we lay at anchor off Rita Atoll and took off our "passengers." As soon as they were off, it was "Anchors Aweigh." Something was up. The Bollinger wasn't stopping for long—again.

Two days steaming up past Kwajalein and a few more Marshall Atolls found us slowly making way into a harbor at Eniwetok—off Parry Atoll—on

Feb. 27. We fueled off a concrete oiler. During movies, topside, that night, an announcement called all watch officers to the bridge. Our navigator gave us some pertinent dope. We were joining a convoy—10–11 ships like us and we got tactical info as to our formation, column guides, radio procedures and were told we were shoving off the following morning, Feb. 28. But he didn't say where to!

We found our unit early that next forenoon and steamed out. I had one of the first watches that day and a few hours out the Captain said, over the bull horn, "The ship is bound for Iwo Jima." A damn simple statement—but pregnant with meaning. I think I was glad. Finally, damn it, we were going where there were Japs. Finally, hell! We'd only been out of the States 15 days!

It's a long way to Iwo Jima. Lots of water! We had a ring of Destroyer Escorts forming a sort of semi-circle around us. Our job was to go in and take the Marines off—when and if the Army moved in to start final mopping up exercises. Well, we left plenty early. The papers will tell you that the time estimated as necessary to take Iwo was a bit presumptuous.

Nine days later we were steaming off Iwo waiting for word to go in. And by God we steamed and waited and waited and steamed! We were as close as you are to Brookings. For a solid week we cruised around in a sort of circle at tractor speed waiting for the need to go in. Nothing to do of course but wonder when a sub would give us a bad time or Nip aircraft would come screaming out of some cloud. The nights were black as ink, for which all hands were thankful. It made maneuvering a problem, with ships on all sides, but it also made sub attack less probable—no silhouette.

The radio in the ward room got plenty of attention. We could pick up our own reports, but we also could get, very clearly, Radio Tokyo's versions of the fight at Iwo. Naturally, they didn't jibe very well. Seemed to be an outright difference of opinion, in fact. Tokyo Rose assured us that any attempts to remove Marines would be squelched. That meant we would be squelched, of course.

But Hell's Bells—on the morning of the 14th—before sunrise some several hours we went steaming right by Suribachi! If I hadn't known it was Iwo I might have mistaken it for a friendly spot. The whole dinky island was lit up like a down-town Christmas display.

Of course, they weren't the same kind of lights. I guess I chose the wrong Holiday. The 4th of July would be more descriptive.

A couple of miles—or less—out from our side of the island, Tin Cans (Destroyers) were lobbing in flares. They would break over the island like star shells some seconds after you heard the Ka-rump as they were started on their way from the cans. This kept up the remainder of the night—and every night. The Nips got no rest. For maybe a second or two there would be darkness, except for truck and jeep lights racing over the hastily built roads the cats had thrown up, then a couple more flares would burst and start lazily floating earthward. Then the small arms and mortar fire would rip out, and Marines would break for cover further advanced. From our anchorage—right damn close in—we could see the shadowy forms of men running, jumping, falling flat. Then the flashes from machine gins, pistols, rifles—would all cut patterns across the dark blotch between them and open sky—Suribachi.

Daylight changed the eeriness of the picture. We could plainly see the tanks, trucks, jeeps, bulldozers—rumbling along apparently oblivious to the roars of infantry and artillery. They were moving supplies, building roads, air strips and all the things necessary to speed up the day of securing the damned rock.

We put our boats over and carried provisions around the sort of half-way bay to other smaller ships. Our big stock of provisions was split up among several smaller craft—DE's and the like. We had two boats equipped to make smoke and stood smoke boat guard every night and day, in case of surprise air attack.

An LST came along side—we unloaded her of her jeeps, howitzers, amtracs, rifles and Marine personnel gear. The big boom would swing over— men would hook on a truck or a jeep and we would tuck them into our holds. We loaded a lot of it at night. If you've never seen ships load in a rough sea— side by side—then I can't give you a very good idea of it. Suffice it to say it's no child's play. It's heavy, tiresome work. The men worked with a will and did a splendid job. We beat hell out of our port side, forward. Two ships clapping in a sea roll—well, something has to give.

In the daytime, in the boats, we sometimes—(one time anyway) got too close to shore, and Jap snipers opened up on us. After plopping a few just short of our LCVP* stern's (3 feet), we took off like gang busters. Something mighty unpleasant about the hum of a bullet over your head! And nobody got sleepy on watch at night. Japs had a habit of swimming off the island at night and climbing aboard our ships—with a few grenades or just to get clear of the rat hunt the Marines carried out all day and night. Fore and aft sentries didn't set down their rifles— and the water around us was scanned with binocs with a fervor.

From the bridge we watched the progress on the beach. We changed anchorage 3 times—were in close on both sides of the Island. Jens and I watched one day while the Marines attempted to clean out a particularly big cave about half-way up Suribachi. The Marines were strung out all the way up the side of the mountain. They grabbed shelter behind rocks, ledges. After tossing grenades in with no visible effect except a puff of smoke rolling out the cave entrance, 3 of them got bolder and stepped up to the mouth, and a

*Small landing craft carried by U.S. Navy transports.

sharp report flashed from the cave. We saw the Marine pitch and fall in front of the opening. His two buddies grabbed for him and one of them got hit. He crawled away—the other one dragged off the first Marine. Stretcher bearers eased their way up. After getting down to a protected ledge, they started carrying the two wounded (or dead) Marines back to the center of the beach. A land mine explosion threw up so much smoke and lava dust we lost sight of the entire group. We quit looking after that. It's not very damned pleasant to see guys blown up—especially when you're sitting in a spot of comparative safety. And especially when you know you're there to take off, and back to safety, as many of those scared but courageous guys who can be crammed aboard your ship. One day more, and those very Marines would have been among the worn looking, hungry looking, hodge-podge clothed group that boarded our ships. The next day we got our personnel load—I can't tell you how many—but enough to jam the ship from stem to stern and bulge over the bulwark. They came aboard at night, and when the skipper announced to them, as they clambered up the nets from an LST, burdened with their rifles, spades, and camouflaged protective gear,—that their hot supper would be served as soon as they had been assigned bunks in the compartment for troops—when he announced that, they cheered like anything! A month on K and C Rations makes a man ridiculously happy to hear news of a hot meal. And I wonder just how many people at home would grumble over the points it takes to buy catsup if they could see battle fatigued men, fresh from horrors on Iwo Jima, pour streams of it over nice thick steaks. And sink teeth, used to chewing hastily on any damned thing out of a ration can, with childish delight into honest to God yankee food! Sure, they ate us out of ship and home on the voyage back—but I don't guess there was a hell of a lot of grumbling from us on that score. They paid us back with tales of Iwo and with souvenirs. My Jap Air Medal, taken from a still warm Jap by an artillery sergeant, paid me back.

So we got the hell out of there a month ago today and headed back with our load. Two days after we left they had a Jap air attack. After sitting there for a week like ducks on a pond—loading our ships—Tokyo Rose's threatened squelchers showed up. But we were gone and so were the Marines!

Except for a middle of the night sub scare, which the DE's took care of with depth charge after depth charge (I don't know how many), we sailed into a friendly port. Then a few days later we sailed into another one. And later still we took the Marines into their home island base. And for my money, the greeting they got from the people and natives—the band and the Native girl dancers—well, they had it coming.

So here we are, sitting for awhile waiting to go out again. And maybe this time we'll be in at the start and put 'em ashore and let somebody else take 'em off. I don't know when or where. But the Japs won't get any rest. And neither will lots of guys like those Marines and like the guys on this ship—we won't get any real rest until the whole nasty mess is over and we can come home.

I love you, Carol Jean—and the day we can be together again with our David boy and the Barber family and the Hoover's and Olmsteds and Barne's and everybody at home—well, that's the day I'm waiting for—and praying for. Keep your chin up—and have what fun you can and don't worry.

I hope Dad enjoys this letter. It's a poor thing, at best, but it's what I remember best. The long days at sea and the humorous and sad incidents that occur every day slip from memory. And the Navy doesn't permit a diary—damn it!

Anyway it wasn't tough for us. The guys that *took in* the guys that *went* in deserve the credit.

Kiss my big boy for me. Wrassle him a litter for his Pop

P.S. I just got your long letter with the poems. Also one from Dad, Mom & Wanda. I hope Lottie's colitis is okay by now.

More later—

Love
Buck

Letter Home from William Bieluch[2]

A sailor aboard another APA at Iwo Jima relates his part in supporting operations, including the onerous duty of manning the "smoke boats."

21 March, 1945

Dear [Dad]

Now that it can be told, I want you to be among the first to hear my account of our participation in the invasion of Iwo Jima. I can well envision your fears and worries over my safety as you surmised that I was taking part in the bloody action about which you heard and read so much in the news accounts at home. If mental telepathy were a reality, I would have resorted to it all the time I was in the danger area to assure you of my wellbeing. While I didn't write to you during our stay at Iwo Jima because it didn't feel natural for me to do so in the light of all the activity going on ashore and about the ship, I thought of you continuously and prayed to God that He deliver me back to you safe and sound. With His blessings I went through the engagement without harm.

Iwo Jima, Japanese for Sulphur Island, is, as you undoubtedly know, in the center of the group of tiny islands known as the Volcano Islands. Sometimes it is called only Iwo. Its location is midway between Saipan and Tokyo, about 640 nautical miles distant from each of the two points. The military significance of the conquest of territory so strategically located is tremendous, and I am proud of the part, small though it was, that I played in it.

My account of the battle, which is by mandate limited to a description of my personal experiences therein, is best begun by relating my feelings prior to D day. With the official announcement of the operation three weeks before, there was generated within me a feeling of tenseness not unlike that which I had experienced before in approaching an important examination in my academic career. The climax of that feeling was reached on Sunday, February 18th, D minus one day, the development being marked in its various stages by our briefing sessions and other last-minute preparations. Our church services that day bore a very solemn note. General Absolution was imparted, and we all received Holy Communion. The sermon was excellent; it was recorded by mimeographing. The services were held in the open on the main deck, and towards the close of Mass we could see some of our escorting destroyers and planes going to the attack of a submarine contacted underwater, our attention having been called by the dull explosions of depth charges.

That afternoon we halted our journey to Iwo to take on an unusual visitor, an officer member of the underwater demolition team that swam into our landing beaches the preceding day. Our final briefing session was called immediately, so that he could recount to us the characteristics of the beaches, surf, etc., all of which he had observed first-hand. As I listened to him talk, I couldn't help but feel that we were already there, although actually we were still over 175 or 200 miles away.

On the eve of the battle, I had to stand the midnight to 0400 security watch. This was not the usual watch. It had a new significance. I considered the watch to mark the end of our usual routine for a while. My security rounds of the ship this time disclosed a small number of men awake in their bunks reading by flashlight. One chap, a crew member, I observed was reading a prayer book. About the middle of the watch, gun fire flashes began to appear beyond the horizon ahead of us. These, I knew, were due to the naval bombardment of Iwo, which was preparing the way for our landings. While these were first observed while we were about 65 miles away, they increased in intensity and frequency as we neared our destination.

Although I sacked in after my watch, it wasn't with the expectation of getting much sleep, for everyone was scheduled to be called at 0415. However, I did sleep soundly for the half hour interval between my relief and reveille, which was a tonic for my feelings, short as it was.

When dawn broke, there it was in plain sight ahead of us. Our part was now to be realized. The feeling of suspense was gone. I was now concerned with the present, rather than the future. The gunfire was terrific, but at this stage it seemed to be one-sided. Little did I realize then how soon I would become accustomed to it. I'm very thankful, though, that I wasn't very conscious of it for long. It does tax the nerves somewhat, even if it's from the distance.

As I intimated before, my part was a very small one. I did not get ashore at all. Those who hit the beach were in the thick of it. Our ship at first stayed 7 1/2 miles off shore, but, after a few days, we moved to within three-quarters of a mile from the beach. Nevertheless, considering the mission of our ship, the part of every man aboard was a somewhat significant one. Each job bore a relation to the whole.

I was one of the four smoke boat officers aboard the ship. We went out on patrol nights in a smoke boat, standing by our ship, ready to cover it with a smoke screen upon signal every time there was an air raid or a probability of such. I went out on smoke patrol eight nights of the ten that we were at Iwo. As I was the only smoke boat officer aboard the ship on the night of D day, I was out on patrol the entire night, from sunset to sunrise, a total of thirteen hours. The remaining nights, the four of us went out in two shifts; I had the second run, from a half hour after midnight to sunrise. During my patrol, only a few raids were made, all of which were very, very small and directed against the beach. While on this duty, I witnessed a lot of fireworks, in a somewhat true sense of the word; the shells of the continuous naval bombardment traced a red path through the sky, while flares kept the island continuously illuminated. I might add that the light of these flares helped our visibility on the water considerably.

Smoke patrol was rugged duty. This was especially true the first few nights, when the ship maneuvered almost continuously, for we had to chase after the ship every time it moved, in order to be close by in the event we received an order to make smoke. The weather was chilly nights, so chilly, in fact, that I had to get a pair of long underwear after suffering for a few nights. We were wet so much by the spray when we tried to keep up with the ship that we could hardly keep our eyes open; most of the time that I was out in a smoke boat during the first part of our stay, the water was rough and whipped up into a spray at even a slow speed of movement through the water. Our rainsuits were not sufficient protection for the drenching we received. And then, one night we had a heavy rain, while at several other occasions we had intermittent showers. After the first few days, the ship stayed at anchor. That made the patrol a lot more comfortable, for we didn't have to move about very much in the smoke boats. Wouldn't you know it, though; when we didn't have to maneuver after the ship, the sea was relatively calm. Smoke patrol was very dull duty, though I had one exciting incident. One morning at about 5:00 A.M. our boat broke down, and we almost drifted into the open bow doors of an LST before we were towed back to the ship by our second smoke boat. The duty was very tiresome; and with all of the activity going on about the ship, I had a devil of a time getting sufficient sleep, although I tried very hard. I can truthfully say that I slept only about half the time that I went in my bunk. I even resorted to stuffing my ears so that I wouldn't hear all of the announcements over our public address system, but that didn't help much.

During a part of the day I did a couple of incidental things. I gave relief to my first lieutenant and his assistant in standing damage control watches. Also, I helped to carry a few casualties to the sick bay as they came aboard. Many times when I had nothing else to do and couldn't sleep, I would go out on deck to watch the action. While our distance from shore originally limited our view of the activity ashore, our subsequent position gave us a ringside seat, although by this time our front had advanced in part beyond a ridge and out of sight. With the aid of binoculars I really got a close view, especially during the later days of our stay.

A few hours after the initial landings, we began to take casualties aboard. At first I felt the sight touch my stomach, but I soon became hardened to it. I had to, in order to get along about the ship. The injured came aboard at all hours, but regardless of the time, the chaplain was always on hand to meet them. It was a magnificent job that he did. And our staff of doctors worked wonders. Many a man will remember them for their work.

Everyone aboard took an interest in the welfare of our casualties. We tried to make them as comfortable as possible by giving them cigarettes, cheering them with our talk, and even writing letters for them. The several deaths that occurred among them saddened us.

The burial services that I witnessed were very solemn ceremonies. Our hearts were filled with the deepest reverence, and our lips betrayed a silent prayer as we watched the weighted bodies slide from underneath the American flag and drop into the water.

Of our crew, only one man was lost, a shoemaker from Washington, D.C., who went ashore on D day with the beach party. No one knows what happened to him; he is counted with the missing. I knew the chap rather well, for he stood security watches under me. In fact, he served with me on D day morning as we neared our objective.

Shortly before D day, I made the acquaintance aboard our ship of a marine Lieutenant Colonel, a Slovak from around Pittsburgh. He told me about his wife, whom he met and married while stationed in Philadelphia, and his two year old child, whom he had barely seen. This officer was killed outright within a few minutes of his landing on the beach on D day.

What few prisoners there were during our stay at Iwo, we took aboard the ship. Upon sight of them within our guard, it was hard to realize the meanness that they carry in battle. Some of these were injured. One was given up as a hopeless case, but, surprisingly enough, he pulled through, to the amazement of our doctors. Ironical, wasn't it, when life means so little to them?

I can now tell you that Marine Sergeant Stanley Rydziel was a passenger on our ship. He came aboard with the troops early in January and recognized me at once. Stanley went ashore on February 22nd, D plus three day, a very rainy day, indeed. I spoke with him just before he left the ship and bade him good luck. He promised to write me some day when he got the chance. To date, I haven't heard from him yet, but it's no wonder, for they're still very busy on Iwo. Even though this dot of an island has now been secured, our forces still have to dig out the remaining Japs from their caves and tunnels.

The grandest feeling I experienced at Iwo was when I saw our flag flying over Mt. Suribachi on D plus 4 day. The significance of this achievement was deep, and it made us all very proud. You can well imagine how we felt when we heard Radio Tokyo a day or two later announce that the Japanese flag was still waving over this volcano. Tokyo's account of the battle was a mass of exaggeration. The American reports from San Francisco, on the other hand, were very authentic. It was really interesting to get a word description of all that was transpiring about us.

I hope you have been following the sequence of the battle in Time magazine. This was written by Robert Sherrod, one of the correspondents aboard our ship, and is an excellent piece of journalism. Nellie is saving all of the issues covering the invasion for me. She is being told to keep the daily accounts from the newspapers also. I would like to read them someday.

Before this operation, I thought the Marines took too much glory for their part in the Pacific war, but after witnessing their toughest and bloodiest fight to date, I don't think they went far enough. They fought bravely against tremendous opposition and made a magnificent showing. History will record this operation as a glorious achievement of the Marine Corps.

In conclusion, I would like to opine some general impressions about my first participation in battle. If there is anything on this earth that approaches hell, it is war. My immediate reaction conformed to the popular feeling that "War is hell." There is no better way to express it. War is unnatural, for it is a wanton destruction of life, God's fruit upon this earth. How I hate the thought that this may still go on for years. Pray to God that there's an early end.

Please don't let this personal account give you any cause for worry or concern in the future. I'll be alright. May God bless you and keep you.

As always,
[signed]

Sailor's letter home: "I enlisted because I liked the nice clean ships the Navy had. Now I know who keeps them that way."

—Sydney J. Harris, Chicago Daily News

A MERCHANTMAN'S TALE

POEM BY IAN A. MILLER—
"MERCHANTMEN LIKE THEE"

Crews aboard merchant vessels often faced risks as grave as those in combat. Indeed, until mid-1943 or so, U-boats lurked in the Atlantic with considerable success. Delivering Lend-Lease shipments to the Soviet port of Murmansk was particularly dangerous because the route by necessity passed close to Nazi submarine bases and airfields in occupied Norway. Here is a poem dedicated to the merchant marine sailors of World War II.

MERCHANTMEN LIKE THEE[3]

Here's to thee, thy wandering heroes—
Roaming o'er the sea—
Gone are you from families loving—
To eternity.

Blazing sunshine . . . frozen ocean—
Ocean winds blow free.

Here's a prayer for those departed—
Wandering o'er the sea.

Here's to thee, thy gallant heroes—
Brave boys of the sea—
Gone are you in battle's glory—
To eternity.

Man the deck guns . . . launch the lifeboats—
In the raging sea.

Here's a prayer for those departed—
Heroes of the sea.

Here's to thee, thy fallen heroes—
Resting in the sea—
Gone are you in stormy tempest—
To eternity.

Blow the whistle . . . bend the flags on—
Welcome home to thee.
Here's a prayer for those departed—
Sleeping in the sea.

Here's to thee, remembered heroes—
Spirits of the sea—
Missing yes but not forgotten—
Resting peacefully.

Slumber quiet . . . sleep forever—
In the rolling sea.

Here's a prayer to those departed
Merchantmen like thee.

By Ian A. Millar

A RED CROSS VOLUNTEER IN FRANCE

LETTERS HOME FROM MARY METCALFE[4]

Mary "ChiChi" Metcalfe was a volunteer with the Red Cross who served in France. In this series of detailed letters she describes her daily chores and, to a greater extent, her off-duty activities. She spent a great deal of her tour working from a "clubmobile," a mobile coffee and doughnut shop. In no small part because of the young women like Mary who served the snacks and chatted with the soldiers, the Red Cross was very popular with the troops, as these letters make clear.

July 20, 1944

Dearest Mommie,

I only have time to write a short note. This is to let you know that "news sometimes arrives" after much waiting around to get over here. We had a wonderful crossing. The weather was beautiful, and the sailors and officers were just wonderful to us. They were so excited to have women to take over. The

officers gave us their cabins, and we slept two in a bunk. The food was marvelous as it always is in the navy.

In the afternoon and evening we had a dance on the deck. We played the
Victrola on one of the clubmobiles and danced to that. It was lots of fun. All
the boys said they would much rather have made the trip than have a 5 day
liberty ashore.

While we were waiting to come ashore, there were lots of amphibious
jeeps or ducks, as they are called, coming along side, so we took rides in those.
We rode right up on to the beach in them and all around, then rolled right
back into the water and out to our ship.

There are two St. Louis boys in the crew, and Mary Pitcairn, Marie Philips
and I had our pictures taken with them, so be sure and watch the papers for
that picture to appear. Also watch all the news reels because they have been
taking pictures like mad since we arrived.

The dust and dirt here are terrific! As we drove from the ship to where we
are, it was so dusty that I had to keep the windshield wiper going in order to
see out the windshield.

It does your heart good to see how glad these boys are to see us. They all
wave and yell like mad as we come along.

You wouldn't believe it possible to see some of these towns. As we drove
along we came through towns that are bombarded to practically nothing. They
must have been such pretty little towns, and now they are just a shambles.

The French people are all so friendly and nice. They wave and smile as we
come along, and when ever we stop they come out with a bottle and glasses
offering us cider. I hope that before I leave I shall have some ability at speaking French.

We are staying at present in an old chateau which was used before us as
some German hqs. The rooms are all barren. We put up our cots and got out
our sleeping bags and are sleeping very comfortably. There are three wood-
en closets in our room, and each one has a German name pasted on it. The
names are Ebentreich, Giesl, and Kühlewind.

Les, Bobby, Jane Phillips and I are in the same room. There are several
wash stands in the house, and to get water out of the faucets we have to pump
a lever in the kitchen to get water up into the pipes. There is one john on the
second floor just below us, but it doesn't work, so we have to use a couple of
little out houses in the back.

Heaven only knows when we shall have a bath again, as there is nothing
any place around here which even looks like a bath tub or shower. The only
way we have of getting hot water is to put a bucket on the stove in the kitchen.

We eat at the mess at 1st Army Hdqs. which is about 5 miles from us.

The mess hall is a big tent with wooden tables and benches, and the food

"Chi Chi" Metcalfe and clubmobile. (Courtesy of the Dwight D. Eisenhower Library, Mary Metcalfe Rexford Collection.)

there certainly beats the K rations we were eating when we just arrived.

Will you call up Mrs. Johnson, Co. 2534 and tell her I saw her son Lewis. He is such a nice boy. We had a grand time, and tell her he looks fine. Tell her to be sure and watch all the papers for the picture of us. The other boy is Brian Walk, and he lives on either Chippewa or Cherokee.

The atmosphere here is so different from England. There is a freer feeling, and every thing seems much more quaint and old worldish than it was there.

I now have something in common with Jack Hall in coming here.

I must go and clean the clubmobile and make some doughnuts, so good-bye for now. Be sure and tell Yvonne at P and P that I am crazy about her country and if I ever have a chance I shall try and find out about her family.

Lots and lots and lots of love to you and everyone.

Chichi

July 31, 1944

Dearest Mommie,

This has to be short and sweet as we are going out to serve in half an hour. Since I last wrote you, we have done some traveling. For three days we went up close to the front to serve some boys who were having a rest of a few days before going back into battle. The first night we arrived in this area we slept in a big stone barn. We took our sleeping bags and threw them down in the straw. There were just four of the clubmobiles that went on this mission; ours, Fran Hacher's, Louise Smart's, and Martha Richrdson's. The driving was something, as we had to drive the last couple of miles with no light at all, not even a tail light to follow. The roads over here are really narrow and rough. There were GIs and officers sleeping in the same barn that night, since we arrived so late and there was no place else to put us.

One of the funniest things over here is the latrine situation. I have to go to the clubmobile now as it is almost time to leave, so will finish this heaven only knows when. It is now Aug. 6th so you can see how difficult it is to find time for anything but work. To continue about the latrines, we have had everything from a slit trench, to one or two seaters with a latrine screen around it to a regular outhouse.

The night after the barn episode we were moved back about four miles, as things were a bit hot where we were. This time we slept in a schoolhouse for two nights. We would get up at 5:30, breakfast at six and then cook doughnuts in a field across the way where our clubmobiles were parked. The first morning we went over and just as we started, here came a complete band. It was a really good GI band, and they set up their instruments and played all sorts of good pieces for us. The second night we were there they had a movie shown for us right in our room when we returned from our movie dispensing. The picture was "Two Sisters and a Sailor" which we really enjoyed. The officers had procured some cognac and sauterur too, so that was nice after a tiring day. I must dress now, as it is getting to be the departure hour again.

Lots of Love,
Chichi

August 2, 1944

Dearest Mommie,

I started a letter to you the day before yesterday but did not have a chance to finish it.

You wouldn't believe it to see how we are living now. We are attached to an outfit, and we serve all the battalions which are attached to them. Our home is a tent called a pyramidal tent. The sides can be rolled up and tied. We sleep on cots with our sleeping bags on top. Our cots are dug into the ground, a little lower than ground level. This is the way everyone sleeps over here if you are camping out. Our latrine is close to our tent, and they made a little sign for it which says Powder Room.

Everyone is so nice to us, and they do everything they can think of for us. There is a one star general in command, and he is most attractive and lots of fun. There is also a very nice young full colonel. The battery commander is Capt. Sperry, and he sees that we get everything we want and need for the clubmobile and ourselves. The general said that he (Sperry) was to be our mother superior. He is so nice about getting everything done for us, and he is quite attractive.

We now have an electric light in our tent and a telephone. They put the telephone in so that we could be awakened every morning. We work in shifts—one has to get up at 5 o'clock to start the doughnuts, the next one comes on at 7:45 and takes over, and the third one has the morning off—this way we have a morning off every third day. We have to start off to serve at about 11:30 as we take in a battalion every day and that consists of about 5 different batteries which are scattered all about. We get home about 10 o'clock at night dirty and thoroughly exhausted.

If the boys were glad to see us in England, you should see them over here. They whoop and howl and have a fit as we drive along. Undoubtedly you have seen pictures of the traffic situation over here, and that is exactly what we contend with every day.

A week ago Sunday, Col. Ruzek and Capt. Roberts came to our chateau in the evening. They had discovered we were here and came to find us. It was good to see them again. We went and served their camp on Tues and then had supper with them.

The next day we were moved up to join the outfit we are with now.

It is now Aug. 7th, and today we moved from the place we were located. Our days consist of the routine I told you of cooking doughnuts all morning. We leave about 11:30 or 12 to go serve a battalion. This means 5 stops at 4 different batteries and a headquarters group. We spend about an hour in each place serving and talking to the boys. An officer arrives from whatever battalion we are to serve, and a couple of us ride in the jeep with him and the driver and the other one in the clubmobile. They have been bringing a GI along to drive the clubmobile to make it easier for us. It is a help, as it is a heavy thing to drive, and it does tire you out on these dusty, shot up roads.

For us it is an unusual sight to see a town that is in fairly good condition. We are so used to seeing almost complete destruction. As we go along, we see German tanks and cars which have been knocked out. In a lot of places there is the smell of death as you ride along. This is terrible. It is amazing all this that we are seeing and doing. It is an experience that we shall never forget, and what tales we shall have to tell you some day. A clubmobile is a mighty important thing over here. Everyone is fighting to have a clubmobile attached to them, from the generals down to the privates. If you could see how these boys just stand and look at us because we are American girls. They just want to look at you and hear you talk and watch you smile. They are all wonderful boys, and we have a good time with them.

We usually don't get back until 10 or 10:30 at night, so you can see the hours are long.

We have been doing our own laundry since in this place we have found no one to do it yet. The dust is so terrific that you can only wear a shirt once. Especially riding in jeeps we get saturated with dust. We wash things in a bucket using water from the clubmobile. I have taken to wearing my shirts rough dried, and they really look pretty good. The clubmobile gets so dirty too after a trip around. As usual there is very little time for anything but work, so you have had no letters. It is a problem trying to work in keeping our tent in order since there is no place to put anything except our suitcases or barracks bags, and as you want to get into one or the other you have to transfer things around.

We have had beautiful sunshiny days and heavenly starry nights for the past four or five days. I only wish we had time to lie out in the sun and get a burn. I have never seen as many shooting stars as the past few nights. It is a real sight.

This is real camping life. It is fun but quite wearing, as we don't get home until at least ten every night, then we have to clean up the coffee urns and get things ready to start off at 5 the next morning.

Our one star general is wonderful to us, as is every one else here. They try to do everything possible to make things easy for us. We have an electric light in our tent and a German telephone. The telephone is here so we can be called at 5 and 7 in the morning. Our telephone no. is "lipstick."

I got a nice letter from Bill Weld saying he had been here since D and 1. I was close to him in the last place but didn't know it until the day before we moved so didn't get to see him.

We have yet to have a bath or shower in France. The only baths we have been able to manage have been in a bucket. It is remarkable how good that feels when there are no other facilities.

I received your 3 letters from the east. I wish you could have gone to Jimmy and Ginny's wedding. Also have received letters from Fantie and Uncle Hugh.

It is again time to wash and dress to go out, so I have to stop. I think that on Mon. and Tues I may have a chance to concentrate on writing a real letter.

Anyway watch the newsreels and paper, and you will know exactly what we are seeing.

Lots and lots and lots of love to you and everyone.

                                                                        Chichi

It is now Aug. 12th.

Aug. 16, 1944

Dearest Mommie,

The day before yesterday we took our clubmobile to an ordnance place to be painted O.D.* like the rest of the army vehicles—also to have it fixed all over. After almost a month of bouncing over these roads, it is quite a wreck. Being grey as it was, it really showed up like a sore thumb, and that is ridiculous with all the camouflaging we do otherwise.

Our tent for instance is against a hedgerow, under some trees, and there is a camouflage net all over it. There are chickens, cows and ducks that wander around in the field outside our tent.

There was a war correspondent here last week named Ruth Cowan. She went with us when we went out to serve and spent the night with us here in our tent. She will write a story about what we are doing so you might watch for it.

Yesterday since our clubmobile was not here, we had a chance to get things a little bit organized in our tent, and in the afternoon we went swimming in a creek way down at the bottom of a hill from where we are camped. It really felt wonderful and was the first real bath we have had.

We had a show here last night which included Dinah Shore. We brought her over to our tent to wash and dress. She really was very nice, and we enjoyed seeing her and talking to her. After all our beautiful weather it had to start raining just as Dinah started to sing.

Yesterday morning who should appear outside our tent but Col. Ruzek. He was on his way someplace and discovered where we were, so he dropped in to say hello. He and Lt. Wieboldt came back last night to see the Dinah Shore show. It was lots of fun seeing them again.

I hope you are seeing all the newsreels and reading all about what's going on over here because that is how you can get the best idea of what it is like. As we drive along we see these French people going back to what was their homes. Their few possessions they push along in baby carriages or carts or what ever transportation they can find. Really you wouldn't believe there could be such complete destruction unless you could see these towns over here. Also there are all the German tanks and cars that have been knocked out all along the road. We are always passing trucks full of German prisoners.

It is marvelous to see how this army works. It is really coördinated beautifully. You know how fast things are moving over here, and you can imagine what a job it must be to keep supplies and everything else moving along just as fast.

---

*Olive drab.

I don't think I told you that one of the battalions we served was almost all from St. Louis. Just as we were about to leave I was talking to one of the boys and told him my name. He said he worked at Straubs and he used to deliver groceries to us on Vernon. He was so excited about it, and we had to have our picture taken together.

The country around here is so beautiful. It is very hilly, and as you drive along you can see for miles. After we took our clubmobile to be fixed and served the Ord. people the other day, we went to that beautiful place that Bud has in his movie reels on his tour through France. To get into the town we crawled through a little door. The cobblestone streets were fascinating. We had hoped to be able to buy something, but there was nothing but very souveniry, junky stuff. We stayed for supper and had the best omelette I have ever put in my mouth. As I was walking along the street I looked into one of the restaurants, and there was Franklin Ferriss. I talked to him for a while and discovered he was with the hdqs. we served when we first came over and were with for the first few days. He says he has been working very hard ever since he arrived, and he looked like it.

I can't remember myself now, but I think the conjecturing was about our three days down in Kent.

While we were in London we stayed at the Grosvenor House too and do we think back on those luxurious days as we lie here in these graves in our tent now.

We are so lucky to be attached to an ack ack* brigade as we are now instead of being with all the other girls and living a dormitory life as they do.

Read the August 6th Yank magazine on pg. 6. The white thatched brig. gen. it mentions is our general. He has more vitality and is a most fascinating person. He likes us and is always bringing us presents. The other day he brought us all some wooden shoes.

One of the boys just brought us a big framed mirror so we can now get a look at our full length for the first time since we arrived on these shores. Last night I wore my red dress with the cut out work around the neck and sleeves. It really feels good to put on a skirt occasionally and the boys say it is so nice to see civilian clothes again.

We are still attached as we were in England, and they are the ones who have put us where we are as they are also part of the First Army.

The last letter I received from you was written July 16th. Our mail comes to the place where the other girls are, and we have to get it from them when anyone goes down that way. I think someone is going tomorrow, and maybe we shall have some more mail.

---

*Antiaircraft artillery.

(Did I ask you to send me another cig. case, tan if possible or any color. Mine is on its last legs. Also I will need some more brown coral nail polish—Chen Yu.)

I think I told you before that we have spent no money except for laundry since we came over, as there is nothing to buy. I wanted to buy you a present when we went sightseeing the other day, but there was nothing worth getting. I guess the best I can do is wish you a happy, happy birthday. I hope you will have a big day and drink a highball or a Tom Collins for me.

I must stop and get dressed for supper now.

As usual lots of love to everyone and especially to you and a happy, happy birthday.

Chi-Chi

BREAKFAST FOR ONE HUNDRED

RECIPES FROM THE WAR DEPARTMENT, "THE ARMY COOK"[5]

Recipe #1. Cakes, Buckwheat

8 pounds flour, buckwheat
4 pounds flour, wheat
3 ounces salt
12 ounces baking powder
3 pounds sugar or molasses
1 can milk, evaporated
6 quarts water
24 eggs

Sift together the flour, sugar, salt, and baking powder. Beat the eggs and add to water and evaporated milk. Turn this mixture into the sifted flour mixture. Then beat into a smooth batter. If the batter seems too thick, add a little more water or milk. Grease a hot griddle iron or clean stove top with bacon rind or clean fat and pour out the batter, a spoonful at a time. Cook until nicely browned on both sides. Serve hot with butter or sirup, or both. Hot cakes should be cooked, a few at a time. If all the cakes required for a meal are cooked before starting to serve, the first ones cooked will become tough and leathery.

Recipe #6. Milk for Breakfast Foods

>15 cans milk, evaporated
>2 pounds sugar
>1 ounce salt

Add sufficient water to make 7 1/2 gallons. Whip well for a few minutes. One ounce vanilla or lemon extract may be added if desired. This recipe will produce a satisfactory substitute when fresh milk is not available.

Recipe #46. Bacon, Fried

>22 pounds bacon, issue, or 24 pounds bacon, breakfast

Cut about five slices to the inch. If dry salt, issue bacon is used, place in a bakepan containing boiling water, boil for 5 minutes, then drain off water. Fry on a hot range or in a quick oven. Drain off excess fat and stir occasionally so that all the bacon is thoroughly cooked. If served with eggs or hot cakes, etc. 10 pounds bacon are sufficient.

Recipe #96. Omelet, Plain

>150 eggs
>8 cans milk, evaporated, diluted with 8 pints water; or 8 quarts fresh
>   milk
>2 pounds drippings or fat
>salt and pepper to taste

Mix the eggs and milk, season, and whip well. Put drippings or other fat into the bake pan, and when the fat begins to smoke pour in the mixture, not more than 3 inches deep, and bake in a medium oven.

Recipe #272. Biscuit, Baking Powder

>16 pounds flour
>3 ounces salt
>11 ounces baking powder
>4 pounds fat (lard or lard substitute)
>6 cans milk, evaporated, diluted with 6 pints water, or 20 ounces
>   powdered skim milk dissolved in 6 pints water

Sift the dry ingredients together three times and work in the fat. Make a well in the middle and add all the milk at once. Stir until mixed. This should make a soft dough, if not, add more milk. Turn out on lightly floured board and knead quickly for not more than 1 minute. The secret of making good biscuit is in handling the dough only enough to mix thoroughly. Roll out to one-half the thickness desired in the baked biscuit, cut out with a biscuit cutter, and place in bakepans just touching each other. Bake in a quick oven (400°–450° F.—9 to 12 counts) for 12 minutes or until brown. Serve hot.

A recent survey made among almost 2,500,000 American soldiers to determine their food preferences revealed that the majority of them like frankfurters more than any other meat, mashed potatoes more than fried, cake more than pie, and that they prefer cocoa to coffee.

—Freling Foster, Collier's

LIFE WITH THE REAR ECHELON

LETTER HOME FROM LOREN FRED[6]

Loren Fred was a corporal in a personnel records unit that worked behind the frontlines in Europe after D-Day. He was a very observant and curious soldier, however, and found much of interest in the people, animals, and landscape of France. Although this letter does not discuss his official duties, it does give a vivid sense of how many Americans experienced foreign lands and peoples in the aftermath of battle.

July 12, 1944

Personnel Section
France

Dear Agnes,

You remember the scavenger hunts that those giving parties used to have? That seems to be what we're having here lately. A good many of the rear echelon are out to see what they can find, and practically all of the 915th personnel section have been having a great time the past few days. Different ones are always losing something, unavoidably, and different outfits are sometimes forced to leave items behind. Then, too, when some unit is moving back for a rest sometimes they discard a lot of things that others can use.

Almost as soon as we got over here two or three started looking for souvenirs. Gradually the others lost their reluctance until now all the section but one has been out looking for souvenirs or something that he could make use of; this one fellow doesn't seem to have enough ambition to get out himself,

Loren and Agnes Fred, seated on lawn, Abilene, Kansas. (Courtesy of the Dwight D. Eisenhower Library, Loren Fred Collection.)

but he is always willing to share whatever someone else finds. Once when we were staying in a house he did look around in the attic, but he doesn't venture outside much.

A good many of the articles picked up are things that the individual or the group can use, such as an extra shelter half, a raincoat, gloves, scabbards, maps, oil, food that can still be eaten, and so forth. Lots of times, though, we're out for souvenirs to keep or send home. Parachute cloth or whole parachutes, many of which we think were used on D-day, are prized finds. In the old house where we stayed once we found several old French books, which several of the fellows are sending home. German pistols and knives are much sought for, but so far no one has had any luck.

Last night one fellow found a small copper skillet with brass handle, coated with soot and smoke. He thought it might be useful to cook something in but when I suggested it would make a fine souvenir he adopted the idea and now won't part with it for a good deal of money or anything else. I would like to have it to send home, myself.

However, I haven't been unlucky myself. I expect I have picked up about as much as any of them. Yesterday I found about 20 fruit bars, which are well liked by most of the men here. I thought everyone liked them, and I don't see why they were discarded, but it was lucky for me. Another fellow got about a dozen.

A few days ago while I was searching through a pile of junk along the roadside (I never thought there would be a day when I would be a scavenger in a junk pile), I found a sock with a wad of something in it which I immediately thought might be money. I didn't really expect it to be, but when I got it out I had found 3,160 francs in French and invasion money. That has been the biggest haul so far, unless a whole parachute is more. I don't expect to approach such a value again; I think this is the only time in my life I ever found any money, at least in a sizeable quantity—never over a dollar before.

There was an article in Stars and Stripes yesterday which contained an excellent description of the hedgerows here in Normandy, I thought. It says, "The hedgerow is more than a mere line of hedges–usually it is a dirt embankment three to four feet high covered with a tangle of bushes and trees which often make it a total height of six feet or more. Most hedgerows are two to four feet thick. In Normandy they bound each field and road and alongside each is a shallow ditch two or three feet deep and about three feet wide." (This isn't always true; sometimes there is no ditch at all, and the size varies. Lots of time there are ditches out in the middle of the fields, too. L.)

The whole countryside is divided into small orchards and pastures, bounded by these hedgerows. I don't know whether one family owns just one parcel of land or several, but if they own only one I don't see how they make a living. Each of the parcels is small. Most of the orchards seem to be apple trees. Cows, sheep and horses are kept in the pastures, with a few turkeys, hogs, geese and other small animals occasionally. Usually in the orchards and some of the fields there is a grass about three feet tall, which the farmer cuts with a very old-fashioned hand scythe as feed for the animals. Usually he cuts no more at one time than he intends to use immediately.

The farm people don't live on separate farms as ours do. They seem to build their houses together in small groups and go out to their fields and farms from this cluster of houses. Sometimes there are only four or five families in a small community, but most of the time these small communities have a name of some sort, so that when you read that such and such a place has been captured it may not amount to much.

The people seem to be almost unbelievably poor. A good many of them still wear wooden shoes, lots of them without hose of any kind. Their clothing is very poor too. Some of the furniture and dishes I have seen in a few houses are a poor grade. Buckets and pails are thin and poorly made. The houses themselves are made of brick and native stone, held together by a poor grade of mortar. Some of the mortar, in fact, is almost mud; some of the house walls seem to be nothing more than dirt too. Occasionally I have seen a house that seems to be a well made one, attractive looking.

Many of the houses, on the farms especially, are constructed as a unit with the barn and sheds. The family lives in one part, wagons and implements are kept in another part, and the animals live in their part—sometimes right next door to the family. They have the run of the yard, of course, which is no different from America. Most of the houses are small. It seems to me that the families must eat in the kitchen and perhaps spend most of their time there. Some of the houses seem too small to have a living room even.

Of course, we have seen two or three chateaus too, with innumerable rooms. They are old now, and may have been fine places at one time, but I can't say that I would care to live in such a place. Ordinary people, such as you and I, never did have such homes anyway.

There are many, many trees around the countryside, as there are in England. Some of the country lanes are lined with trees and bushes; sometimes the branches are so heavy overhead that the sun (when there is one) hardly shines through. The hedgerows are more brush than hedge, and are not trimmed as those in England. There are not the fancy designs in trees either. In one place I saw a row of trees along one side of a lot, about ten feet apart, whose branches had grown up to form a solid row all along the line. This row had been trimmed square along the sides and top. That is the only instance of any trimming at all I remember seeing.

There are good roads over here, along the main routes. They are paved with asphalt or macadam and even concrete, and wide enough for two or three vehicles. The country roads are nothing but dirt, though, and when they're wet they really are slippery.

Wood seems to be a scarce item here, as it is in England. As I said before, houses are stone (a few have thatched roofs, not as attractive as some of those in England). One thing that surprised me is that some of the telephone poles are made of concrete, tall and slender and rectangular in shape.

I suppose there are automobiles, but so far I haven't seen any. If the poorer people did have any the must have been stored long ago because of the lack of gas, or perhaps the cars were taken over by the government or the Germans. Most of the people seem to travel by bicycles, which don't look like much. I think the French ordinarily must have good bicycles, though, for as a people they go in for bicycle tours and bicycle racing. Some of the people travel by riding in a two-wheeled, high-wheel cart which I think is called a tumbrel. These are in various grades, from the poorer ones used for work, to the fancy ones made especially for riding purposes. All I have seen seem to be pulled by one horse.

Practically all the soil I have seen so far is terribly poor. I guess the people get out of it only what they put into it, necessitating the use of some kind of fertilizer. Most of the farms seem to have a manure pile, which doesn't help the already poor sanitation; in fact, I doubt that the people know what sanitation is.

Cows are not brought into a barn or even the home lot to be milked, but the people go to the field and milk them. I have seen them come back with their pails of milk, which usually has a good deal of dirt floating around in it. The cows look healthy enough—some of them, really, are fine looking animals—but I have decided I would forego getting any of the milk because of the dirt. Some of the fellows have bought a little milk, and it tasted very good, which doesn't mean that it is. We were warned about drinking milk over here, because of tuberculosis. The cows seem to be all right, but I don't care for the dirt. Some of the fellows insist the milk is perfectly good because the cows look all right and the milk tastes good, but we were warned that the people may have developed an immunity that wouldn't help us. I don't believe everything the army puts out, but I think I'll wait until later for milk.

Back to the soil again, it doesn't seem to be very porous. As much as it rains here, the ground doesn't seem to soak up much water. It gets very slippery on top but down about a foot it is almost dry. I've noticed that holes filled with water don't drain either; the water just stands in them.

Tree roots have surprised me too. In digging we have found it very easy to cut roots in two. They seem to be very soft. We can cut them with the small entrenching shovels we have, with ease. Back home it usually was quite a job to cut through a root of any size, as you no doubt know.

There is a farm near where we are now that has some of the most unusual hogs any of us ever has seen. Their ears are almost a foot long and about six inches wide. When the hog lies down and brings his ears together, they cover his whole face.

Most of the men left right after breakfast this morning on another souvenir hunt. There are only three of the ten of us left here now. They really are going wild over this. It has been a good opportunity for me to get a good letter written though, and I still have most of the day to go out myself.

It may sound as though we don't do anything else, but we still are keeping up with our work. It just happens that this is a slack period.

I had intended to answer some of your letters this time, but I have been wanting to write most of this for some time, and this was a good chance. I may have forgotten some of it, but not much, I guess.

You can see, no doubt, that I'm able to get around as well as ever. I'm feeling fine. I think I have lost a slight bit in weight, but that won't hurt me.

With love,
Loren

Big-eared Norman hog. (Courtesy of the Dwight D. Eisenhower Library, Loren Fred Collection.)

ENTERTAINING THE TROOPS

An important morale booster for the men and women in uniform was entertainment. All the services presented movies and live shows for the troops, whether they were in training camp or deployed overseas. People with show business experience, including the finest actors, musicians, comedians, singers, and directors of the day, entered the service for this very purpose.

Letter from Lieut. General Jacob L. Devers Accompanying Program Notes of Irving Berlin's *This is the Army*[7]

The following is a letter that was included in the program to a London production of Irving Berlin's This is the Army, which was presented all over the United States and in Great Britain, too.

TO OUR ALLIES:

In initiating an overseas tour of Irving Berlin's "This Is The Army," General George C. Marshall, Chief of Staff of the United States Army, personally imposed two stipulations: First, that the soldiers of our Allies, as well as American enlisted men, should see this Army show free of cost; and, second, that all monies realised from the tour of the United Kingdom should go to British service charities.

Several performances will be given exclusively for Allied troops, and one-third of the house for each public performance will be reserved for soldiers; while all funds from the purchase of tickets by officers and civilians will be handled by the British Service Charities Committee.

Also, it should be made clear that the one hundred and fifty men who make up the cast are soldiers. Following their tour of Great Britain, they will be sent to Africa to play before Allied soldiers, then will join America's fighting forces.

If you find "This Is The Army" entertaining, it will have served an important purpose. Entertainment is an essential to high morale, a fact which is understood, surely, throughout the British Empire, where astonishing esprit stood alone, for a time, against the barbaric effort to conquer the civilized world.

Also, I hope "This Is The Army" will play a part in cementing international friendships along the grim road to eventual victory.

> *Jacob L. Devers*
> Lieut. General, U. S. Army,
> Commanding.

Letter from an Army Movie Theater Manager[8]

A theater manager who entered the armed forces to continue his occupation for the benefit of the troops writes to an old friend serving at the front in Europe. Stationed at Camp Croft in South Carolina, the author is a prime example of a draftee who, despite his years of training and service in the military, remained very much more "citizen" than "soldier" as he performed a necessary function to keep up morale among the troops.

March 4, 1945

Afternoon Hank—

How's everything in Germany these days? I guess you are more or less out of snow and knee deep in mud. Me, I'm knee deep in telephone calls—I'm C.Q. and this being a fairly nice Sunday seems as if every babe in town has some guy she has to get in touch with immediately. Just like it use to be with you when you was going to W.V.—man about town. Wonder whatever happened to that June Storey.

I am going to be a Great Uncle, Hank—you remember that little tike we used to call Junior. He's going to be a poppy just like you and that makes me a Great Uncle—some stuff huh. He is also on his way over to visit Germany. He read about it in the travel news and the Infantry decided to give him his opportunity so he is on his way. If I can just stay on this side a few more months I'll have a monument built in my honor in the school yard as being the only local man of the community who fought the entire war in the states because I don't know anyone else from home who has been so lucky.

I'll tell you a secret, fellow, but be sure not to repeat it—this is restricted dope. I'm home sick. I just want to be a civilian again. I want to eat at a table with linen on it and dishes without grease. I want an ice box with beer on ice so I can have a bottle when I feel like drinking it. I want to wear a white shirt without a tie down the main street with bed room slippers on. I haven't been dressed in civilians since November 30th 1941—that was the last Sunday I was home before War. One gets ideas like this every once in awhile. All bull aside the one thing that has me mad about being in the Army is my shoes—I had five real good pairs of shoes and four not so hot pairs and someone used them to pieces while I've been in the Army.

Here at Croft everything is normal. I'm still in the theater business. I guess Gene is in the same racket. Helen wrote some time ago that he was working in a booth. You buy a theater, Hank, and Gene and I will operate it for you. I had expected to see the Miss of the family next month but we are so short of men that I doubt if I'll be able to make it. She'll be quite a daughter when you get home and I hope that will be damn soon. I got a letter from Helen the other day and she said that Stevie and Snuffy were taking turns taking bites of bread.

I'm all cleared up with the Company. The front office wrote me a letter clearing all of my post war worries so far as employment goes. Every day I spend in the Army goes as if I was working so my pay, pension, and other benefits are to my liking now. I'm afraid we're in for a big strike in the mines again this Spring. Lewis hit out with a lot of demands this week and within a month everyone will be raking the miners when this thing should have been brought up months ago and settled before the contract expired. Every year it is the same thing.

That Major who used to be my C.O. and was one of our clerks back in civilian life is out of the Army now—wait until I see him the first time. He entered the Army as a Major (CMT) in April of 1941 and stayed at the same rank for nearly four years so you can have your own opinion. He was the one who jipped me out of my furlough and lectured me thirty minutes for being out of uniform when I had just fallen thirty feet off a pole. The saying goes—Will you remember tomorrow as you think of me today. I'll jangle up my daily reports so bad that he'll be until midnight getting them straight for consolidation.

Well, Hank, I've written nearly two pages and I haven't said a thing but then there isn't much I know. I hope you got through the worst part of the winter without gathering too many aches from the many nights in the fox holes and I sincerely hope you're spending the coming winter home at Reel Ave. Here's the best of luck to you and I do wish you the best. With the coming of Spring you'll be very busy there and I hope it ends quickly.

I'll see you in a couple of weeks—
your pal—
Dunn

WACS

A Certain Reputation

When women served in the armed forces in World War II, there was almost always some controversy, and no women were more numerous or controversial than the WACs. The Women's Army Corps (originally the Women's Auxiliary Army Corps) eventually included hundreds of thousands of women who were given clerical staff jobs in order to free up men for combat roles. Many Americans—of both genders—placed little faith in the motives and conduct of women in uniform, but the WACs' performance of duty belied the popular stereotypes and contributed importantly to victory.

These brief excerpts are references to the nefarious doings of the WACs. Such stories were oft repeated but seldom verified. Like their sisters who attended college, women in the armed forces faced slander and calumny when they attempted to join what had heretofore been an overwhelmingly masculine domain.

DIARY OF CASIMER PRUNCHUNAS[9]

We left Fort Dix on the afternoon of December 17, 1943 and after an all-night trip, in a day coach, reached Camp Patrick Henry in Virginia the following morning. During the night, we passed through Washington, D.C., Philadelphia, Fredericksburg and Richmond.

This camp was located among very tall pine trees and could not be easily spotted from the air. The barracks were made of wood and were made to house fifty men. Showers and toilet facilities were OK. Chow was served cafeteria style and the food was OK. The mess hall was very large and quite a few times, a trio entertained us during mealtime with some hot jive.

There were plenty of theatres around and I just about saw a movie every night. And all of them were late pictures..

All that we did at this camp was calisthenics, short hikes, gas drill, cleaning of personal weapons and have a lot of inspections. And in addition we were issued a lot of new equipment and a new type of gas mask. . . .

The only fun some of the boys had was with the WAC's. It wasn't hard to get one into the woods for a little sexual intercourse. Most of them looked like old bags anyway, and had probably joined so as to get a little now and then. And here, as the soldiers had no place to go, they were getting plenty.

It wasn't an uncommon sight to see a couple hundred soldiers waiting for the WAC's to come out of their barracks after dark. And from this point on, my conception of a WAC was pretty low.

It was also rumored that the girls working at the PX were selling it at $7.00 a throw.

LETTER HOME FROM ERVIN J. COOK (JULY 12, 1943)[10]

. . . Incidentally, we have some WACs stationed here. You should see the boys race to sit next to them in the show. The girls seem to like the attention. Don't worry, your husband doesn't give them a second look because I don't think much of them. I've heard too many wild tales concerning their morals.

The Life of a WAC Officer—Letter to a Friend from Edith M. Davis[11]

The commander of a WAC detachment in Paris writes to a friend.

29 October 1944

Sunday
France

Dear Betty:

When did I last write to you? Or better, when did *you* last write to me, Betty Pig? A long time ago, methinks.

At any rate, wasn't I in England, either way? We've been so doggoned busy the past few weeks that it's hard to keep the record straight. Be that as it may, we're now in la Belle France, and it's really la Belle. Haven't had much opportunity for sightseeing or shopping, but there's certainly an air about this country that England never had. I've been here on and off since the fall of Paris—crossed that bit of Channel five times in as many weeks—that's what comes of having so many useful interests in life. Once I flew through such a storm that I decided no matter where I landed I'd stay—so here I be.

The officers have graduated from the Nissen hut to a very charming French villa. That's if you like small and finicky French furniture of the Marie Antoinette type. We have everything, including a French maid who puts the furniture back, no matter how we rearrange it. But we fooled her, by dragging down an enormous green velvet sofa from the attic. It took three Army officers to get it down, and by god, she can't get it back! Americans have no taste at all—that, we are sure, is her personal and private opinion. Our villa boasts a hot water tank, which is more than one can say for most French plumbing.

There are five of us here, WAC officers all, so we ration the bath by each taking a turn as duty officer up at the barracks, which involves being away overnight, hence no bath. We also boast a little electric stove, which enables us to have a bit of home cooking now and again. A drink, a log in the fireplace (if one can get a log), the radio—and presto! we have all the comforts of home.

This morning I attended mass in one of the world's famous cathedrals, mostly because some of my WACs were to sing in the choir, first time American voices ever rang out in those sacred walls. It was exceedingly lovely, except that I knelt for interminable hours on cold marble. What price the saving of one's soul?

The grass in England was always green, but here the red and gold of autumn colorings are reminiscent of western Michigan in October, perfectly gorgeous. Probably a forerunner of colder weather to come, but how we love it now.

Harold is in Holland or Belgium, I'm not sure which. I have missed him in Paris on at least three occasions—that's war. Don Scott is in Holland. His dad, Pa Scott, died suddenly last month. Did Florence call you? I felt dreadful about that—like a break-up in the family.

How's your mother? And Barby? Do write.

Love,
Edith

The Life of a WAC Enlisted Person—
Letter Home from Mildred Karlsen[12]

A WAC writes from Paris to her sister.

4 November 1944

Paris, France

Dear Leona:

You're really a good egg to keep writing me so faithfully when I so seldom answer, but don't think that I don't appreciate it. I really don't have much time for letters during the day, and it's too cold in my room at night to hold a pen. Your long letter arrived yesterday and a nice letter from Ann Beach, which made the first two letters for about two weeks. I just now wrote Ann a letter and will write you and Mom and Pop today if I have time.

I started to write to you last night in bed, but my room-mates came home in a rather delicate condition, and I had to put one of them to bed. These French Boilermakers are too much for most of these gals. A French boilermaker is a drink consisting of one part cognac and one part champagne. You go along okay for a while, and all of a sudden it hits you. And what a blow. Many a night have I staggered to bed because of those things. I don't get sick though, and poor Woody did last night. She kept saying, "Karlsen, I don't feel so good." I knew just what she meant. Woody is leaving for the States to go to O.C. School, and if she stops in Chi, she will give you a ring. She's really a swell kid.

Was off last Thursday and had a swell day. My pal, Bigley, has a Jeep assigned to her now by the General she works for, and we went to Versailles to see the Palace and the Gardens and the Temple of Love. The gardens are beautiful, and we saw the house that Marie Antoinette had specially built for one of her lovers while Louie sweated it out in the Palace. There are lots of fancy statues and fountains and stuff, and I understand that during peace time

WAC Mildren Karlsen Morris with friends at social event. (Courtesy of the Dwight D. Eisenhower Library, Mildren Karlsen Morris Collection.)

everything is lit up with colored lights at night. I wish I could see these things when the war isn't going on. I think I'll go to lunch now and will continue this when I get back.

We didn't have a very good lunch—hot dogs and dehydrated cabbage. I don't go for dehydrated foods very much. We don't get hot dogs as often in France as we did in England. For a while in England, we had hot dogs practically every day in the week. In general, the food is okay here, and when you stop to think the boys at the front are living on K and C rations, nobody should ever complain.

Well, tonight there will be hot water in our joint again, and I'm going to try to leave here a little earlier than usual and go home and soak my weary, filthy bones in a tub of nice hot water. Leona, you just don't appreciate the little things in life until you don't have them for months on end. The faucets in our bathroom are labeled "Froid" and "Chaud," but they both give out with ice water. Our bathroom would be nice if it had ever been completed—it's sort of blue and gold and white, but all the plaster isn't on the walls. When I stop to think of all the kinds of places I've lived in since I joined the Army, I grow weak with laughter. I guess the best place yet was the tent town in England at the end. And this business of digging through a barrack bag each time you want to find a sock drives me nuts. I wish you could have about a week of this, just so you could appreciate what you have in civilian life. All the letters I get from people back there say about the same thing: "How I envy you." All they think about is traveling all over Europe—they don't know how we travel. I came to Paris in a ten-wheeled truck—nice smooth riding vehicle—I thought my insides were all disconnected by the time we got here. The roads aren't so good because not so long before they were sort of shot to hell.

We also have a hot plate in our room, and each night one of the girls makes noodle soup. We heat the water in two canteen cups, and evidently the night before she didn't wash out the cups, because I heated some water last night to wash in and I smeared noodles all over my face and neck before I realized what was wrong. So I had to wash all over again in cold water and went to bed and shook for about an hour. The breeze sure blows through that place. We wash little things like stockings and pants—my pants aren't so little, though, I think they got the pattern confused with a shelter half, and hang them on hangers from the chandelier. With all the doors and windows closed, the clothes sway in the breeze, so you can see how cold it is. I wonder if they forgot to turn off the air conditioning.

And when we "undress" for bed, we take about an hour to put all the clothes on. I always take off everything I wore during the day and then put on an altogether different outfit. Long drawers, long shirt, wool socks, flan-

The WAAC Rookie Recipe

Take one enrolled member, slightly green. Stir from bed at an early hour. Soak in shower or tub daily. Dress in olive drab. Mix with others of her kind.

Grate on sergeants' nerves, toughen with physical training, add liberal portions of baked beans and roast beef. Season with wind, rain and snow. Sweeten from time to time with chocolate bars.

Bake in 100-degree temperature summer and let cool in below zero winter.

Will serve 130,000,000 people. Serve in place of one soldier, sometimes two.

—WAAC Bulletin

nel pajamas, sweater, robe, etc. Yesterday I was issued two more blankets, so now I leave off some of the things.

I ordered a doll to be sent to Penny for Xmas; let me know if it gets there okay. I don't know what the thing looks like except that it's 18 inches tall. Holly will get one too, and Robbie should get some kind of stuffed lamb. They have pretty dolls here, but I'd be afraid they'd be broken by the time they arrived.

I don't know what else to say now. Tonight I shall probably hang on a good one because it's Saturday night and that seems to be the thing to do and I haven't had anything to drink for two or three nights now except an occasional glass of champagne. Write me as often as you can and I always like to hear about Penny. I wish I could see her and Blackie play together. My love to you and Max and Penny.

Mil

A WAC in Africa—"A Day in the WACery"[13]

A DAY IN THE WACERY

Would you like to walk into a Wackery? To you a place where WACs make their home. If you would, here is a bird's eye view of what takes place any day between the hours of six-fifteen AM and 11:00 PM.

Six-fifteen on the dot some one comes in, turns on the light and calls, "Time to get up." We are divided in what is known in the Army as SQUADS. One squad to a room. As usual, I am high and dry in the last room. The squad leader starts her morning call, just like a mother hen. She calls each one by her name in hopes of getting her up. But as we have fifteen minutes to pull up the legs of our pajamas, slip on our fatigue dress, sox and sneakers, run a comb through our hair before we have to report down stairs, we stay in our bunks, where it is nice and warm, for ten minutes. As for steam heat, we are now in the army and take things as they are.

Six-thirty the whistle blows, and we must all be there for roll call. We WACS pride ourselves on our neatness and our spick and span appearance. But pity our poor hides if some fine morning we should have "high powered" visitors at that hour. For when that whistle blows, one sees many strange things. The girls are running from every direction in hopes of getting their proper squads, in time for their reports. Along with running, they are either putting on their dresses or sweaters, as well as trying to make their pajama legs stay up above their knees so they won't show.

The next move is for chow, and as usual some of the girls forget there is a war and they can not go in and order anything they want. Also they forget

they are in the army, and we are getting a great deal more food than some of
the boys that are really doing the fighting. However, here are some of the
breakfasts that are put out in the kitchen. Toast, butter, jam, sausage or eggs
and coffee. French toast, fruit juice, jam or syrup along with coffee. Bacon
and eggs is another dish that is served with buttered toast. Then the cooks are
good enough to make hot cakes which include all the trimmings. And there
is always just plenty for every one. Could one ask for more?

Then back to our rooms to clean up around our beds, for if everything is
not just so, that "GIG" sheet* is like a black cloud hanging over our heads until
we get everything just so again. After inspection, every one runs to look at
the gig sheet to see if they are restricted that night or not.

Then we take our showers. Well I really do believe that this is the busiest
or should I say the noisiest time of the day. As for hot water, well I guess I
must be dreaming, as the only time we see that is when we wash our mess
kits after each meal. So in we go, turn on the water, making more noise than
a bag of monkeys. A little imagination plus the noise heats the water enough
that by the time we are soaped it is lukewarm.

Next comes the dressing act, in which every one must look just so. And
pity the girls that are blessed with toilet water, as that is something we can't
get over here. It is, "Can I please borrow some of your Yankee Clover, or some
of your Old English Spice?" The proud owner who is so big hearted and will
not say no just passes around the bottle.

When next we are seen, we look just like we have stepped out of a band
box. Uniforms always pressed just so and each and every hair right in its place.
Then to our different offices we walk so proud and spry.

The next rush comes between eleven-thirty and one, when once again our
food is ready, and back to the Wackery we go in army trucks. Our cooks, God
bless them, certainly strive to make our meals just as if they were fixed at
home. We have our hot meal at noon, which consists of meat, potatoes, a vegetable, bread and butter, either home made pie, cake, cookies, doughnuts or
fruit and a drink. Now what else would one want?

After eating, up stairs we go and "fix" our faces once more, then the trucks
are at our door to take us back to work.

Before we know it, it is five o'clock and the time to fold up and call it a
day. We take our own sweet time in walking home and try and see something
different every day. Of course we are always looking forward to the mail we
hope to get when we do get there, as well as once more chow.

---

*WACs could earn "gigs," or demerits, for rules infractions or other behavior not up to
standards.

Then the evening's pleasure. Due to our being the only W.A.C.s in this African town, we are indeed the most popular ones around. Some thing every evening. They have dances and movies for us, and we are allowed to have the boys come and see us in our day room twice a week.

Then comes the happy hour of ten, when a very lady-like voice from down stairs calls up, "Ten o'clock girls and you know lights out please." But if one wishes, one can go in the day room and read or write letters, as bed check isn't until eleven. Then every one must be in her bed and down for the night.

Now this is just one day of the goings and comings at the WACERY. Of course we each have our time off every week, and if we have been good girls and have a pass coming, we are given this pass, along with a smile from our officers to enjoy ourselves, but be sure and be back on time. Though we are out on our own more or less during these hours, we still do not let our hair down. For we must always remember our place, position and our duty, as we are here for work and not for play.

So maybe now you can picture us African W.A.C.s in our Wacery. If so, I hope it is at our best.

You relatives and friends, pull for us W.A.C.s in North Africa, while we here, far from home, will not only pull but will work to finish our big job that we may all be together again.

I think by this time you will understand how I feel about my life in the W.A.C.s, and I want you to believe me when I say I LOVE it here all the time.

Recognition—Citation to Accompany the Award of the Bronze Star Medal[14]

JEANNE E. BETCHER, A-220117, Sergeant, Woman's Army Corps, United States Army. For meritorious service in direct support of military operations from 1 April 1944 to 1 April 1945. As the enlisted person in charge of the administration of highly classified matter for this headquarters and its lower units, Sergeant Betcher displayed outstanding integrity and steadfast devotion to duty. The selection of Sergeant Betcher for this position was based on a splendid record in other important sections where her duties were accomplished with marked accuracy and tact. Sergeant Betcher's position assumed particular importance in the weeks prior to the invasion of the continent and much credit is due for the smooth flow and efficient handling of the many plans and documents relative to this important military operation. The exceptional manner in which Sergeant Betcher has met the responsibilities placed upon her has been a notable contribution to the war effort. Entered military service from New Jersey.

There are so many women in the army now that when a soldier sees a uniform coming down the street he has to wait till it gets within 20 feet before he knows whether to salute or whistle.

—Bob Hope

■ SOURCES

1. Ensign G. Barber, U.S.N.R., U.S.S. Bollinger, APA 234, to Mrs. G. Barber, April 20, 1945, "Carol J. Barber Papers" File, World War II Participants and Contemporaries Collection, Dwight D. Eisenhower Library, Abilene, Kansas.

2. William Bieluch to Father, March 21, 1945, William C. Bieluch Papers, World War II Participants and Contemporaries Collection, Eisenhower Library.

3. Ian A. Millar, "Merchantmen Like Thee," "Memorabilia" File, George B. O'Donnell Papers, World War II Participants and Contemporaries Collection, Eisenhower Library.

4. The letters in this section are from Mary Metcalfe to Mother, July 20 and 31, and August 2 and 16, 1944, "Letters July–Sept. 1944 (1)" File, Mary Metcalfe Rexford Papers, World War II Participants and Contemporaries Collection, Eisenhower Library. For a more complete look at the wartime adventures of "ChiChi" Metcalfe, see Oscar Whitelaw Rexford, *Battlestars and Doughnuts: World War II Clubmobile Experiences of Mary Metcalfe Rexford* (St. Louis, MO: Patrice Press, 1989).

5. The recipes in this section are from War Department, Technical Manual No. 10-405: "The Army Cook," June 9, 1941, "Army Cook Books (1)" File, John T. Bradley Papers, World War II Participants and Contemporaries Collection, Eisenhower Library.

6. Loren Fred to Wife, July 12, 1944, "Letters (1)" File, Loren Fred Papers, World War II Participants and Contemporaries Collection, Eisenhower Library.

7. Included with Mary Metcalfe to Mother, August 16, 1944, "Letters July–Sept. 1944 (1)" File, Mary Metcalfe Rexford Papers, World War II Participants and Contemporaries Collection, Eisenhower Library.

8. Lt. Dunn to Henry Novak, March 4, 1945, Stephanie Salada Papers, Private Collection, Pittsburgh, Pennsylvania.

9. Casimer Prunchunas, Diary, "Diary (1)" File, Casimer Prunchunas Papers, World War II Participants and Contemporaries Collection, Eisenhower Library.

10. Ervin J. Cook to Wife, July 12, 1943, "Letters to Wife, July 1943" File, Ervin J. Cook Papers, World War II Participants and Contemporaries Collection, Eisenhower Library.

11. Edith M. Davis to Friend, October 29, 1944, "Correspondence" File, Edith M. Davis Papers, World War II Participants and Contemporaries Collection, Eisenhower Library.

12. Mildred Karlsen to Sister, November 4, 1944, "Scrapbook (3)" File, Mildred Karlsen Morris Papers, World War II Participants and Contemporaries Collection, Eisenhower Library.
13. "A Wac in Africa II," Elizabeth Blazek Papers, World War II Participants and Contemporaries Collection, Eisenhower Library.
14. "Bronze Star Citation," n.d., "Jeanne Betcher—Correspondence (3)" File, World War II Participants and Contemporaries Collection, Eisenhower Library.

FIVE

SINCE YOU WENT AWAY

For a majority of Americans, one of the most difficult aspects of the war was the chronic separation from loved ones. Spouses, sons and daughters, siblings, and lovers marched off to training camps and often ended up overseas or in some remote corner of the United States, too far for visiting. At the very least, normal familial contact was reduced to sporadic and unpredictable visits. Letters, photographs, and packages became the inadequate but all the more precious currency of their relationships then, and it was not unusual for family members to write to one another nearly every day, for months or even years.

Those at home tried to write of commonplace things and local news to ease the homesickness and bewilderment of their loved ones abroad, adding the occasional notice of marriages, births, illnesses, and deaths of family, friends, and neighbors. The story of the dog's latest escapade or Friday night's high school football game takes on an added poignancy when we appreciate them as the tenuous threads that connected a young person with the only world he or she had known before the war. Useless and arcane trivia about Aunt Mary's gall bladder and the baby's first words offered a beloved diversion for the faraway soldier and provided an anchor for the youth struggling with the timeless problems of growing up.

For those sent to strange lands by the war, letters home were the place to describe new experiences, muse about foreign peoples, or pass the time between mundane and repetitive tasks. Often the nebulous promise of the future lurked in the thoughts of that generation that now found itself caught up in the whirlwind of world events. Most often the soldier's confidante was a spouse or perhaps a fiancée, but it could be anyone, from parent to former schoolmate, who had traditionally filled the role of friend.

Most revealing of all are the letters between husbands and wives, for even a casual perusal of such correspondence quickly makes it clear that both the leavers and the left had to adjust to life alone by taking on added burdens. A young wife had to learn to pay the bills and cut the grass, and a young husband had to learn how to care for his clothes, make his bed, and get to work on time. But much harder to develop was the psychological strength and moral self-reliance to manage, without one's life partner, the challenges and stress of a world turned upside down. Add culture shock, altered lifestyles, and the loss of the calming stability of traditional family life for those who left home, and we have the makings of psychological trauma—and on a national scale. Many relationships failed to survive the strain, but the real wonder is that so many did.

The topics discussed are generally ordinary and petty; we find few literary masterpieces among the reams of correspondence cranked out by the enforced separations of the day. To judge these documents at face value, however, is to miss their historical, and very human, significance, because for many people these letters were also their only lifeline to their past lives and to sanity. Read in this context, the letters become captivating literature and beacons to the human spirit.

LETTERS TO A WIFE

LETTERS HOME FROM ERVIN J. COOK[1]

Ervin Cook was a newlywed when he left the United States for his tour with the U.S. Army Air Forces in England. His letters to his

*wife suggest the wide range of experiences and emotions that
became so commonplace for Americans during the war.*

*In this letter from his training school, Airman Cook attempts to
help his spouse deal with a pair of lives put on hold by the war. It
is a blend of philosophizing and recounting the familiar.*

March 24, 1943

Dearest Barbara:

Hello! Honey, I hope you're feeling better these days. Honey, you know I think
your trouble is that you don't find enough happiness in every day living. Sounds
funny, but maybe I think you live too much in the future and in the past. You
wanted me to give you a talking to, so here I go. Ever since I can remember,
you have given me the impression that things at a certain time were not too
good. In other words, you weren't completely happy, but you always thought
that soon in the near future everything would be rosy and turn out perfect. In
other words, you are living just for some future date and in the meantime just
putting in time waiting. The future never comes completely, for nothing ever
turns out perfectly or as you had pictured it. Then all that time you were waiting, putting in time as it were, is wasted. I don't mean that you couldn't be
working hard, but even if you were working 24 hours a day, it would be wasted time if you couldn't find something interesting, humorous or anything that
contributes to a state of happiness. We are all inclined to be that way, but it's
a hard thing if done too much. The first week I was here at Maxwell I started
out that way, and it was a pretty miserable week. I'll tell you how I got a hold
of myself. I just started to convince myself that I loved the place. I found enjoyment in little things that happened during the day. I found working hard helped
and not thinking too much about the things I didn't like around here. It just
seems like one thing leads to another, and soon I found I was very happy. And
I am not kidding, because I feel that I'm very happy even though I could have
a lot of reasons not to be. I have an advantage over a civilian because here we
have to hit the ball, while if we could have a lot of spare time we wouldn't be
as happy. I know I'm much happier here than Nashville because at Nashville
we had too much time to think about things.

I know you're working hard and it's hard to keep your spirits up, but try to
do your best, because I do want you to be happy even if we are separated. You'll
probably have a tough time getting anything out of what I've just written, but
it's hard to write stuff like that. Maybe we can talk it over someday, eh!

So Black Bottom's going to have kittens? Well, now, which is the nicest
cat? I still like my old mangy one.

Everyone in the squadron had to apply for some position as a cadet officer. You see, when our upper class leaves, we have to have fellows step into
the cadet officer jobs. Of course, there are just a few fellows who will be selected officers out of the bunch. I applied for Supply Sergeant, but I hope I don't
get it. It takes up too much time and cuts in on the studies. Sometimes it happens that a furlough is given between Pre-Flight and Primary, but you wait
and see, our bunch won't get any. I got a feeling we are going right on through.
Gosh, it's time for bed already. Honey, you know I love you only. I think you're
the best and finest wife a guy could have. I want that chin up, now, or I'll come
home and spank you, you stinker. What a wonderful thing it would be to sleep
with you again. Good night, sweet.

All my love
Ervin

*Cook reveals his homesickness in this letter, which also gives a quick
look at life on an American air base in England.*

July 3, 1944

My Darling Barbara,

No mail for me again today, but there was very little mail that came in the
squadron today.

I am sitting next to our oil stove, and the rain is coming down steadily outside. We haven't been using our stove, mainly because we were too lazy to go
down and get the oil. We finally worked up enough ambition the other day
and got a jeep to go down to the line, and we got about 25 gallons of oil. It
should last us a couple of weeks.

Yesterday (Sunday) we had some war orphans visit us. Our group has
financed six of them with enough money to keep them for five years. The girl
our squadron is keeping is about ten years old and smart as a whip. They lost
their parents during the blitz. The fellows made quite a fuss over them and gave
them a ride in a plane. They are only able to visit us once every three months.

I never have been as homesick and lonesome for you as I was last Saturday
night. I thought that after we had been separated awhile it wouldn't be so bad
once I got used to it, but I miss you more and more as the days go by. I don't
think I ever fully realized how much you meant to me and how much I needed you as I have over here. I love you so terribly much, and I realize now how
much our love has grown since we were married. Darling, I wish I could take
you in my arms and tell you just how I feel tonight.

Let me see now, where was I? I am still doing not much of anything, which
I find very pleasant and agreeable. I don't know whether I told you or not, but

my Pop's birthday was in June and I bought him a book which I am sending to him from both of us.

I don't imagine your Dad had much of a Father's Day the way things are,* but you tell him I'm thinking of him and wish I was back there to get in his way!

I sure hope your Mother is out of the hospital by now and kicking up her heels. Give her a kiss for me! (Do you mind?)

Well, "honey doll," take care of yourself and keep remembering I love you and I am being a very good boy.

Yours always
Ervin

The loneliness continued for Ervin and, undoubtedly, for his bride at home, too. Here he shares a few light thoughts but also some plans for the much-anticipated but imponderable postwar years. It is difficult to imagine the number of times young men and women must have tried to envision their future, post-military lives. For the citizen-soldier, that longed-for period was always in mind but excruciatingly distant. It was all too common an experience among the generation that had to put its life on hold "for the duration."

August 16, 1944

England

My Darling,

I received your Aug. 7th letter this afternoon in which you told about going to the carnival. It sure sounded like a lot of fun. They have them over here, but there is no comparison, they are so small and stinky. So you went to the strip tease! Too bad I wasn't there to see it, you know how interested I am in "Art."

It is quite warm this afternoon, and I have half a notion to go to the beach for some swimming, since I've already done my work for the day.

As far as I can tell, we are going to keep on flying until the war is over, which I hope is soon. Seems to me that someday the law of averages will get us, but I don't give a damn, at least it doesn't worry me anymore. We've been very lucky and fortunate, maybe it will hold out for awhile longer. The constant good war news is a wonderful stimulant to us.

I hope to gosh that both this war and the Pacific war will be over by a year from this fall so I can start to school. I'll be 24 next year, which will mean I would

---

*Cook is referring to the illness of his wife's mother.

be 26 by the time I finished school. We are both still very young, but the years are sure whizzing by. Oh hum and no family yet—am I a man or a mouse?

Darling, the past when we were together seems like a wonderful dream now, and it was just a few months ago. Whenever anyone talks of going home, they might as well be talking of going to the moon, it seems so far off. Sometimes I wish I would get hit so I could be sent home, but I guess it's not right to think things like that.

Honey, I do love you so much and dream of holding you in my arms again. You're my one and only, and don't forget it. Just a second, I want to give you a big kiss! Hmmm wonderful, you haven't changed a bit. Well sweet good-bye for now. All my love always.

                                                              Ervin

Ervin talks a bit about the British people here, but this letter is also of interest for its look at attitudes toward gender in the World War II era. In addition, it illustrates the pangs of loneliness that plagued American servicemen and servicewomen the world over.

August 20, 1944

England

My Darling,

Well, I just got back from work, and I had quite an interesting day. There was no mail from you today, but not much came in. I got lots of mail from you last week, so I'm happy.

Last night the boys and I went into town to see a stage play. The name of it was "The Druids Rest," and it wasn't so hot. It was supposed to be a comedy, but we found the English humor too dry for us. Another things is, it's hard to understand the actors when they talk fast because of their accent. After the show we went to a nice hotel for dinner, and did we get taken. It cost us $2.00 apiece for dinner, and all it amounted to was fish and french fries. I guess we were paying for the nice surroundings. There are a lot of nice hotels in town because it is a big resort center. This is the most modern town I've seen in England, reminds me a lot of home.

There is a little boy who comes around to pick up our laundry, and his mother does the work. He brings it back in 24 hours, I don't know how his mother does it so quick.

You know the people don't hardly get paid anything for working over here. This kid said his sister made 3 shillings a day working in an office. That's 60¢ a day. I've looked at the ads in the paper, and most average jobs pay $8–$10 a week. I don't see how people get along with prices so darn high. Most jobs are long hours, especially factories. They work from 12 to 15 hours a day.

You wanted to know something about the girls over here, so I'll tell you what I know. All girls over 18 must either be in the Service or holding some kind of a job. Once they have one job, they cannot leave it. Generally the girls are stinky looking, they don't hold a candle to our American girls. I've been told that most of the nicer type girls are in the Army or one of the Services. The girls in the land army really have to work hard and long. They work in the fields from sun up to sun down, which is usually 15 hours. I've seen some nice looking girls in Land Army uniforms, kinda' feel sorry for them. We had a trial at the base in which an enlisted man was accused of raping a Land Army girl. It was an open trial, so most of the boys were there. They said it was a scream. The girl's panties were exhibit "A," and they kept waving them around the court. I guess it turned out to be more of a show than anything, and the boy was acquitted. Some fun, eh!

Did you see the picture I am enclosing, in Life?* I thought it was good, that's what you need when I get home! Boy, would I like to be with you tonight, I'd neck the pants off of you. Gee, I miss you something awful, Honey. Here's lots of kisses. Goodnight, Sweet.

Love
Ervin

The girl friend, worried a little by newspaper stories about soldier marriages "down under," demanded of her hero, "What have those Australian girls got that we haven't got?"

"Nothing," he wrote in reply. "but they've got it here."

LETTERS TO PARENTS AND SISTER

LETTERS HOME FROM BRUCE CARSON[2]

Although the separation of spouses was the most obvious personal difficulty caused by the war, other families suffered as much

---

*This reference is to a page from *Life* magazine, which contains a photograph of a woman on a chaise lounge wearing a "breakfast coat" (looks like a housecoat) "for girls who like to sleep nude."

from the disappearance of a son or daughter. Here an intellectual young reserve naval officer, fulfilling his patriotic duty by serving in the administrative forces in the Pacific, makes some erudite and insightful remarks to his family about politics, aesthetics, international affairs, and life. One imagines that these letters took the place of the evening conversation over a cup of coffee in the living room or around the kitchen table.

13 April 1945

Philippine Islands

Dear Family,

The news that President Roosevelt had died came to us in the Philippines just as we were getting up this Friday the 13th morning. He died at 0535 Philippine War Time.

Death of a man is difficult enough to believe if one has known him in all the alertness of life. Death of one who has become as much an institution and a symbol as he was a man is even more difficult to believe.

All morning over the radio have come the voices of commentators and announcers in an unending procession, with late bulletins on the inauguration of President Truman, biographies of Roosevelt, eulogies, commentaries on what the Death means to this country and to the World.

I believe Truman will make a good president. Pressure of circumstances would force any honest man with a conscience to do his best. The question then becomes merely the academic one, Is his best good enough?

His best won't be nearly as good as Roosevelt's. He is unknown. His prestige is merely the prestige of office. He has not the personal contacts, the familiarity with foreign heads of state that Roosevelt possessed. Roosevelt as a man was certainly one of our chief physical assets, especially in international affairs.

Truman is no such asset. He has not the personal aura of Churchill nor Stalin, nor that Roosevelt had to such a great degree.

Domestically I believe Truman will fare as well as would Roosevelt, had he lived. He will have the loyal support of all genuine Roosevelt friends so long as he gives evidence that he deserves that support, and Roosevelt's detractors are not likely to be as bitter nor as bigoted against this unknown newcomer as they were toward Roosevelt himself. The policies will probably be much the same. A slight trend to the right will be inevitable, because all of the force of Roosevelt as a man and as a symbol had to be exerted at times to salvage programs of a liberal character. Truman won't be able to bring this last, necessary ounce of pressure to bear upon the issue.

Internationally, I believe we are reduced to a second line power, if we consider Russia and Britain as first line powers.

I believe that Churchill and Stalin will determine the peace settlement in Europe, with the United States acting merely as a reinforcing echo to Britain or as a balance of power between the two blocs of interest.

Unless Truman grows in stature in the next two years, Russia and Britain will probably outline the peace in the Pacific also, with ourselves having merely a slightly amplified voice in the settlement.

Fortunately, our military forces and our military leaders have grown in prestige from victory to victory. With Wilkie and Roosevelt silenced in death, with Cordell Hull old and retired, we have only two non-military figures with international stature. These are Wallace, who was rejected by his party and is hamstrung by political enemies; and Herbert Hoover, in retirement, but still remembered for his earlier successes in international affairs, and respected for his experience in and out of office. We would do well to use both these men to the fullest of their capabilities.

Marshall, Eisenhower, and MacArthur are world figures today. They, more than our state department, are our best guarantee that our military interests at least will not be neglected nor over-ridden. They speak their specialty with the weight of the world's largest and most powerful armored machine behind them.

Stettinius and Truman speak as office holders whose commitments cannot be counted upon unless ratified by congress and public opinion. They will have great influence as officeholders. But even Roosevelt would have been handicapped by his unstable tenure and his inability to positively commit his nation to a particular course. How lesser men will fare under the same circumstances is not possible to predict with exactitude, but the general trend seems obvious.

In the short run, I believe we shall have to depend largely on Churchill to represent our interests internationally. I think that Churchill will feel obligated to Roosevelt to do just that. Britain's and our own interests do not always appear to coincide, but they never actually oppose and therefore can be reconciled. Whether Truman and Stettinius will see any wisdom in Churchill's advice or will go along with him in a pinch, I can't guess. I think they would best serve our countries' interests by doing so.

My constitutional law is a bit vague, but if memory serves me faithfully, Stettinius automatically becomes vice-president. In that case, I would like to see either Wallace or Hoover as Secretary of State. Preferably Hoover, since paradoxically enough he would come in with fewer enemies personally.

The Democrats, I am afraid, will be a little put out to find Stettinius, a Republican, running the Senate. And labor will undoubtedly look askance at the ex-president of U.S. Steel and a Morgan partner so close to the White House.

I believe that the influence of Roosevelt and of his works will guarantee that this country will not retrogress too far on the road to conservatism; and I hope, but can only hope, that isolation, economic as well as political, has been ended through his efforts.

Roosevelt quarried the block and outlined the figure. Someone else will have to finish the work and determine whether we have a masterpiece or the too customary disappointment on our hands.

I suppose Americans everywhere feel the same sadness at Roosevelt's death. It is no different here, I'm sure, and no different in any area overseas where soldiers, who by and large are strong Roosevelt men, are assembled. Even those persons who hated Roosevelt as a man and thought his policies were inimical to the American way of life will miss him now as a symbol of American greatness in international affairs and as a stabilizing and reassuring entity domestically.

We never appreciate the importance to us of great men as symbols until these great men die and we must find someone to take their place.

*The Omnipotent One**

Sharing thoughts with a recently married sister, the officer hints of the ever-present longing for an end to war and the chance to lead a "normal" life.

5 July 1945

Oahu

Dear Dorothy,

Your success in managing to eke out something approaching normal home life against the efforts of all deities (animal and vegetable, pre-historic and brass-hatted) is refreshing to behold, even from a distance.

How does civilian domesticity agree with you?

All the flitting from pillar to post that you and Vern do is of course inconsequential. If you wish, you can pretend you are married to a traveling salesman who needs you to demonstrate his wares. Or more romantically and perhaps appropriately, you might be some gun moll, on the lam from authorities, trying to find a safe place to set up a tepee with your two-gun Joe. Anyway, I hope for a while at least you two are able to forget your military connections and perhaps have a personal pre-view of the post war world and living conditions.

---

*A somewhat flamboyant signature, but Carson always used it in his letters to his parents.

So far in my thirty-eight years of post-womb traveling,* I have managed to avoid the blurb-iferous sovereign state of Texas. (I haven't always been fortunate enough to avoid certain vociferous exiles from that realm, however.)

Still, when you cut away the desert, the heat, Mexicans, negroes, and black-widow spiders, there must be something for everyone to be talking about, so your banishment to that wasteland ought to be pleasant enough. Do you mind if I envy you not much, but just a little?

Just returned from five days' relaxation on the "big island" of Hawaii.

Vern and you ought to try that place for a honeymoon. It's just about ideal.

I was almost tempted to try out the place myself, maritally speaking, but sanity prevailed, so I will save my wild oats to sow in the best traditions of mother's family, until I reach fifty-five or ten years after I'm past caring, which ever comes sooner.

> As ever
> *Bruce*

A FATHER'S LETTER TO HIS MARINE SON

FATHER TO GEORGE W. DINNING[3]

A mixture of generalities and small talk makes up this letter from a father to his son, a Marine platoon sergeant in the Pacific. But between the lines one can sense the blend of pride and anxiety that so many parents must have felt.

May 21–45

Dear Geo

How are you, old fellow? You are sure giving those yellow bastards hell now, but you marines sure do a good job all the time. I do hope you are ok. I saw Joe Wyatt the other day, and he wants me to come over to his home for a chicken dinner, and I may go. I think Steve will be home soon. He deserves it, as he has been in about all the different countries.

It sure has rained here a lot, and we had some hail to-day, but I think things will clear up soon.

Geo, please write, as you don't know how I feel. I am so nervous, as you can tell by my writing, and if you will just write, I know I will get over it.

---

*This phrase is confusing, as records show Carson was twenty-four years old when he wrote this.

Well, old boy, good luck and write. Hope you are ok.

Good Nite, Geo

Dad

will write more next time

A FATHER'S LETTER TO HIS SOLDIER SON

M. R. NOVAK TO HENRY NOVAK[4]

A father catches his son up on the family and local news from western Pennsylvania. Busy with the wartime task of building landing craft, the father nevertheless finds the time to relay stories of relatives and his own recent hunting adventures.

Friday, Jan. 7th, 1944.

Dear Henry:

I am very sorry that I do not write to you any oftener, but you should realize that after working all day in the dust, smoke and grime, I am pretty well tuckered out when I come home and I do not feel like doing anything else but sleep. However, I will try to write to you as often as possible.

Your letters are very much appreciated here. I think that you have learned how to write a letter. They are getting better and better. Keep up and you may end up as a correspondent.

As far as we are concerned, we are doing pretty well, or at least as well as could be expected. Johnnie had a touch of flu and spent the New Year's Holidays in bed. He just got up yesterday and went to school.

We had some miserable weather here. One day the temperature is about zero and the next day it starts to rain. We did not have a white Christmas and even now, there is no snow on the ground.

Yes, Gene was home for seven days and he overstayed his time. He thought that he had a full seven days at home and did not read his furlough papers. I had him to the plant on Thursday and showed him both the LST's and the DE's,* and when we came home, he was showing mother the extra rationing for his staying home and just by luck or intuition, I had asked him to show me the furlough papers and there as plain as could be it said that, "P.F.C. Eugene N. Novak, shall report back for duty on or before Jan. 6th,

---

*The elder Novak worked at a shipyard building land craft (LST: Landing Ship, Tank) and escort vessels (DE: Destroyer Escorts).

1944." Well here it was six o'clock P.M. Jan. 6th, and Eugene was still at home.
I lent him the car and told him to dig out as fast as he could. I know he did
not make it before 12 o'clock Thursday, but he said that if he could get there
before reveille, every thing will be O.K. If it were not for me he would have
been one day A.W.O.L. Of course I do not know how he made out till we
hear from him. He said he would write a letter as soon as he got to camp and
saw his superior.

Yes, we do feel better if we see one of you home but what I cannot and
will not understand is why there are so many young boys and men deferred
who do not have any dependents and are as sound physically as well as you
are. Just look at poor Ed! Just after eleven weeks' training, he had to go on the
high seas. Of course, we are proud that none of our boys are any slackers or
cowards, but I doubt very much that when you come back, you will be treated any better than those that stayed at home.

I am glad that you are good with the rifle or machine guns. After this is
all over, perhaps you will be able to hit a few more rabbits and squirrels than
heretofore.

We just heard the news that Marie Bradfield had another baby girl. Of
course this is no news!

Helen, the "Pee Wee,"* Mrs. Sheppard and Jean, spent the New Years with
us, and Sunday we went to their house for supper. We had really good baked
ham. Stephanie is getting along fine. She is strong and husky, and she is getting used to me. I have bounced her up and down for a few minutes at a time,
and she really likes it. I only regret that I cannot see her as often as I wish.

You do not have to grin and enjoy yourself at my misfortune while hunting. If the damned thing would have dropped right on the pipe line, I would
have been 50 berried out because there were six strange witnesses right on the
pipe line. [?] Just by sheer luck that none of them saw the trail of blood and
they thought I never hit the deer. Of course you have to understand that I shot
it on the run, while it was jumping the creek and that I meant to shoot the
biggest deer I saw. That and the gutting of two deers made me very nervous,
and although I had some more shooting, and standing shots at that, I missed
all of them. We had lots of fun while it lasted, but counting lost wages, the
two deers set me back no less than 100 bucks. But hell! This was the only vaca-
tion I had during the last year. The doe hunting was very dangerous this year.
There were 1500 licenses issued for McKean County, and from eight o'clock
until 11 o'clock, there was not a second that a shot would not have been fired.
Most of the surrounding counties were closed and you can imagine what 1500

*Henry's infant daughter, Stephanie.

hunters can do in one county. There were a good many men that served in the last war, and they went out from the woods as fast as they could. It was just the same as the first year I went deer hunting with Bill Latzkus. None of the bullets came any too close to me, although I heard them overhead, but they came pretty close to Adolph and "little Joey." And remember this was not an open season for domestic turkey.

Esther and Little Eddie are doing fine. The little bum is hollering at me if I do not pay any attention to him. As long as he is awake, he wants me to play with him and you know, I am not as young as when you were a little tyke.

We will send you a box of food as soon as we make some Polish sausage with some of the deer meat in it. Do not expect it right away, because the meat was just ground yesterday. We will try to have it for you for your birthday, that is Jan. 19th.

Vernon Lodge, son of James Lodge, manager of the Boys Club in Lawrenceville, was killed in action in Italy. He was in the Air Corps. You ought to know him. They lived at 1212 N. Highland Ave., in one of the Equitable houses. We have worked in their house.

In conclusion let me say that I expect you to do your best in the service. As I told you before, I do not like a quitter.

Best of wishes and lots of love, we remain

Your loving parents, brothers and sister in law also your little nephew.

per Dad

A POPULAR SONG

"KEEP THE HOME FIRES BURNING"

Keep the home fires burning,
　　While your hearts are yearning,
Though your lads are far away
　　They dream of home;
There's a silver lining
　　Through the dark cloud shining,
Turn the dark cloud inside out,
　　Till the boys come home.

WRITING AFTER THE LIFTING OF CENSORSHIP

LETTER HOME FROM HAROLD PORTER[5]

A difficult part of writing home was dealing with the censorship of letters. Although necessary for security reasons, censorship imposed dual hardships on the letter writer: certain topics simply could not be discussed, which meant that some basic aspects of life overseas could not be shared with the folks at home, and there was a loss of intimacy because of the knowledge that words intended for one person were going to be officially read by a third party. The lifting of censorship after the war, then, was met with great enthusiasm by the homesick troops still overseas.

23 May 1945

Dachau

Dear Mother and Father,

Here are some facts, until now, restricted. Just thought you might be interested:

Kilmer was my P.O.E.* camp—at New Brunswick, New Jersey.

I was 10 days at sea, landed at Marseille Nov 6, traveled on the S.S. Mariposa, which, though unescorted, was armed with 17 guns plus depth charges.

About Jan 1, during a German push, our hospital was the only American installation, except infantry and artillery units, for miles. We were fully resigned to being captured within a matter of hours, but the 100th Division was rushed up and saved the situation.

Military information heretofore verboten: U.S. winter footwear and handwear was sadly deficient—when compared with either the allies or the enemy.

Our winter camouflage was deficient or non-existent—except in newsreel pictures. The Germans were very superior in this respect—as they have been in all camouflage.

The German Royal Tiger tank and their 88mm were two weapons we had no counterpart for—though the Germans have had them for nearly three years. Infantrymen complaints over our lack of similar weapons were bitter and nearly reached the mutiny stage in some instances—though you at home were carefully left ignorant.

---

*Port of Embarkation; that is, the port from which Porter sailed for Europe.

We were periodically bombed while at Sarrebourg by a single plane—he seemed to be after the railway station which was close by. Eventually he hit it—and blew all the windows and doors out of Leone's house.

At first we used to "shiver" out the raids in the air-raid shelter, but later on we got so used to them we would go up to the roof to watch the ack-ack* display.

If there's anything else you want to know about what I haven't been able to tell you about before, ask me now. Because as soon as we are alerted for the C.B.I.** theatre, strict censorship will again be enforced.

Love,
Harold

A young lady received an envelope addressed in familiar handwriting from one of our far-flung army outposts. But instead of the expected letter, she found inside a slip of paper saying simply: "Your boy friend still loves you, but he talks too much." [Censor]

—Collier's

WARTIME ROMANCES

While the war stressed or even ripped asunder many a relation-ship, it also generated numerous new friendships, liaisons, and romances.

Letter from Pat McNabb to Joan Flor⁶

6 February 1944

U.S.S. Belleau Wood
At Sea

Joan Dear,

Surprise, huh? I didn't say a pleasant one, but you'll have to admit that these California attorneys are most devious. If you read beyond this point, you're

---

*Antiaircraft artillery.
**China-Burma-India.

going to have to hear the story, so here goes: Lt. Potts, our Photographic Officer aboard, is in constant correspondence with Phyllis Pinckney of Glasser-Gailey (say, this has complications already, doesn't it?) and the aforementioned firm had a Christmas Party, and you were in attendance at said party at which was taken a lovely picture of Phyllis in company with Miss Flor—picture sent via Pinckney to Potts to Patrick. Immediately persuaded Potts to send out general alarm for name and whereabouts of the creature finally designated as the recipient of this incoherent letter. May not be orthodox or conventional—but the least you can say for me is a commendable "persistence." If I have been offensive—forgive me. Months out here makes one a little unaccountable—and I was such a pleasant individual (really) before leaving the mainland.

Seriously, your picture was exceptionally attractive—and I've always liked the unusual, so I without justification or apology hack this out thinking it may be transferred and taken to some port for mailing.

Previous to official connection with the Navy, I had a law office in Westwood Village, Los Angeles, although spending last two years in the East as a legal advisor to a business corporation in Baltimore and Washington, D.C. Now I roam the seas as an Aviation Officer aboard this carrier. Details of our activities, of course, are censorable—so I cannot enlighten you as to "doings" or whereabouts.

Spent the last 10 days in the States before my departure westward in San Francisco. Lived at the Fairmount—and how I envy you in being there this minute. Our existence may be exciting and hectic—but we'd give much to spend even a few days in your good city—and, please admit, Los Angeles isn't the most undesirable place in the world.

Since our schedule is rather monotonous as regards "entertainment," mail is the highlight of our routine. Like kids at a circus—we jump up and down, whistle, and run from staterooms to Post Office in our eagerness for home-front news.

Been out over 3 weeks now—and haven't slightest conception of when we'll return to port—much less where. If you aren't completely disgusted with my approach, seat yourself and give forth with the latest concerning the west coast. Builds morale (or moral, as most of the enlisted men put it). Charley is a grand guy—and sends his regards—he won't get over missing the Christmas party (and frankly he wouldn't have gotten over it had he been there). Yes, you photograph well—now do I get an answer?

"Pat"

Pat McNabb and Joan Flor were later married.

Letter from Mary Metcalfe to Mother[7]

Mary "Chichi" Metcalfe was a Red Cross volunteer who served GIs in France. She drove a "clubmobile," a truck for providing coffee and doughnuts to troops near the front lines. This letter furnishes a view of those duties but also details a young woman's infatuation with one of the many soldiers she met.

Nov. 10, 1944

Dearest Mommie,

Since our clubmobiles were still not operating we discovered where our Brigade had moved and got in touch with them. Bibby talked to the Gen. after I had talked to Sperry, who was coming to see me on Thurs. The Gen. said they were having a party Wed. night and they would send for us.

On Tues. night the GI (like 1, 2, 3 not 9) section, which is the personnel section of the army, gave a party for us. The party was for Vicki, who was leaving us the next day to go back to the states to be married. Greg is in this section, by the way.

On Wed. afternoon Capts. Sperry and Ellis arrived in the General's car to take us back for a couple of days. While driving there it started to snow and never stopped even when we left to come back Fri. noon.

We didn't arrive until about 7:30 Wed. night so we had supper, then the Gen. let us use his room and bath room to take a good hot bath and get dressed for the party. We danced, sang, and drank beer. It was such fun seeing all our old friends again. Les didn't go with us because she was just getting over a cold.

We stayed in a pretty, quaint, little country hotel with the officers. There were three other R.C. girls there from Group E. They had just arrived the day before with the Brigade for two days, and they left Fri. morning to go serve all the battalions under the Brigade. They will not be with the Brigade all the time as we were since the battalions are so scattered around now it would be impossible to cook, go out and serve and get back the same day.

On Thurs. Bibby and I arose about 11 o'clock, took a hot bath and spent the afternoon wandering around and resting. That night the girls were serving coffee and doughnuts to the enlisted men. Bibby and I went over to talk to the boys, and they were just as glad to see us as we were to see them. We had lots of fun seeing and talking to them all again. Back across the street to our quarters where I spent the rest of the evening talking to Capts. Sperry and Bornshever, listening to the radio and drinking a little cognac.

Don't worry about me drinking too much. I don't like to drink too much. We got a ration of liquor last week, a bottle of cognac, one of armanac and one of benedictine, the works for 350 francs or seven dollars. Imagine that! I haven't any of mine left now because I took it up to the Brigade and left it as a present.

We came back to our old stone barracks, leaving the Brigade at noon on Fri. It was a beautiful ride with the snow all over the ground and the pine trees. To get there and back we were in France, Luxembourg, and Belgium.

On Sat. we made and served doughnuts at the base. Sat. night we went into town and had a good dinner at a hotel there.

When we were in Belgium a couple of months ago we served some engineers who were reconstructing a bridge which had been blown out. Whenever engineers build a bridge over here they put up a sign on the bridge saying "such and such a bridge constructed by—engineer battalion, company—." When this bridge was built, the engineers put up their sign and it said all I put above "_____ and Clubmobile Group A."

Capt. Sperry was down there and saw the sign and had pictures taken of it and sent each of us, Les, Bibby and me, one of them. Wasn't it nice of the engineers to put us on their sign, and wasn't it nice of Sper to send us the pictures!

Sunday afternoon we left to come on our present assignment which should be fascinating. I'm wondering if I might run into Warren Elmer. I don't know who he is with, or if he is in France.

I think we shall be here for about two weeks or more. Our whole group is on this assignment, but we are in two different places. The clubmobiles here are Martha Richardson's, Helen Longshore's and ours. Either Pussy Crocker's or Jean Hacher's will join us in the next couple of days. They went on a 3 or 4 day assignment just before we left to come here. There are also two other clubmobiles from K group which came today, and we shall all be serving here.

We are in a little bungalow type of house which is divided in half. On our side we have an entrance hall with a lavatory on one side and a room with a sink in it on the other. There is a living room (unfurnished), Les and I are in one room, Bibby in one room, and Helen, Marie Philips, and M—* Eberle in the other.

There is one bed in our room which I have my sleeping bag and blankets on. Les has a cot with Bibby's air mattress on it. Bibby got this air mattress by a stroke of luck. When she was on the Paris to Cherbourg supply run, she left her sleeping bag. When the other girls came back from Cherbourg, they brought what they thought was Bibby's sleeping bag. When she unrolled it she discovered it was not hers, but there inside was this wonderful air mattress. They are wonderful to sleep on! I wonder if you could find one for me and send it?

---

*Illegible in the original.

Now, to tell you something about "this Sperry man!" His mother died when he was 5 years old. His father married again when he was 7. Since his step-mother was only 25, they did not pay much attention to him, and he was left more or less to his own devices. I think that as a child he was hurt and developed an inferiority complex from not having attention or any family life. He said that when he was young and anything went wrong, home was the last place he would want to go. He apparently never did like or get along with his stepmother. He lived in Aurora, Ill. which is about 40 miles outside of Chicago.

I believe he went to Northwestern for a year. When he was 20 or 21 his stepmother and father decided to live in a furnished apartment, and since they didn't get along so well, she told him he better get a room someplace for himself. At the time he was a sales manager or asst. sales manager for some company. Sometime later his grandmother died leaving him her house. He sold the house, and with the money he and a friend of his bought a trailer and went out west. They traveled around living in the trailer, working by doing almost any job when they needed money. He loves skiing and horseback riding, and has worked quite a lot on ranches. He was in the cavalry, went to paratroop school where he broke his ankle on the first jump so he couldn't be in that, went back to the cavalry, and since they were not coming overseas, he joined the Brigade, but he is technically still in the cavalry. He met the Gen. someplace in the states just before the Brigade was coming over and said to him "How can you go overseas without a cavalryman in your outfit?" The Gen. apparently thought he couldn't, and so he brought Capt. then Lt. Sperry along as his aide. It is just since they have been here in France that Sper became battery commander of the Brigade and so a capt.

He was all set to be married to a nurse a couple of years ago in the states. They had planned their leaves to be married. She had put in an application to be an air evacuation nurse, but a long time had elapsed and she thought the application was not going to come through. It did come through, and they were married and had just three days before she had to leave. Apparently she decided their marriage would not work out. I asked him if he thought it was entirely her fault, and he said he did everything he could, and under normal circumstances he thought it would have worked, as it wasn't a spur of the moment thing, but they had known each other for a long time. He hasn't heard anything from her for 13 or 14 months and he doesn't know whether he is divorced or not.

I have told you all the nice things in other letters that Sper has done for us. He went out of his way doing nice little things not only for me, but for all three of us. Everyone in the Brigade likes him immensely. Les and Bibby both like him very much. He is a very frank and honest person. We always have lots of fun together, talking and laughing, especially by ourselves. I think and everyone else does too that he loves me, and he does act as though he does. I like him and could very easily love him, but where does it all lead? When will this all be over, he has no money, and he has nothing or no kind of a job to come home to. This is one of those many screwy things that happens in war times. There is no solution, and there is nothing to do but wait and see how everything comes out.

Now you know about as much as I can tell you about my captain. Please do not publish this to most of St. Louis, Greenwich, etc.

I must get up at 6:30 A.M., and it is now 11 o'clock so I must be off to bed. Les and I were thrilled to get your and Mrs. Allen's letters telling of her trip to St. Louis. I know you must have talked your heads off. I wish I could have been there to hear it all. Lots and lots of love.

Chichi

"You have never kissed so wonderfully before, Laura. Why is that? Because we are in a black-out?"

"No. It's because my name is Vera."

LETTERS FROM A LOVING HUSBAND[8]

W. HILDRETH TO HIS WIFE

These two letters are from a thoroughly depressed and disillusioned soldier to his closest friend and confidante: his wife. How many more people must have felt as he did but could not or would not commit their sentiments to paper?

24 May 1944

Italian Front

My Dearest Dolly,

I am somewhat calmed down from the wearied frenzy of my last two letters—I've been getting some rest, and with rest comes a kind of repose. I am a very fortunate man. In less than a month I shall have the most precious gift possible. And I have a wife whose serene guardianship of my life is a comfort to me "beyond all mine infirmities." Occasionally my vision of these two wonders is

Portrait of Hildreth and wife. (Courtesy of the Dwight D. Eisenhower Library, Martha C. Hildreth Collection.)

clouded by present brutality—and I lose some faith. But I can always return to you, and you are better than life, stronger than death.

When time has passed I shall have something to say of this war. Never have I felt more strongly about anything. If I can say one thing clearly, for people to listen and feel with me, it is this: there is nothing on earth so frail or so priceless as a human life, and it's taking must have better reason than war offers. "We know nothing better than to live." I love you very dearly, ma chère Dolly,

W.

3 June 1944

Italian Front

My Dearest Dolly,

That I cannot write more often in these trying days is a constant thorn in my side. I know that you must read the papers and wait so hungrily for these few letters to tell you that all is well with me. And when I do get a chance to get back to the battery and write, my constant thought is: this letter may be the one she reads just before the baby comes.

I have had two packages—one of cigarettes, the other with the cake and this stationery. But no letters for more than ten days. The services of supply just can't keep up with us.

My darling, things are a little better with me now. Hellishly, one can get hardened to the sights and smells of a battlefield. Only at the back of the brain a voice repeats: this is unnatural and not a part of life. And all of the consciousness returns to the reality of your miracle—there is no death in that.

I seem to be living ages long these days. Have I ever known anything else but this constant weariness and surge of conflicting emotion? Will there ever be a peace for me? I want to remain changeless for you, Dolly, but I can see the changes in myself even as the days pass. You get something twisted out of your insides by all of this filth and sewage. You are shocked at first, profoundly—and it goes on—you can't close it out with anything—no doors to shut, windows to close. You have to live with it. So you do. Your mind splits. Part of it guides your feet and puts food in your mouth, looks and smells. Most of it retreats back to the "time before." It has to. We are not, God bless us, butchers.

I want so to wring out my heart to you—you who have so completely the heart I once had. Perhaps I never shall be able to tell you—for to tell is in some measure to relive. Written words are too cold.

I don't care anymore that a kitten is lost outside a Virginia post office. Because the whole world is lost somewhere between the Hell of earth and the promise of Heaven. And irretrievably lost. No one can redeem what has been lost in our souls for having sinned thus against ourselves. Our children have the right to spit on us for what we are.

Darling, hold me so close tonight. Never before have I had so much need of you.

I love you.
W.

From a wife's letter to her soldier husband at Fort Bragg: "When I start to write to you, my heart holds the pen."

A WARTIME RELATIONSHIP

LETTERS FROM BETTY KLEIN TO GEORGE W. DINNING[9]

Love conquers all, the truism goes, as it did for Betty Klein and George Dinning. Having repaired an earlier, broken engagement, the two confronted their enforced separation with renewed commitment to one other. Betty wrote her George often, and she never failed to express her undying devotion to him.

8 Sept 1944

936 Highland
Apt 3
Bremerton Washington

My Dear Dinning,

Just got back from swimming, and it was so much fun. I swim on the average of twice a week—Gotta get some exercise—well, I could always change to classified labor and dig ditches. Ever since I've been in Bremerton I've been famished so the Lieut sees me eating 8 hrs. a day—so he said I could be a 3/c* Garbage Inspector (sorting garbage)—why 3/c why not 1/c and he said 'cause I wouldn't know edible garbage from inedible garbage. Sounds like I was vaccinated with a Victrola needle. Gee whiz, it's great to be 21, Dinning. Figured I could get away with anything at the office, but now they expect me to act like an adult.

A day like today is quite interesting at the office. You know these movies you see where there are Captains and Admirals, Generals, etc. around a big, long table, deciding the fate of a nation? Well, that's the way one of our sales looks. Disbursing Officers and Representatives from all these big Companies in the East plus a couple of Captains sit around this table, and little Betty sits at the end of the table and records each bid. It is conducted somewhat like an auction sale, only each bid is sealed in an envelope. The amount of money

---

*3rd Class.

enclosed is what I record with the price bid per lot. Each bid is worth several thousand dollars. An awful lot of Jews are represented, and they really get excited. Anyway, to be their only Secretary is a great deal like court reporting. It's fun, Dinning.

The mighty President was in Bremerton about a month ago, and this time I got a better look at him. Last time he was here he just drove by and guess my heart was in my mouth for months. Jack Benny and Jimmie Lunceford were also here. Hope your diet is half way civil. Tonite we had steak—stringbeans—stewed tomatoes—grape and pear salad—coffee and peach upside-down cake—I think that supply of peaches should be just about depleted by now. Got my hair washed this evening, too. It is long now, Dinning—always in the way. Someday I will get desperate and put it on top of my head. I have no new clothes worth raving about—just the same Betty 1 year older; and still very much in love with you, Dinning. Darling, I wish I could pray—I wish every thing would be okay—I wish this didn't happen. Dinning, I wish I were married to you—I love you—so very, very much.

Betty

Dinning! Close your eyes—I love you. . . .

2 January 1945

My Darling Platoon Sergeant,

Well, Happy New Year! Wish you a happy Easter now, too—then I won't be belated again. The man I love made me so happy tonite. Your Christmas present was wonderful. Pay attention while I tell you. The package was 12" long—6" wide wrapped with green paper on the outside and white tissue paper and white ribbon on the inside with a card "Merry Christmas from George." It is without a doubt the most beautiful scarf I have ever had. It is 70 inches long and 20 inches wide—a very rich color a bit deeper than pink—closer to flame. It is quite sheer with tiny silver sequins all over it that sparkle and glitter—honestly, it's just dreamy! Ruby said it makes me look like an angel, so you can imagine how dainty and nice it would have to be. It will go so well with my flame formal, but gee I wish you could see it—you would like it, dear, honest you would. Anyway, I need a platoon sergeant to guard it for me so these room mates don't possess it.

Ruby just brought me some punch—made with grape juice—well, Ruby is a sweet girl and I like her and she's brilliant and she's thoughtful and I like punch—but darn it that stuff makes my teeth purple and hang it all I'll have to brush my teeth and I just did on Christmas.

New Year's Eve wasn't very "wet" in Bremerton, as the following day was a work day in the yard and anyway it was Sunday and then too—just before payday and anyway Betty doesn't drink every night of the year, so it was as exciting as New Year's Eve on an island—what am I saying.

Why don't you come over and hang my mirror—I'm not much of a carpenter, even though I have 7 uncles that are architects. Dinning—how many invitations do I have to give before you'll oblige? Now look–You are cordially invited to 936 Highland, Bremerton, Washington, 1 April 1945 (RSVP)*—and don't forget your appointment for Christmas 1945—ah! the life of a private secretary. What do I have to do to rate a Platoon Sergeant?? I wonder what it would be like to be in the arms of a platoon sergeant—to be kissed by a platoon sergeant—to be held real close and be loved for ever and ever and ever.

Thanks for the priceless gift, dearest—I love you.

Your Betty

Now I want a little tiny pin with a Platoon Sergeant's insignia on it—No! I want a platoon sergeant. I'm so much in love.

25 April 1945

Darling Dinning,

Your first letter from Okinawa Shima was here this evening—It was like a diary, only 50 times more interesting. It is quite apparent that censorship regulations are not so rigid now, which is no doubt quite a relief.

Told Ruby you said you lost 5 toothbrushes, and *did* she laugh. "What a couple you two will make." She's afraid we'll fight over the bathroom—think she's right there. Someone said the Japs are great big fellows, and I thought they were tiny. Which is generally so? If and when Germany falls—there is plenty of excitement expected over here, which I really don't understand. I wish you could see the memos and the orders ". . . a minimum of loss of lives and Government property is demanded." . . . Don't see how anyone could celebrate, knowing about the loss of lives in the Pacific.

Simply can't get over how interesting your last letter was—think how interesting you yourself will be. You've seen so much. Will have so many things to talk about. It's going to be great to see you, Dinning—Be real brave for me.

Do you remember I love you I love you I love you I love you I love you I love you I love you I love you I love you I love you I love you I love you I love you and do you remember my eternal pride for you—remember our ring—remember to come back to me.

Betty

---

*Ironically, George Dinning would be invading Okinawa on that very date.

As much as Betty loved George, things changed. Betty wrote religiously to George until July 1945. Then there was a six-week gap in their correspondence, broken finally by the following letter.

13 September 1945

Dearest Dinning,

It is a most unhappy girl that is writing these words. Have been unhappy for so many months, Dinning. My decision was certainly not a result of your having to be away for so long, as you had no control over that. My love for you was deep and most sincere until a month ago, at which time I got another ring. I am hoping that marriage may take the place of this horrible feeling of being alone. I regret very much having to hurt you, Dinning—the nights I spent crying myself to sleep are evidence that it hurts me, too. I guess a guy has to have an awful lot of understanding to read a letter like this. It's difficult to write, too, as there is that constant longing for you that I don't think I will ever be able to dismiss.

I will be living at 936 Highland Apartment 3, so it's okay to send my class ring there. It would be nice if you could visit us when you get back.

If only I could know what I am doing—everything is so terrible.

Love you,
Betty

Dinning remained in the U.S. Marine Corps for another twenty years. He later married.

■ SOURCES

1.   The letters in this section are from Ervin J. Cook to Wife, March 24, 1943, "Letters to Wife, March 1943" File; July 3, 1944, "Letters to Wife, July 1944" File; and August 16 and 20, 1944, "Letters to Wife, August 1944" File; Ervin J. Cook Papers, World War II Participants and Contemporaries Collection, Dwight D. Eisenhower Library, Abilene, Kansas.

2.   The letters in this section are from Bruce Carson to Family, April 13, 1945, "Bruce Carson Letters 1945 (1)" File; and Bruce Carson to Sister, July 5, 1945, "Bruce Carson Letters 1945 (2)" File, Richard Lowitt Papers, World War II Participants and Contemporaries Collection, Eisenhower Library.

3.   Father to George W. Dinning, May 21, 1945, "Letters from Mother (1)" File, George W. Dinning Papers, World War II Participants and Contemporaries Collection, Eisenhower Library.

4. M. R. Novak to Henry Novak, January 7, 1944, Stephanie Salada Papers, Private Collection, Pittsburgh, Pennsylvania.
5. Harold Porter to Parents, May 23, 1945, "Letters May 1945" File, Harold Porter Papers, World War II Participants and Contemporaries Collection, Eisenhower Library.
6. Pat McNabb to Joan Flor, February 6, 1944, Joan Flor McNabb Papers, World War II Participants and Contemporaries Collection, Eisenhower Library.
7. Mary Metcalfe to Mother, November 10, 1944, "Letters Oct.–Dec. 1944 (1)" File, Mary Metcalfe Rexford Papers, World War II Participants and Contemporaries Collection, Eisenhower Library.
8. The letters in this section are from W. Hildreth to Wife, May 24 and June 3, 1944, Martha C. Hildreth Papers, World War II Participants and Contemporaries Collection, Eisenhower Library.
9. The letters in this section are from Betty Klein to George W. Dinning, September 8, 1944, "Letters from Betty Klein 1944 (1)" File; January 2, 1945, "Letters from Betty Klein 1945 (1)" File; April 25, 1945, "Letters from Betty Klein 1945 (3)" File; and September 13, 1945, "Letters from Betty Klein 1945 (4)" File, George W. Dinning Papers, World War II Participants and Contemporaries Collection, Eisenhower Library.

SIX

THE
ARSENAL
OF
DEMOCRACY

D espite the justifiably celebrated feats of American arms, the nation's greatest contribution to victory was probably its production effort. The United States manufactured munitions and other war materials in abundance. For instance, American shipyards built over 85,000 naval vessels of all types, from small ramped landing craft to massive battleships and aircraft carriers. And this figure does not include wartime merchant shipping construction during the war, which aggregated more than 50 million deadweight tons. These are scarcely imaginable achievements, considering that a single 10,000-ton tanker contained sixteen miles of pipe, which required 5,300 cuts, 5,700 bends, and 17,000 welds to acquire the proper shapes for installation, or that a single B-24 necessitated the assembly of more than 100,000 separate components. And yet the U.S. economy also produced civilian goods, foodstuffs, and myriad other necessities. To be sure, the manufacturing of some consumer items, such as automobiles, was temporarily discontinued so that production facilities could be used for war work. But civilians had to eat, wear clothes (especially work clothes), and get some modicum of enjoyment from their off hours, or popular discontent could undermine the entire war effort. Many items became scarce, but Americans generally maintained their basic standard of living.

Not only the United States but, through Lend-Lease, all the other partners in the victorious alliance benefited from the remarkable American production achievement. Aside from the well-documented assistance supplied to the major coalition partners of Great Britain and the Soviet Union, U.S.-made goods turned the Free French into a battlefield force of real moment, fed starving refugees, and rehabilitated the transportation infrastructure of Iran. From Algiers to Murmansk to Bhamo in the deep recesses of Upper Burma, the Allied effort was touched to some degree by the enormous output of American factories.

Industrial facilities and shipyards themselves thus were in a sense a certain kind of field of battle and the workers were warriors. Reducing absenteeism and improving labor efficiency became not only desirable business goals but patriotic duties. The dismal employment situation of the Great Depression years was soon forgotten amid the sudden labor shortage following Pearl Harbor, and women, as well as the elderly, immigrants, and other minorities, found unprecedented opportunities for work. This change in the labor force was the foundation and harbinger of social change that would become one of the defining characteristics of the ensuing decades of American history. In the end, the nation's striking transformation into the "arsenal of democracy" affected more lives than did the sacrifices of the battlefields.

A SHIPYARD WORKER'S LETTERS TO HIS SON[1]

LETTERS FROM M. R. NOVAK TO HENRY NOVAK

News of home and family is scattered among references to war work in this series of letters from a shipyard worker to his son in the field artillery, who was himself a shipbuilder before he joined the army. Father and son had been contractors before the war but had found much more profitable employment in the new government-built yards for producing the ships now needed in large quantities, especially destroyer escorts, for protecting the

Atlantic convoys, and LSTs, for supporting the many amphibious operations in both major theaters.

Thursday, March 23rd, 1944.

Dear Henry:

We received your letter a few days ago and were glad to hear from you. On the other hand, we were surprised and saddened that you are ready to go across. The least they could do is to give you at least a week of leave before you go. Helen told Mother that she expects you home this weekend and we earnestly hope that you come. We saved some "kielbasa" and I have a crock-ful of "kosher corned beef," which can be cooked on short notice. We would have a regular feast.

I was almost certain that you would end up in the Field Artillery. Your Grandfather and all his brothers as well as your great grandfather served in the Russian field artillery, so you ought to feel at home.

Your father is getting along as best he can. I am as efficient as the work-ing conditions will permit me to be. All the DE's* are in the river now and we are launching two LST's** every week. There are a whole lot of changes on the new batch of LST's. They are more efficient than the ones you worked on. No elevator for unloading and therefore the unloading can be done in less time. They have now their own conversion plants to convert sea water into fresh and a whole lot of other changes that would take me a few hours to explain to you.

All the men that you bowled with want to see if and when you come home. They want me to call them up as soon as you land home.

We hope that what you say about all three of you coming back home is true. That is our most desired wish.

Well, I have to sign off, because last week I was transferred to the second trick and it is now one o'clock P.M. and I have to start out for West View. So far I have nobody to drive me and have to ride the street cars.

If we do not see you before you leave, we wish you the best of luck and may a lucky star guide you in all that lies before you.

With sincere love,

Your father, mother, brothers and sister in law also little Eddy.

per Dad.

---

*U.S. Navy designation for destroyer escorts, a small warship useful for fighting sub-marines.

**Designation for "landing ship, tank," a particularly valuable type of landing craft.

Soldiers saying goodbye to families before embarking on a bus. (Courtesy of the Dwight D. Eisenhower Library, Kristian P. Frost Collection.)

This letter makes explicit reference to the efficiency of mass production methods, the secret behind the U.S. production miracle.

Sunday morning, Aug. 6th, 1944.

Dear Henry:

We received your letter dated July 20th, last Thursday. It was two weeks on its way.

I have written to you before since you are in France and according to your letter you did not get it.

We are glad to hear that you are well and we fervently hope that you will come out of this mess sound and healthy.

Here at home, everybody is well and as happy as the circumstances permit. Your Helen and Stevie* are the same. We saw them last Sunday and again last Friday. We may see them today again. Today I am going to the Hill District, to buy some herrings, smoked fish, wieners and if I can pick up some hard Jewish summer sausage that won't spoil in shipment, I will send you a package if I am permitted to do so.

---

*Henry's wife and his daughter of toddler age, respectively.

Yes, I am still working on the Island, building some more L.S.T.s. We put them out much faster than we did, say two months ago. They put the bonus system in operation and some men are getting as high as thirty hours extra in a week's time. I am putting in the plumbing in troops' quarters in both sides and doing it in three days' less time than before. The new boats are a big improvement over the ones that you worked on. They are better arranged and are better armed. I like my work if it wasn't for the fact that it is too hot in summer. For the last two weeks, we did not have any rain and when that steel gets heated, it stays hot worse than hell itself. We got some rain last night and cooled off some but not much.

Dan Morgan got a letter from you in two sections. Section two got here first and the first got here one week later. Lois and Art McKenneys have a baby boy, two weeks ago. You ought to see Art going around like a peacock! So is Grandpap Silverman. Fred Slanina got two letters from you. Stella, Stanley's wife, had a baby girl.

The garden is much better this year than last year. We are eating tomatoes for over a week and also fresh corn. The potatoes are not so hot, but we may get enough for our own use. If nothing happens, we will have a good many bushels of field corn.

Ed is well and made the trip to some place in Africa, but from there his ship sailed somewhere else and not for home. Ester got a letter from him yesterday. Gene is still in Valley Forge hospital. They are trying to straighten his thumb and limber it up so it would bend at the first joint. He may have to submit to another operation.

Well, this is about all that I can think to write you now, so I will close with our best and sincere wishes. Be good and take good care of yourself.

Your loving parents, brothers, sister, in law and nephew.

per: Dad

V-Mail was a wartime innovation to save shipping space. The V-Mail letter was photographed, and a snapshot-sized print was sent to the addressee instead of the full-sized letter. This V-Mail letter provides some family news and some hints of the productivity and versatility of the U.S. shipbuilding industry during the war.

Sunday, Sept. 17th, 1944.

To: Pvt. Henry R. Novak, 33706421
Btry. "C" 552 F.A.Bn. A.P.O.230
c.o. Postmaster,
New York, N. Y.

From: M. R. Novak
R.D.#7, Bellevue,
Pittsburgh, 2, Pa.

Dear Henry:

It is two weeks since I wrote you a letter. In the meantime, we received one
from you, dated Sept. 1st, and were glad to hear that you are well and kicking.

Ed came home the night of Sept. 4th, and will stay here till coming
Wednesday. Eugene came last Friday night and will leave Monday night. We
had a nice party on my birthday. By the way, I thank you for your birthday
greetings. The party was mostly a family affair. We had Helen and Stevie here,
Walter Brandt, Saul Silverman and his family and Mirriam Rickert.

I told Ed to write you a letter the first day he got here, but you will realize, that with the parties and visiting here and there, he did not have the time.
He says he will write you as soon as he returns to duty. Mother wants to thank
you for the nice birthday letter that you wrote her. I forgot to mention this in
my last letter. Pausel Walter Pawlak came home and Ed, Eugene, Mother,
Wally and Esther are leaving for New Kensington right now. Just now, little
Joe Urban came in and we will go to see Mrs. Przeklasa, so I will interrupt the
letter right here. Well, Joey and I had a couple of "Yehudis," as he calls them,
a couple of Duqesnes,* and here I am back home. Nobody here but myself.
Will have to water all the animals and feed them. After this is over, I will warm
up some veal stew and eat.

Johnny played his first scholastic game of football yesterday. Mother, Ed,
Esther, Gene and Wally went to watch it. Of course, I had to work. They
played Avalon High. According to their account Johnny has saved the game
for West View. You know how it is after such an event. They talked about it
all night and as soon as they got up. I did not understand a word of it. All such
things are Chinese to me. Well anyway, they enjoyed it, and that's all I care.
At the same time, I cannot get an hour's work out of John in a whole week.
He is always thinking of the game. Practicing every blessed day.

I am working as usual. I think the present contract for the LST's is coming to an end. We will begin to build mine sweepers. There were so many of

---

*A popular brand of beer in western Pennsylvania.

the LST's built that after the war is over, I will buy one and convert it into a floating entertainment palace, with bar, dance hall and other accommodations. They ought to sell for a song. I will anchor it at Sixth Street Bridge.

Well, this will be all for tonight. I have to go to bed in order that I would be fit to put in some steam piping in an LST tomorrow. Be good and remember that we all miss you as bad as ever. With best of wishes for good luck and good health, we remain as ever,

Your loving parents, brothers, sister in law and little nephew.

per Dad

P.S. There is nothing wrong with little Eddie's leg. Will grow out of it.

> "It has been rumored that you are receiving money for playing football here. Is that true?"
>
> "Yes, sir. But I have to make money. I'm putting my mother through welding school."

AMERICAN LEGION PUBLICATION

"VENEREAL DISEASE: SABOTEUR OF WAR MANPOWER"[2]

Whether viewed as a medical problem or a consequence of immorality, venereal disease also becomes, in an industrial-age war, a problem likely to undercut military and economic effectiveness.

VENEREAL DISEASE: SABOTEUR OF WAR MANPOWER

Together, syphilis and gonorrhea are responsible for the loss of more man-days to the armed forces and industry than any other single cause of disability.

In the first World War, 7,000,000 man-days were lost to the United States Army because of syphilis, gonorrhea and other venereal diseases. A total of 338,746 fighting men—the equivalent of 23 divisions—received treatment for venereal infections and were lost to service for varying periods of time.

Exclusive of administrative expense, the Veterans Administration had spent by June 30, 1940, $82,043,500 to care for disabilities caused by venereal disease contracted in the last war.

In the present war, of the first 2,000,000 men examined for military service under the Selective Service Act, 100,000 were rejected because they had syphilis. They were young men needed by their country on her fighting front. But they were out of action before they had even been issued a uniform.

From 1940 to 1942, inclusive, according to the United States Public Health Service, newly-contracted venereal disease infections were responsible for 329,500 Servicemen being incapacitated for a total of 4,175,000 days.

Syphilis and gonorrhea are probably the most insidious saboteurs of production. The havoc they cause by attacking manpower on the home front is far more devastating than any attempts of Axis agents on our production lines.

Then there's the sad case of the kid who couldn't tell the boss his grandmother died—she was working there as a riveter!

LIFE AT THE OFFICE

LETTERS FROM BETTY KLEIN TO GEORGE W. DINNING[3]

In these letters from a woman to her Marine fiancé are, intermingled with bits of news and expressions of affection, descriptions of life in a shipyard management office. One can see the glass ceiling for women workers and the problems of getting competent staff members, caused by the dire shortage of labor.

5 February 1945

My Darling Dinning,

It wasn't much of a weekend—didn't really do anything any more than sleep. Guess that's good, only some day I want to know why I feel exhausted Monday morning after having slept almost my entire Sunday away. Also got a few suits pressed, so I don't feel so guilty.

I wish I were a boy so my new understudy wouldn't irritate me. I'd overlook all her faults and feast upon her beauty, but darn it I'm a girl and it's terrific. I take a contract over to her desk to teach her how to make them. I explain in detail for 10 minutes, and then she looks up and says, "Guess who I got a date with tonite"—I try desperately to continue my instructions only to have her say, "Guess where we're going tonite." It's plenty difficult to teach someone that's enthusiastic, but when she doesn't care and doesn't listen, I'm sort of at a loss just what to say. Every day I think I shall try a new approach to try to make things look a little more attractive. What do you do with men that absolutely have no savvy—and look like they never will have? Never have believed in mixing social life with business anyway so think I will start a campaign for my dear understudy to try to get her mind on her work. Know something? Women defeat me!—Well, men do, too. I can't see, for example, how come my marine wants twins when just one boy or one girl would give him more misery than he bargained for? You're pretty brave to anticipate it. There is no doubt about their eyes being brown, and I am confident the boy or girl would be extremely handsome or good-looking if you were his or her father. He would be real tall and dark and fascinating—wouldn't he, Dinning? Would have curly hair and beautiful teeth. I will teach him manners, and you will teach him calisthenics and math and how to brush his teeth. Doesn't it make you a little afraid??

Sunday Ruby's younger sister arrived from St. Paul to live with us. Her name is Delores—just 18 and is she ever a beauty. Blonde—imagine! Guess she will be a key-punch operator in the yard.

Got quite a jolt on Sunday when Ruby and Lovell were gone—received a phone call from San Francisco. It was a friend of Lovell's that decided to talk to me since she wasn't here. Golly, I wonder how it would seem to talk to you from San Francisco. It will be so wonderful. Wonder who will be the most excited. If only you knew how much I'm looking forward to that homecoming and how much I want it to be beautiful and to result in love that will last forever and ever.

Love you my darling,
Betty

7 February 1945

My Darling Gunnery Sergeant.

Can you tell that I'm always thinking of you? Isn't it registering somewhere? If not, I've simply got to invent a machine for the purpose 'cause you simply must know about something that is so important. Wrote to the other two people I love tonite, too—my dad and my income tax collector; both of which were financial. Since it was the end of my fiscal year, I decided to let Dad know about my intimate relations with my bank book. I shall be quite proud to get a few of his suggestions for "Methods of Improvement." Think he will discover that his daughter has become pretty mercenary, and that ain't good.

Yesterday was the most important day of my career. Mrs. North was in Seattle, and the Lieutenant was sick, so they left me alone with the office. Could have given you the whole scrap yard. It got pretty hectic as it was the day of a big sale, and I took 14 bidders to the conference room with the Disbursing Officer. It was fun, though. Today I completed the monthly reports which were a direct cause of insomnia. Feel that I can actually breathe now. The only thing that I don't like is my understudy. If she doesn't get to work on time one of these mornings, I think I shall lower the boom on her. See, I told you I'd get tough.

What are you doing with my Gunnery Sergeant? Are you keeping him especially for me? The kisses are very definitely reserved for you, Dinning. Have no desire to have it otherwise. Are you ever going to have a problem teaching me. It will be so wonderful, won't it, Dinning? The thing that hurts is when I look at people all day and expect them to suddenly be you. Sometimes you are so vivid in my memory it seems that if I say your name you'd answer me. All I can think about is you—all I can hope

Your Betty

24 February 1945

Dinning Dear,

Why don't you get an emergency leave—come home—marry me—and see that I get some sleep. Last nite I think I got about 1/2 hr. Ruby stayed with the Lawrences and so—no room mate. Think I wake up about every 8 minutes—imagining the darndest things. By morning was a nervous wreck. I want a Gunnery Sergeant for protection. That's not unreasonable, is it??

The letter I got this week from you was a pretty one—even when you're in a hurry, they're perfect and seem to always arrive when they're needed the most. I wish I could be there with you—now while you're reading this would be fun to watch your smile—would you—just for me—Love you, Dinning. You were supposed to be at the office with me today, but you must have had another appointment.

Mrs. North took off to Tacoma again—leaving me alone again with that cussed office. Someday they'll be sorry—I'll sell some battleship or something. The strife between my Lieut. and supervisor is so juvenile, dear. They scream at each other from 8 to 4 until I almost tell them to shut up so I can think. The argument on Friday got pretty violent, so she felt she'd get revenge by going to Tacoma. Think they should both be spanked. Got such a kick out of one of our bidders. Just before the sale, they all stand around and smoke and argue and rib each other and naturally they include me in their teasing. Mr. Sidell said—"Say, Miss Klein—that ring—is that still the same fellow you were engaged to when you first came in this office?" And I told him it was, and he wanted to know what I was waiting for—when I told him you were overseas—he sat down and in 2 minutes all those bidders were over there—listening to the story of your life. That proves I get more attention in the office than outside the office.

This is resulting in a week end letter—I take out time to sleep and eat and talk. Now I'm at work Monday morning. Sunday was so pretty, so we took a few pictures out on the lawn in front of Lovell's house. The afternoon was spent going for a hike to Manette—kinda silly, isn't it?

Got to release a car now, so I'll be talking to you again real soon. Love you, Dinning—honest I do.

Your Betty

This chatty letter nevertheless contains some somber news about the shipyard. It reminds one of the very real hazards of heavy industry and that war brings risks even to those thousands of miles from the fighting.

25 March 1945

My Darling Dinning,

Have been lolling here on my bed almost all day—just thinking about you—my attention was diverted this morning, however, when I made my way to church.—Palm Sunday and it was beautiful. Lots of new bonnets already, too. Easter—just a week away—was planning on wearing green and gold but can't get away to Seattle just now so will have to forget about it—anyway, you won't be here, so I don't much care how I look. Hope I won't lose interest in everything by the time you get back—it's the best I can tell that I'm really in love, though.

How long has it been since you've had chicken? That's what we had late this afternoon, and we enjoyed it pretty much, as ordinarily we just don't eat the things that take that long to prepare. It makes the evenings so short, and none of us ever accounts for Sundays. Did you know that your fiance was the laziest girl in the N.W.?

Ruby just brought me some ice cream with chocolate on top. She's 100 times sweeter than I am. Can't see why some fellow doesn't take her away and marry her. Her younger sister is just 18 and has plenty of charm. When you meet her, you'll wish you would have met her before me. Gee, I think everybody is wonderful, don't I?

Think they will have to paint a skull and crossed bones on the Pier—There have been 5 lives lost down there during the past year. This week another fellow fell from the top of a crane over the Pier on down to the pavement. Don't think I'll be a brave Marine, as just hearing about these things makes me wince.

Sailor posing with two children in yard. (Courtesy of the Dwight D. Eisenhower Library, Dennis and Jane Medina Collection.)

How I wish I could be there with you to watch you work—no, that isn't the reason—was just thinking how beautiful it would be to have your arms around me and never—ever—let me go.

Waiting for you—

Betty

> Since Pearl Harbor 150,000 workers have been killed on and off the job; 69,000 persons killed in traffic accidents; 112,000 killed in accidents in the home. Think of it! Almost one third more than the total number of our military personnel killed in World War II.
>
> —Philadelphia Record, November 1945[4]

AMERICAN LEGION PUBLICATION

"SPARE TIME"[5]

Here is a wartime affirmation of the significance of home-front production.

SPARE TIME

In total mobilization, recreation is a resource of war. It is no more a frill, a frivolity, than munitions, food, or manpower. Fun, play, entertainment for workers in off-the-job hours is time gained on the job to turn out more bombers, more ships, more tanks. Recreation is a hard-boiled necessity in these times, an investment in our Number One asset—human resources.

People working at the intensive tempo of war plants—and living too often in overcrowded quarters, and in towns that may be alarmed by the problems strangers bring—traveling long distances to and from work, seek and need release from tension at the end of the work shift. The high intensity that war production demands cannot be maintained beyond a certain span—the rest of the time the pendulum must swing back to those interests and activities that body and mind normally crave.

As war towns boom and living grows more complex, as homes lose men and women to the services and to the war plants—as life becomes one-pointed to the single end of victory—it becomes imperative that society safeguard workers with decent food, adequate housing, and proper recreation, to guard against human waste that is just as much a casualty on the home front as on the battlefront.

There is no real separation between fighters and workers—everybody is fighting in one way or another, everybody working. The fighters, let's put it, are at the top of a pyramid; the rest of us make up the base supporting the top.

The pyramid is no stronger than its base. The soldiers are fighting the common enemy. The workers are producing the ammunition for their guns. There's no distinction between them. They are all part of one effort. Workers must be as physically fit—and their morale as high—as soldiers. As the Army and the Navy equip and safeguard the fighters, communities need to equip and safeguard the workers who live in their midst. Among none of those in the pyramid can we afford human waste—not in soldiers, not in workers, men or women, not in youth, not in children.

Service men, happily, are fairly well provided for. Workers and their families, less glamorous, have had limited opportunities. Their needs in communities where they have crowded in unprecedented numbers either are unrecognized or pushed to the rear by priorities, psychological or material; in some cases by indifference, in others by sheer bewilderment because of catapulting community problem.

But war workers are people! They may spread over a wide range in some respects, but they are all pretty much alike in their relish of those golden moments for relaxing play when the time card is punched and the work shift ends. They have fairly common impulses and desires, which include play.

But there are differences. Uncle Joe, 60, when he leaves the drill press, may like to sit in the shade of a tree with his pipe and whittle. Jinny, his granddaughter, 20, will choose the hilarity of juke-box dancing after a hard day's riveting, and why not? Between Uncle Joe and Jinny there will be a wide range of interests according to age and sex, where workers live, what kind of jobs they do. Nor are workers to be separated from their families—all are included in recreation.

"All work and no play"—everybody knows what that does to Jack at any time. This old proverb was never more true than among today's Jacks and Jills on the war production line; machines whirring, spinning; electric hammers pounding; pulleys moving and giant cranes swinging; tools cutting, punching, polishing to the thousandth of an inch—life and death hanging upon the turn of a hand.

And many of these Jacks and Jills, with a long inheritance behind them of the hand-made, are comparative newcomers in gearing to the tempo and drive of the machine. Many of them are new workers, still shy of the monstrous machines, the roar of noise, the Vulcan fires of the furnaces. This is the sensitive human machine under strange, unaccustomed pressures. And the machines the workers operate are speeded as machines have never been speeded since they were invented, to the end that there shall be freedom once more upon the earth.

No frontiers separate work shift from living shift. The man who makes bombers and the woman who welds steel plates for ships or planes doesn't stop living when they lay down their tools. For many, the real problems begin when work is done—the problems of living. Unsolved, they pile up, taking toll of efficiency and, sooner or later, of the output of the job.

"The way people live and the way their families are cared for is bound to be reflected in production," said the manager of Henry J. Kaiser's Vancouver's shipyards. "If members of the family are sick, the worker worries on the job or stays home to take care of them. If workers have no recreation, they get morose. You have to treat workers like human beings, not like machines."

Wages are not the one incentive needed to keep workers at the peak of production. Facts prove that. Even patriotism isn't enough. They must have some chance to be human beings, have places to go in time off, to entertain and to be entertained, to dance or enjoy themselves according to their age and taste. Young or old, they need to get together.

Above all, while workers toil for victory, recreation offers them one of the few areas of freedom left in a world mobilized for war. This sphere of freedom they cherish, not for themselves alone but for their children as well.

For lack of this essential, mobilization of workers is slowed up. People don't want to work in places and under conditions where they are cut off from normal interests, or where their families and children are deprived of them.

The tense worker is a poor worker, the tired worker a liability. Often over-fatigue leads to illness. "Accidents and illness snatched 484,059,000 workdays away from the Nation's war-pressed industrial output in the year just ended," says Carl Brown in *Nation's Business,* January 1943.

"The effect on production was the same as though enemy bombers had knocked out for the entire year 1,861 industrial plants, each employing 1,000 men and women. . . . The manpower loss equaled the services of 1,800,000 persons from the year's start to its end." Of the five simple rules advocated by the Institute for Life Insurance to reduce accidents, illness, and absenteeism, one is "play some every day." But in order to play, there must be places to play and facilities to play with.

A Detroit industrial concern spent a million and a half dollars for mechanical safety devices of all kinds in its plant and only $50,000 for recreation. Yet good recreation is actually one of the soundest safety devices.

Elaborate care is given to the maintenance of machinery in industrial plants lest a wheel or a tool get out of order and slow up production. Maintenance of the human machine is more likely to be neglected. Human engineering is as important as mechanical engineering!

Absenteeism among war workers is one of the factors, along with shortage of workers and raw materials, which slows down production.

Many absences could be prevented if provision were made for wholesome recreation at normal intervals and some thought given to helping workers meet off-the-job problems.

The primary cause of absenteeism, of course, is sickness and the closely related factor of overfatigue—most likely to prevail among new workers. Along with good food and proper housing, release from emotional strain through recreation is one of the preventives of both fatigue and illness.

Morale is a vital factor in production. Workers may get jittery, turn out poor work, when for too long a stretch they can't do the things they are used to. Workers are sometimes homesick, they may suffer acutely from the unfriendliness of a strange town and strange ways of living. Recreation of the right sort can provide new interests to help replace the old. It can do much to keep the lives of workers balanced and normal.

Most women workers have double jobs. It is hard to be both plane maker and home maker. Off hours from the machine usually mean "on hours" over the kitchen sink or the washtub. And large numbers of women also at this time are new workers, not broken in to the strains and pressures of work in plant or shop. Statistics show that women are ill more frequently than men; by the very nature of their physique they are more easily tired.

As women take over an increasing volume of war production, special provisions should be made for their relaxation and recreation, both inside and outside the plant. Where women, either workers or the wives of workers in war plants, are newcomers to the community, they need the integrating influences of hospitality and the opportunity for normal pleasure and sociability. Above all, mothers who must work need the assurance of satisfactory care of younger children and programs of after-school recreation and activities under safe supervision for older children.

Recreation facilities are sadly overtaxed or lacking in most war towns. There's not enough manpower to keep up playgrounds and tennis courts; not enough cars or busses—or gas—to take people to the places where they can have fun. Steel for equipment goes into tanks and planes and ships; the bounce has gone out of the balls for lack of rubber; priorities of one kind or another edge in on recreation: all this in the face of the primary fact that lack of recreation definitely means a lag in production, disturbed family and community life.

Perhaps the chief factor, however, in the whole picture of recreation for the worker, is the unawareness of communities that recreation is an actual and vital part of the war production program. In many places a lot of people are doing a little something in the way of recreation, but in few places has there yet been a thoroughgoing all-out mobilization of resources, with a well-planned program, under trained leadership.

Out of workers' pay envelopes can come the recreation fee and the club dues, but the pay envelope, no matter how sizable, cannot build ball parks and play fields, gymnasiums, and club rooms; cannot buy good recreation leadership. It can pay for the purchasable entertainment, but that is scarce in boom towns. The many-sided recreation needs of workers, which are part of the recreation needs of the whole community, can be met only by total mobilization of resources—by all groups working together.

The difficulties of meeting the clamoring need for recreation for war workers in the face of war restrictions and priorities, with the many problems involved, throw leaders back on ingenuity to "use what you have." It gives a prod to good American initiative and ingenuity which never yet have failed when face to face with an emergency. If our soldiers and marines could lick Japs from their foxholes of Guadalcanal, our war industry communities won't fail to down the difficulties involved in providing decent recreation for the home-front soldiers of production.

Absence makes the war grow longer.
—Curtiss Wright aircraft plant poster

AN APPEAL TO BUY WAR BONDS

FROM EVAN GRIFFITH TO THE FARMERS OF KANSAS[6]

Farmers, too, did their part for the war effort, often despite equipment and labor shortages. Here is a well-considered appeal for farmers to use their wartime profits—from their first profitable harvests in a generation—to support war production and improve their postwar situation.

August 3rd, 1942

War Savings Staff
Topeka, Kansas

TO THE FARMERS OF KANSAS:

Your own sons and neighbors are fighting on foreign battle fields to hold back the Japs and Hitler. Millions of other American boys are being trained for overseas service. These men cannot fight bare-handed. They must have guns and tanks and ships and planes—which cost a lot of money. We must supply these war implements in a hurry. We must win, and the sooner we win, the fewer American boys will be killed.

Farmers, like all Americans, have obligations to meet and families to support. Crop failures have occurred frequently in recent years. Some sections are just now recovering from the effects of drouth and depression years. This year, again, adverse weather conditions have hurt some localities. Farming in Kansas certainly has not been profitable for everyone every year. Still, the Kansas farmer has kept his faith in the "good earth" of Kansas—and that faith now is paying dividends. It appears that farm income for Kansas this year will be more than in any year since 1929—and I am writing to ask you to buy all of the War Bonds you possibly can. You can buy these Bonds through your banker, postmaster, building and loan association and many of our merchants.

You help win the war . . . you're backing the boys in the service . . . when you buy War Bonds.

War Bonds are the soundest investment on earth . . . you are always guaranteed at least what you pay for them, plus interest . . . War bonds can be cashed in at any time after sixty days . . . they are a liquid asset, like wheat in the bin.

We all realize that we can't buy cars and tires and farm machinery . . . but we can convert Bonds into cash for farm machinery and other necessary articles when the war is over and these articles are available again.

I know that the Kansas farmer is intensely patriotic. I know that each of you will do everything you can to help win the war. I know that every Kansas farmer will invest every extra dime and dollar in War Bonds.

Please accept my sincere thanks for your patriotic cooperation in this program. It means so much to the ultimate success of our fighting men and the entire war effort.

> Very sincerely yours,
> *Evan Griffith*
> State Administrator
> War Savings Staff

■ SOURCES

1. The letters in this section are from M. R. Novak to Henry Novak, March 23, August 6, and September 17, 1944, Stephanie Salada Papers, Private Collection, Pittsburgh, Pennsylvania.

2. "Venereal Disease: Saboteur of War Manpower," prepared by the National Law and Order Committee, The American Legion, n.d., "American Legion Publications (6)" File, World War II Participants and Contemporaries Collection, Dwight D. Eisenhower Library, Abilene, Kansas, p. 6.

3. The letters in this section are from Betty Klein to George W. Dinning, February 5, 7, and 24, 1945, "Letters from Betty Klein 1945 (2)" File; and March 25, 1945, "Letters from Betty Klein 1945 (3)" File, George W. Dinning Papers,

World War II Participants and Contemporaries Collection, Eisenhower Library.

4. National Casualty Company advertisement, *Philadelphia Record,* November 3, 1945.

5. "Spare Time: A War Asset for War Workers," Federal Security Agency, Office of Community War Services, Division of Recreation (Washington: U.S. Government Printing Office, 1943), "American Legion-National Headquarters, Government Pamphlets (2)" File, World War II Participants and Contemporaries Collection, Eisenhower Library.

6. Evan Griffith to the Farmers of Kansas, August 3, 1942, "Government Material" File, Linda Kuntz Papers, World War II Participants and Contemporaries Collection, Eisenhower Library.

SEVEN

IN THE WAR'S SHADOW

T he battles raging in Europe and the Pacific filled the headlines, and Americans began learning of strange and distant places, with names like Guadalcanal, Cassino, and Myitkina. Radio and newsreels brought many of these places to life for the average citizen. But John and Jean Q. Public, holding a demanding job or two, had mortgage payments to make and children to feed and educate. The war was a powerful distraction and an interruption in their daily lives, but those lives went on nonetheless.

Still, one could never leave the war behind completely. Rationing became a way of life, scrap drives and air raid drills prevented those on the homefront from ever forgetting there was a war on, and much of the workforce found employment in war industries. Commuting habits changed because of the shortages, and so did residential patterns, to say nothing of property values. Life became more complicated as parents tried to find day care for their children while they

211

reported to new, wartime jobs, perhaps at the plant making artillery shells, and life's pleasures became simpler and more infrequent. Bulging paychecks were little consolation when rationing limited what civilians could buy, and some of the finer things could not be obtained at any price.

After awhile the young began to think of wartime as normal. Young men were seen rarely, and then only in uniform. A train trip was anticipated with relish, and riding in an automobile was positively an adventure. Franklin D. Roosevelt was president and had always been so. Paper, tin cans, and rubber tires were never thrown away. Vegetables from a Victory Garden were part of everyone's diet, sugar was scarce and butter unobtainable, and adding color to the margarine had become part of the daily routine. Everyone was called upon to make sacrifices "for the duration," and that usually meant giving up the company of a brother, cousin, or uncle who had gone to war. Men's suits did not have lapels, and young women drew lines on their bare legs to simulate the seams of nylon stockings. Sweets were treasures to be hoarded and savored. The grownups were always at work, and the children had to amuse themselves— and mind their older sisters.

War in the industrial age had too many facets for Americans to ignore it, even when they sought to escape its oppressive demands and hardships for just an afternoon or a weekend. The clothes they put on in the morning, the food they ate for breakfast, and the way they got to their jobs all reminded them that there was a war on— and that was just before eight o'clock in the morning. Without presenting any direct military threat to the United States, World War II was nevertheless the principal arbiter of the nature and quality of American life for four years.

AIR RAID DEFENSE

The North American continent saw virtually no combat activity, but the war intruded into the American consciousness in other ways. After Pearl Harbor, civil defense suddenly became a priority, though the danger of an actual attack, along with the concomitant public anxiety, waned fairly quickly. Still, precautions against air raids had to be taken.

American Legion Publication— "Air Raid Precaution Services"[1]

In certain phases of the Nation's defense women will play an important part. In England, the "Women's Voluntary Services for Civilian Defense" has proven itself invaluable for diet and canteen services; in the operation of communal kitchens; as Air Raid Wardens, messengers, ambulance drivers; for home services such as attending the sick and part-time household relief; as telephone and radio operators, auxiliary police and in first aid work. In the conduct of classes for the education of the civilian population in matters of care and protection in case of emergency women can play a large part. In many localities throughout the United States the American Red Cross, long recognized by the American people for its humanitarian and emergency relief work, offers courses in first aid and auto mechanics which should be extremely beneficial to civilian defense volunteers. . . .

As many persons as possible should be trained as leaders, in order that reserves may be available.

Wardens may be either men or women. In the case of male wardens, for national defense reasons, local authorities making assignments should give consideration to a minimum age of from thirty to thirty-five years. Men who are likely to be called under the Selective Service System, or required for other military or naval service, should not be chosen. Former police and firemen can possibly render more efficient service with the separate emergency auxiliary setups of that nature, which of necessity also will be organized. Care should be taken to avoid the withdrawing of essential employees from industries engaged in national defense work. Such citizens, if they desire to undertake extra duties, could best be trained primarily to act within their places of employment, and, being trained, could be available to supplement the public air raid warden service if necessary in case of extreme emergency.

British experience has shown that women adapt themselves readily to warden service. No age restrictions need be applied to women volunteers other than the obvious need to avoid those who are too young to occupy responsible positions, and whose age, or physical condition, make them unsuited to such duty.

It is clear there is every likelihood of a considerable number of persons selected for air raid precaution service in peace time becoming unavailable from one cause or another when an emergency actually occurs. Consequently the number to be trained should be substantially greater than the number immediately required. A reserve is essential, and the larger the number of persons trained in peace time, the larger will be the proportion of the population who, in time of war, will know how to take care of themselves and others.

Experience in England has also shown that the required number of wardens will fluctuate considerably, according to the density of the population,

from one warden post of five or six members in a small rural community to
an average of one warden for every four or five hundred persons in a popu-
lous center. . . .

Reader's Digest Publication—"A Hobby Goes to War"[2]

All over the country air-minded youngsters are transforming a hobby into an
essential part of America's war effort. Instant identification of an approaching plane is a matter of life and death to combat flyers, and is equally important to seamen, gunners and civilian spotters. They can learn to recognize
planes only by studying real ones or three-dimensional models—pictures won't
do. So early this year Secretary of the Navy Knox asked the country's youth
to produce 50,000 model planes in a hurry (500,000 may be needed).

The response was lively. "I am 14 and though this sounds young I can say
(with caution) that I am very skillful," wrote one model-plane builder from
Iowa. A girl wrote: "I am 15 and have been building model planes for six years.
I can build models as exact as anyone."

The navy's Bureau of Aeronautics and the U.S. Office of Education supervise
the project with the aid of local authorities, who help insure that the models will
pass rigid inspection tests. The young model builders have already received spec-
ifications of 50 types of United Nations and enemy planes. As new types of ships
are put into the air, they also will be copied. The models are built on a precise
scale of 1 to 72, one inch representing six feet of the plane. They are painted black
to promote recognition by design and outline rather than by colors or insignia.

The importance of the youngsters' job is illustrated by the use of the models at such training centers as Anacostia Air Station, District of Columbia.
Here naval aviation cadets peer through an eyepiece into an oblong box, two
feet square by eight feet long. As a model is moved through the far end, the
box is lighted for a second. The cadet must identify the plane in a flash. The
models are also studied through the standard ring sight on aerial gun mounts
for training in range estimation as well as plane identification. A model seen
at 70 feet appears exactly like the real plane seen at just under a mile.

Eventually models will be distributed to civilian plane spotters.

The draft officer surveyed the young man before him. "You've
been put in 1-A," he said in a judicial manner, "and you will report
at 9 o'clock next Monday morning." Then he unbent slightly. "Got
any tires you'd like to sell?"

—Army & Navy Journal

LIVING WITH RATIONING

Americans had to adjust their diets and lifestyles to deal with the wartime shortages of various commodities, from foodstuffs to gasoline and automobile tires. Emerging from an era when money might be in short supply but sugar or butter never were, citizens rapidly became acquainted with rationing. Even after the Axis nations surrendered, rationing remained in effect for some items well into 1946. More than just a shortage of familiar goods and services, rationing meant adjusting one's thinking about the most mundane of matters, as these letters from a divorced woman to her son reveal.

Letters from Mother to George W. Dinning

A mother describes to her son her belief that rationing is part of a general change in social standards and that the war has created a society where the old values seem to have been left behind.

Wed. morning Sept 19—'45[3]

Hello there my Marine—Well it's a rainy morning—Every one was hoping for a *dry* fall so the corn will get a good *drying* out, so it won't have to be stored away wet. We have to help feed a lot of hungry nations, and the old weather man will have to be on his toes. Rations are lifted off all canned goods—we have more meat, but it's still rationed. Butter is down to 12 points—paper says sugar mite be scarce in the future. I made some yellow tomatoe preserves so—sonny boy, just imagine some hot biscuits and butter with those preserves when ya come home—have some watermelon pickles, too. Shoes might be freed from the ban soon—However, none of this has hurt any of us. I think it's large families maybe that were hit hardest—at that I don't believe anyone has been hurt. If PW's have gone thru what they have—we surely can let up. The trouble with people at large: they are mostly "gluttons," and it drives them "sane nuts" [?] to have to do without. Well—nylon stockings are to come back but just a few at first. I can just see the women grabbing "theirs." It's quite a show also to see them, as the papers say, when "soap powders or flakes" are advertised. They knock down and drag out, to get their share, and I hear that some women tell another this, "I didn't need it but I thot I'd get one more pkg on my shelf—you never can tell when you'll need it." Well, there's a limit to even laying up for a rainy day, isn't there, Sonny? The papers are full of drastic and fanatical things people do and think. Well, some of this might be "human nature," but there's a limit even to that. There's a gang of some kind of worshipers that let snakes bite them, and they tear their hair and shout to the Almighty to cure them, and all such as that. Then there's a woman in Indiana who claims the Bible and Christ is just a myth or fairy tale and religion should-n't be mentioned in schools and that *her* little boy *can't* go to school if they teach such *"stuff,"* etc., etc. Well, I know my childhood days were enjoyed very much by the teaching of all this. Of course it wasn't stressed in the schools, but was sorta "understood" that *it* was the *basic* standards to all our other learn-ing—Reading, writing and arithmetic—being taught for our progress for the financial side of our future. I'm afraid the "conquered enemies" are going to have a chance for a comeback at us—orally—if not another war, saying we do not practice what we preach. Our missionaries have already, long since, had a hard time trying to bring the "true light" to many nations. I was active in that work down in C'ville, so I know. There is also a picture of 2 men in the paper this morning saying the world is to come to an end tomorrow, or before Sept 30 and we will all go up into space like an atom had hit us and we'll float and we'll float around in space *forever.* The atom won't let us come down. The future is *not* in our hands. We are taught to live by the good. *All* people—other than maybe the ones no better than to worship idols—*know* right from wrong, but some find more pleasure in doing wrong than the right—no matter what it costs them in later life—thus the world gets in an awful fix. Say, I didn't mean to preach a sermon, but this is actually what's going on and more, too. Did I tell you, George, that *Frank* is back from the navy and has his old job back at the desk down stairs? He was asking about you boys and said he thot you were always such fine boys and Jean, he thinks, is a grand girl. The 6 yrs we've been here everyone knows how you've carried yourselves. Of course, you and David wasn't here very much but know you.[?] He was saying how you and Stevie, down in the drug store once was trying to get the colors straightened out. Stevie was asking you, "Now, what's this one, George," etc. Say—What do you know? Jean just called and said that someone called her that Stevie's name was just mentioned over KRNT this morning that he had arrived in the States. They also named the Iowa boys. Jean and I had WHO on—shoot—Well, I've had 2 calls congratulating me on his arrival. One lady from Red Cross, Mrs. Cotton, and the Rossers are here in a hotel. So—I'm waiting for *him* to call. I can't hard-ly wait. First thing this morning I looked at the time table, and it said the "Queen Elizabeth" was arriving today.

That's what I was wanting to tell you about the time table. I wrote last nite and told you he was on the high seas but mite be delayed on account of a storm. Now, Sonny, I'll be watchin' and waitin' from you and *your* furlough.

Can't you have one first, even if you do have to go to China?

So long sonny boy and keep your chin *up*.

Lots of Love from

Your Mom.

How's "Sgt George" "the pig"? Well, Sonny, I heard Stevie's name mentioned—in with DM boys coming home. Gee, it sounded good—I've been pretty busy now all day—was fixing a chair again with new cover so finished that and now a bit of ironing. I'll go and mail this now. Bye again, Dear.

Isn't this pretty paper? Bob's folks gave it to Jean for her birthday. I snitched it out of her box. Ha—but I know she won't care—as long as it's for you.

This family clipping I am enclosing lost their Daddy in war, and their mother died about 2 mos. ago. She asked that they not be separated, so this couple adopted them, and now this mother died recently, so another couple has taken them. I said if I had the health I would have liked to have done it.

I'm sending some clippings later.

> *This letter speaks of ball games and family visits and finances, yet it is clear that even two months after Japan's surrender, the war was still shaping the lives of the family's scattered members.*

Wed. Oct 3—'45[4]

My dear Scotch Marine in China—How are you and the chinks making it? Bet they're glad now "amelicans" come along. Be careful with those nips still over there. Don't have a thing to do with them. Bet you'll think I'm funny for "giving instructions." You've had so much in all your travels! I believe that you're going around the world—but don't go over in Palestine—guess they and the Arabs are having it out and out. Well, dear, this has been a beautiful day here so thot I'd get out and shop around. I'll have to have a picture of me in my new outfit and send you. Also of Stevie and all of us. It rained so that we didn't get to take a picture. Wished I had the first day now, as I've had a film all ready for a long time. He is to meet Margie tomorrow in Cincinnati, O., so hope they'll both be back soon. Depends on what Stevie takes up and where.

George—Jean was counting up what she's paid you and in 3 more allotment cks, she'll have paid you $900.00. Dad doesn't give me a cent, so seems you children are keeping me. So our financial affairs are *still between you and* Jean and I, altho Dave knows *where* we were getting most of the money. So nice of you, sonny boy, and Jean and Bob both appreciate it, too. If ever you come home and want to know how your money was spent, we'll have a nice get together, but I think you know pretty well what everything in a wedding would cost, altho it didn't cost that amount, and it was a lovely one, too. Traveling, etc. are included, the honeymoon trip and O., I'll not go into detail. Stevie and Margie or Dave and Janet all have been good, too. Guess *I'm* thoroughly dependent on my children. Dave says, "When are you coming down, Mom," almost as soon as we got off the train the other nite when he and Stevie and I met. So I said soon as I got a fall outfit. Think Jean is to go, too, and take in a ball game with them at Iowa City. They want Margie and Stevie to stop off on the way here, so we mite all be there together. He generally gets my ticket both ways, and of course I'm being fed while there. Takes a little off of Jean. Did you get to hear the World Series today? Cubs won 9 to 0 at Detroit. I thot if it had been played in Chicago, Stevie would have gotten to see the game. We didn't get to take any pictures while Stevie was here. It rained so. Wish now I'd taken advantage of the first nice day and gotten one of him in his uniform. He looks nice and sure is one to "swoon" over—as Mary Ellen said when she saw you. Ha—Proud Momma, eh! Well, dear, so long for now. Write and tell me all about your trip. I see where the Marines only have to have 60 points to get out—of course, if you're counting on staying in, I don't know when you'd get a furlough. Seems you don't get any at all and always have to go "tuther" way. Well, we'll all keep waiting. Anyway, hope it's by Xmas. Goodnite, dear sweet boy—Lots of Love from Mom.

Letter from Daughter to Henry Novak[5]

Standing in line, worrying about heating fuel, balancing potential future needs against present-day shortages—these were all part of living with rationing.

MARCH 28, 1945

To PFC. Henry R. Novak 33706421
Bty C 552nd F.A. BN.
A.P.O. 230 c/o Postmaster
New York, New York

From H. Novak
Reel Ave.
Perrysville, PA

Dear Daddy,

Well it has been a whole long year since you have been gone. Little did I think when you left that nite that you would be gone that long. I only hope it isn't another year until you get home. I don't think it will be. Gosh it's hard to realize that a year has passed. I think I miss you more and more every day. Didn't get any mail today. It was another nice day. Stevie and the kids were playing all day outside. I took Stevie up the street and we went over to see Patty Gow. We were there for about a half an hour and neither one of them said a word to each other. Sam brot 4 1/2 tons of coal today. He asked how you were doing. You can only get 80% of the coal you got last year. The coal we got today doesn't count on this year's, so we should have enough. I hope it doesn't get cold again and we will have a good supply to start out next winter. Tonite I did something I never did before. I stood in line for cigarettes. I have a few packs on hand but have to get them when I can. The line formed at the cigarette case clear to the Catholic church. Tonite Ed, Helen and Jean Gillespie tonite. That is Aunt Annie and Uncle Frank's daughter and her husband and girl. They moved to Bellvue. Ed has stopped here several times before. You met him once or twice. Stevie was good today. She plays with the kids for awhile and then comes home to see if I'm still there. If she can't see me at first she starts yelling for me. They thot she was as cute and looked just like me. Well must say goodnite for now. I love you. Love and kisses,

Sis and Stevie

Newspaper Article—"Points for Fats Start Tomorrow"[6]

Not only was rationing ubiquitous; it could also be downright complicated. A newspaper article details a new wrinkle in the nation's rationing program.

December 12, 1943

POINTS FOR FATS START TOMORROW

Mrs. Angeleno, along with housewives all over the country, has been storing her kitchen grease these days so she'll be "in the fat" when the O.P.A.'s new plan for exchanging two meat ration points for every pound of salvage grease that is turned in goes into effect tomorrow.

The idea, heartily endorsed by the War Production Board, which is clamoring for grease for munitions, is reported to have been originally suggested by Mrs. Lincoln Berri of St. Louis, a stenographer. She is given credit, despite claims of about 13,806 other persons throughout the nation that they thought it up first.

Since the O.P.A. announced that it had cooked up the new plan, salvage officials here report that not enough grease has been turned in to spot a small size vest.

But, they say, watch it flow in come tomorrow.

Letter from Mother to William H. Herbert[7]

And then there was always the possibility of other complications. . . .

"P.S. Guess what happened to your 'poor old Mother.' I left all the ration books on the counter at Slapman's Grocery, and somebody just took them. It looks like we won't have much to eat at our house until I can get them replaced, and that takes anywhere from two weeks to two months."

Married women who flirt with the butcher are playing for big steaks.

MAKING DO

Rationing was only part of the solution to wartime shortages. Americans also were urged to stay away from the black market, change their habits or manage without certain items, and "make do" with what was available for the duration. Living this way often required skill and ingenuity as well as effort. It is no wonder that most citizens, whether in the armed forces or not, whether working in a war industry or not, believed they were doing their part for victory.

Publication from the Cotton Spool Company—"Make and Mend for Victory"[8]

Here are a few excerpts from a commercial publication by a sewing company that depict "making do" with clothing as a woman's patriotic obligation. Although the company had a financial stake in getting this message out, the government trumpeted the same view, as is seen in the quotation of the Office of Price Administration pledge. Most citizens agreed.

CONSUMER'S VICTORY

"As a consumer, in the total defense of democracy, I will do my part to make my home, my community, my country ready, efficient, strong.

I will buy carefully—and I will not buy anything above the ceiling price, no matter how much I may want it.

I will take good care of the things I have—and I will not buy anything made from vital war materials which I can get along without.

I will waste nothing—and I will take care to salvage everything needed to win the war."

CONSUMER DIVISION
Office of Price Administration

It's up to you to keep the home fires burning, to see that you and your family stay easy-on-the-eyes. Fortunately, you can be patriotic and pretty both. It's easy to teach an old wardrobe new tricks, to resurrect the skeletons in your closet and bring them up to date. Come on, take those old knockabouts and turn them into knockouts, keep that glint in Uncle Sam's eye and still do your stint towards Victory!

. . . When you are using pins, wear a small pincushion held at the left wrist with an elastic. In this way, as soon as pins are removed, they may be salvaged very easily. Pins are hard to get, and if you pick them up and save them you are helping the war effort.

. . . You've no idea how quickly wilted wardrobes respond to kindness. Try the needle-and-thread treatment for that "just stepped out of the bandbox" look. Your girdles will keep you in shape indefinitely if you apply First Aid in time; with skillful mending your stockings will outlast all their contemporaries; and a judicious—and gallant—patch will keep many a dress going to a ripe old age.

. . . **Alterations and Restyling:** For external use only: a thimbleful of dressmakers' tricks guaranteed to take years off your clothes in the twinkling of a needle's eye. Nobody will ever guess the age of your coat if its hem swings straight and true, or dream your dress isn't this year's vintage if its shoulders are smooth, its collar trim. Follow these simple as ABC directions and watch your tired wardrobe put on new airs, snap to attention like brave and pretty soldiers *for service.*

. . . Clothes may make the woman but nowadays there's no doubt that accessories make the clothes. It's no trick at all for a dress to have nine lives. You can give last year's dress a new lease on life, make every costume pay extra dividends with a little needle and thread trickery.

At 9 A.M. a simple crepe dress looks trim and business-like with neat white collar and cuffs. At 9 P.M. the same dress, glamorized with a frothy dickey, a new belt, a gay little hat, may on occasion wear a fresh-as-paint party face. Many a woman with a well deserved reputation for chic has only a few basic costumes on which she has learned to ring endless changes. It's good fashion sense and smart dollars and cents to s-t-r-e-t-c-h your wardrobe with a versatile collection of easy-to-make accessories.

A polka-dotted hat and bag; a pair of red gloves and a matching calot or an inch of scarlet flounce peeping out from the bottom of a skirt; a necklace and earrings of bright crocheted stars; a set of buttons salvaged from a bureau drawer or made with a few bits of odd yarn change a dress so your best friend couldn't recognize it.

. . . Chances are your closets have their quota of old coats and suits, too good to give away but too antiquated in cut to come out in the open. Every home has its collection of tired dresses, shirts weak in the collar. And nowadays many have a number of suits—made of precious priority wools—drooping forlorn and unworn on their hangers while their owners are wearing Uncle Sam's latest models.

If you only knew it, there's probably a whole winter's wardrobe for you and your family waiting to be rescued from the moths. Frocks, rompers and sunsuits for your small fry, blouses and underwear for you out of old shirts; a snug reefer for Junior out of an old suit coat or pair of flannel trousers. Pinafores and bathing suits emerge like painted butterflies from the chrysalis of old dresses and the tailored suit you've always had your heart set on is yours for the making out of a man's suit.

There's probably no satisfaction to equal the thrill of making something out of nothing. It takes only a little wit, time and patience to turn total losses into handsome profits!

American Legion Publication—"Conservation of Natural Resources"[9]

The American Legion exhorts Americans to live frugally in this excerpt from its booklet on conserving resources.

The fundamental strength of our nation is based not alone upon its standing army or the size of its navy but upon these combined with the available resources which in time of war form the base of supplies and in times of peace are the foundation which gives stability to American homes and communities.

Our people should be as greatly concerned about the losses and wastes in our own country resulting from thriftless exploitation and ill-advised practices in using renewable natural resources as about any similar damage that could possibly be done by a foreign enemy. Careful use of resources also favors a continuous opportunity for employment to citizens of this nation. It contributes to contented people who have something to protect and defend in times of invasion. An adequate area of good agricultural land properly managed also provides an abundance of food to keep the people physically fit. It may therefore be said that the strength of a nation is based upon a large quantity of natural resources quickly available at moderate costs.

It isn't so much the rationing,
Or taxes, or talk of inflation;
The problem worrying most of us,
Is this thing they call the duration. . . .

BALANCING WARTIME NEEDS

READER'S DIGEST— "ESSENTIAL CIVILIAN NEEDS WILL BE MET" (BY ELSIE MCCORMICK)[10]

In addition to the tremendous demands of the military forces, the "arsenal of democracy" had to continue to meet the needs of the American people. How much could people do without? And what items were not truly needed in this time of shortages? These were complicated questions, given the wide array of necessities for family life in the industrial age. Inevitably, miscalculations or some poor choices crept into the government's management of wartime production. The result was dire shortages of some items and services to which no one had really given much thought before the war—but which were now essential.

By last spring, war demands had made such inroads into essential civilian supplies that something had to be done about it. In many parts of the country such homely but necessary articles as diapers, denim work clothes and garbage cans had almost completely disappeared. Safety pins were so scarce that in some towns policemen collected them from door to door for maternity hospitals. Dairymen were killing cows because they could not get milk cans. Rope was so scarce that some ranchers in Oklahoma threatened to break into a store and take a supply frozen by priority regulations.

To help the forgotten men and women on the home front, the War Production Board last April organized an Office of Civilian Requirements, and placed at its head soft-voiced but iron-willed Arthur D. Whiteside, president of Dun and Bradstreet. Under him, the OCR has fought vigorously to relieve shortages that might damage health, morale, and efficiency.

The OCR can claim allotments of raw materials for making essential civilian goods, have them sent to manufacturers, and then so earmark the goods that, except in a real emergency, not even war industry or the armed forces can take them away from the ordinary buyer. Its sphere includes practically everything except food, fuel and rubber.

One of the first emergencies faced by OCR concerned the American baby. The 1942 diaper supply had been 10,000,000 yards less than requirements and the birth rate was zooming. The looms that had made diaper cloth were busy turning out cotton bags for farm produce and army supplies, as substitutes for the burlap that could no longer be had from India. In addition, war factories were buying diapers in huge quantities for use in wiping off machines.

The OCR allocated enough looms for diaper production to bring the supply to near normal and forbade the sale of the cloth for factory rags. Meanwhile, clearing the Mediterranean sea lanes has opened the short route from India and the first shipments of an order for 850,000,000 yards of burlap are on the way.

Sixty percent of the safety-pin supply had been taken for the hospital needs of the army and navy. In addition, the batiste once popular for infants' clothing was being used in balloons; and baby carriages were being bought up by munitions plants, where their soft springs assured the safe handling of sensitive explosives.

The OCR doubled the allotment of steel for safety pins; captured some material for baby clothes; and arranged for the manufacture of more baby carriages. Reports from the field soon indicated that the new carriage, using only six pounds of steel, was not a success. Mothers were overloading them with groceries crammed in alongside the baby, and the wooden wheels buckled. The OCR has now claimed more steel for each carriage. In addition it has provided for twins, overlooked in the original order.

The OCR is one of the few government agencies that doesn't smother its public under questionnaires dreamed up by desk men in Washington. Its field investigators talk and listen to war workers, farmers and housewives all over the country, in informal, friendly fashion. It receives hundreds of letters describing cases of individual hardship. It has 21 "listening posts" throughout the country to spot local shortages in the early stages; it then rushes the needed articles into that area.

One important thing learned by the OCR has been the disastrous effects of irregular ice deliveries and the breakdown of mechanical refrigerators. The consequent spoilage of food—wasteful in itself—has meant more garbage, which, coupled with the scarcity of garbage cans, brought a dangerous increase in rats. Lack of spring wire led to a shortage of rat-traps.

The OCR is having refrigerator repair parts made by smaller war plants not working at capacity. Since the number of refrigerator servicemen has dropped from 16,000 to about 5300, local draft boards have been asked to defer such workers for several months. Meanwhile the electrical industry has begun a program of training new men.

The garbage cans, it turned out, were being bought by war plants to hold tools, small machine parts and greasy rags. Now plants no longer buy garbage cans on priorities, and the OCR is claiming more galvanized iron to help tide over the shortage. And the amount of steel for rat-traps has been almost doubled.

Cutting the umbrella output to 30 percent of normal resulted in illness and absenteeism among the millions of people who used to ride in cars but now often wait in the rain for buses. So the shortage of umbrellas is being relieved.

More steel wool is going to be made, too, because OCR investigators found that housewives often complained more about this shortage than any other. In homes where the kitchens serve as living rooms, rows of gleaming pots and pans are a great source of pride. The steel wool to keep them shining will be made out of wire scrap, not needed as war material.

The fact that more silver-plated flatware is to be manufactured will be good news to restaurant owners. Purchases by the army and navy, and diversion of the industry to making everything from Ranger knives to magnesium bombs, cut the total for consumers to about one sixth of normal. The pinch was felt chiefly in factory areas where thousands of people were establishing new homes. Thefts of cutlery from restaurants became so common that some eating places were severely handicapped.

No steel has been claimed for needles. We have never made needles for hand sewing. Our entire supply came from England and Japan and we are still getting needles from both countries. The Japanese needles are reaching us from indirect sources.

The OCR has successfully avoided clothes rationing. Many textile mills are being put on a three-shift basis, and enough material for essential needs is now assured. Luxury garments will be scarcer than cheap ones. There are fewer rayon dresses because rayon makes a good parachute for fragmentation bombs or for food supplies and ammunition floated down to isolated outposts. Dresses of heavy, solid colors are being replaced by prints and pastels, because the coal-tar derivatives from which dyes are made are in demand for TNT, synthetic rubber and aviation gasoline. There is no real scarcity of cosmetics. The OCR regards them as important morale items, and maintains their production.

By working with manufacturers and with other WPB departments to simplify styles and use substitutes, the OCR has also released large amounts of materials for the armed services. For instance, the 27,000 varieties of door-knobs and other forms of builders' hardware of prewar days have been reduced to 3600. There are now 6000 fewer styles of incandescent lighting fixtures, and only one type of domestic gas stove. Your dentist's choice of burrs for drilling teeth has been reduced from 75 to 24.

Substitutes developed by WPB's Office of Production Research and Development, with the help of about 200 laboratories throughout the country, include waterproof baby pants, an efficient kitchen utensil cleaner made of bamboo and reeds, a coiled rawhide bedspring, a hairpin made of wood, and an all-clay stove.

The OCR is not trying to maintain civilians in their accustomed style. But Mr. Whiteside believes that without things necessary to keep the home front in a state of health, efficiency and high morale, the way to victory might be seriously impeded.

DOING YOUR SHARE

THE MACARTHUR CLUB PLEDGE

Buying bonds to help underwrite the war effort was another patriotic enterprise during World War II. All sorts of plans were devised to increase the purchase of war bonds.

THE MACARTHUR CLUB PLEDGE[11]

In honor of General Douglas MacArthur and his brave troops and in support of all our beloved soldiers, sailors, marines and airmen wherever they may be fighting, suffering and dying for the cause of freedom and for my protection, I most solemnly pledge myself to faithfully perform the following obligation, total disability or dire poverty alone preventing:

To set aside each and every day, so long as my Country is at war, the sum of ten cents and a silent prayer for victory. Every thirty days from my beginning I shall convert these savings into United States Defense Savings Stamps which, in turn, I shall convert into United States Defense Savings Bonds each time my stamps total $18.75. These will I hold and keep until God gives us the Victory.

Insignia for men: Loop of narrow Flag ribbon through the buttonhole of the left lapel of overcoat and jacket. For women: Same buttonhole loop or small Flag red bow worn on left side of dress and coat.

For additional copies of this pledge address
The American Legion, Department of Delaware
Citizens Bank Building
Wilmington, Delaware

EXPERIENCE OF A SOLDIER'S FAMILY

Sooner or later, all families experienced it or knew someone who did.

Letter from Jack Kammerer to Brother[12]

Written in a childish scrawl by a young Marine, this note to a kid brother was sent in January 1945, shortly after the author had turned eighteen. A few weeks later, he would be storming the beaches at Iwo Jima.

Hi Bunny,

How are you today. I am fine. How many wittle wabbitts do you have now? I'll bet you build a snow man every day. How is Kay, Judy, Sue, and Maxine? I bet you're sure big. I'm sending you a clipping. I wrote to my girl tonight. How is Mamma and George? Are you saving any money? I have a whole bag of Hersheys tonight and wished you were here to help eat them. Write me a letter soon. Tell all the kids hello.

Your Big Brother
Jack

A Telegram from A.A. Vandergrift to Mr. and Mrs. Julius W. Kammerer

The most dreaded figure in wartime America was the Western Union messenger.

KA7 83 70 GOVT=WASHINGTON DC 8 907P
MR AND JULIUS W KAMMERE (PARENTS)   1945 MAR 8 PM 9 58
351 NORTH HYDRAULC ST WCHTA=
DEEPLY REGRET TO INFORM YOU THAT YOUR SON PROVATE JACK

Jack Kammerer's mother holding his portrait (after Kammerer's death). (Courtesy of the Dwight D. Eisenhower Library, Hal Ottaway Collection.)

D KAMMERER USMCR WAS KILLED IN ACTION 20 FEBRUARY 1945 AT IWO JIMA VOLCANO ISLANDS IN THE PERFORMANCE OF HIS DUTY AND SERVICE OF HIS COUNTY. WHEN INFORMATION IS RECEIVED REGARDING BURIAL YOU WILL BE NOTIFIED. TO PREVENT POSSIBLE AID TO OUR ENEMIES DO NOT DIVULGE THE NAME OF HIS SHIP OR STATION. PLEASE ACCEPT MY HEARTFELT SYMPATHY. LETTER FOLLOWS=

A A VANDEGRIFT LIEUT GENERAL USMC COMMANDANT OF THE MARINE CORPS

A Letter from Lieut General A.A. Vandergrift to Mr. and Mrs. Julius W. Kammerer

Arriving within days of the telegram, the letter from the commanding officer (in this case, the commandant of the Marine Corps) removed the last hope that some terrible mistake had been made.

10 March, 1945.

My Dear Mr. and Mrs. Kammerer:

It is a source of profound regret to me and to his comrades in the Marine Corps that your son, Private Jack Darrel Kammerer, United States Marine Corps Reserve, lost his life in action against the enemies of his country and I wish to express my deepest sympathy to you and members of your family in your great loss.

There is little I can say to lessen your grief but it is my earnest hope that the knowledge of your son's splendid record in the service and the thought that he nobly gave his life in the performance of his duty may in some measure comfort you in this sad hour.

Sincerely yours,

[signed]

A. A. VANDEGRIFT,

Lieutenant General, U.S.M.C.

Commandant of the Marine Corps.

Mr. and Mrs. Julius W. Kammerer,
351 North Hydraulic Street,
Wichita, Kansas.

Included among Jack Kammerer's effects was a pocket bible with holes in the pages caused by shrapnel from the artillery burst that killed him.

■ SOURCES

1. American Legion Combined Manual, "Air Raid Precaution Services," revised January 1, 1942, American Legion Vest Pocket Series for Civilian Defense, "American Legion Publications (1)" File, World War II Participants and Contemporaries Collection, Dwight D. Eisenhower Library, Abilene, Kansas.
2. "A Hobby Goes to War," *Reader's Digest* 40, no. 242 (June 1942): 60.
3. Mother to George W. Dinning, September 19, 1945, "Letters from Mother (1)" File, George W. Dinning Papers, World War II Participants and Contemporaries Collection, Eisenhower Library.

4. Mother to George W. Dinning, October 3, 1945, "Letters from Mother (2)" File, George W. Dinning Papers, World War II Participants and Contemporaries Collection, Eisenhower Library.
5. Helen Novak to Henry Novak, March 28, 1945, Stephanie Salada Papers, Private Collection, Pittsburgh, Pennsylvania.
6. "Points for Fats Start Tomorrow," December 12, 1943, "Rationing" File, Elmer Lewis Papers, World War II Participants and Contemporaries Collection, Eisenhower Library.
7. Mrs. George Fowler to William H. Herbert, May 20, 1945, "Mar.–July 1945, Europe" File, Henrietta Cragon Papers, World War II Participants and Contemporaries Collection, Eisenhower Library.
8. *Make and Mend for Victory,* Book no. S-10 (The Cotton Spool Company, 1942), Diane McCluskey Papers, World War II Participants and Contemporaries Collection, Eisenhower Library.
9. "Conservation of Natural Resources: A Community Service Program of the American Legion," distributed by the National Americanism Commission, American Legion, n.d., "American Legion Publications (6)" File, World War II Participants and Contemporaries Collection, Eisenhower Library.
10. Elsie McCormick, "Essential Civilian Needs Will Be Met," *Reader's Digest* 43, no. 258 (October 1943): 64–66; condensed from the *Baltimore Sunday Sun.*
11. "The MacArthur Club Pledge," prepared by the American Legion, n.d., "American Legion Publications (3)" File, World War II Participants and Contemporaries Collection, Eisenhower Library.
12. The documents in this section are from Jack Kammerer to Brother, January 23, 1945, "Correspondence (1)" File; and Telegram, A. A. Vandegrift to Mr. and Mrs. Julius W. Kammerer, March 8, 1945; and A. A. Vandegrift to Mr. and Mrs. Julius W. Kammerer, March 10, 1945, "Death of Jack Kammerer" File, Hal Ottaway Papers, World War II Participants and Contemporaries Collection, Eisenhower Library.

EIGHT

COMING HOME

When the shooting finally ended in August 1945, millions of Americans were scattered overseas, from Iceland to Australia. Most simply wanted to go home, to shake off the trappings of military life and get back to families and careers, or, in many cases, to get back to starting them.

Much still needed to be done, however, before they could leave. The subdued Axis nations were to be rebuilt as trustworthy allies in peace. Thus, the Allied nations undertook, with the support of their occupying forces, to remove the militarism and fascist tendencies that had crept into the Axis nations' behavior, to punish those responsible for the aggressive and inhumane excesses of the past decade, and to provide the incentives—and often the wherewithal—for instituting democratic traditions in political life, achieving economic recovery, and returning to the more constructive elements of national cultural legacies. This task would take some doing, and some time.

Two GIs with water buffalo and Filipina girl. (Courtesy of the Dwight D. Eisenhower Library, Daniel Weimer Collection.)

Contact with foreign peoples naturally increased during the years of the postwar occupation. Former enemies and allies alike were encountered, studied, and remembered. When it was time to go home, this generation of Americans had had more personal contact with their fellow citizens of the world than has any other generation before or since. What they saw and experienced in Europe, Africa, and Asia became the basis of U.S. popular attitudes about foreign behavior and, consequently, about what American foreign policy should be.

Most servicemen and women were not thinking about future U.S. foreign policy, however, as they waited out the weeks and months before they could go home. Awarding "points" for length and nature of service, the armed forces established a priority system for getting the troops back to the United States for demobilization. Limited shipping space suddenly made every "point" crucial for hundreds of thousands of these citizen-soldiers waiting to become just citizens again.

They were not quite sure to what they were returning. Expecting a repeat of the brief but sharp postwar depression that had settled in after the last great conflict, they considered their options and their plans for the future.

HOW IT LOOKS FROM HERE

LETTER HOME FROM BRUCE CARSON[1]

In early 1945, most Americans understood that the end of the war was probably not far off and began to assess their chances of getting home soon. Here a reserve army officer confides some of his plans and his estimates of the situation to his family.

29 April 1945

Philippine Islands

Dear Family,

The San Francisco conference is on,* Russian and U.S. troops have met in Germany, and "VE" Day looks to be no more than a month or two away.

All good news.

The war over here is going more quickly than could be expected, but too slow for most of us.

The army rotation and furlough policies in the Pacific area accentuate the slow pace of the oriental end of this global war.

For instance, in the Central Pacific Area (under Admiral Nimitz and Gen. Richardson), a man had to spend 3 1/2 years overseas before he could be sent back to the states. Having served forty-two months, one then had to wait one's turn, wait for all the men with more than 3 1/2 years who had been held back for lack of transportation or because their outfits considered them essential.

While all this was being perpetrated against the Army, the Navy felt picked upon if any of their men was away from the states for more than one year.

This resulted in a certain lack of inter-service cordiality at the lower personnel level.

Of course it is hard to say who if anyone is to blame for the fact that a man has to and had to spend so much time overseas and why furloughs, even emergency furloughs in case of death of parents, were something you heard about but never expected to see.

Transportation has always been short out here. (The navy had its own and was consequently only slightly handicapped.)

Men were needed here. Replacements were slow in coming, most outfits going to the higher priority European Theater.

---

*A reference to the preliminary discussions of the United Nations Organization.

This is the orphan side of the world so far as military personnel is concerned. Oahu had some glamour, of course, but less than England; and the coral atolls and the tropical jungles, which were the alternatives, had nothing.

Everyone here is hoping that the end of the war in Europe will make possible rotation of the many men with close to four years overseas, the discharge of men over thirty-eight, and a more liberal policy on furloughs and rest leaves.

We're taking all rosy statements with a certain skepticism, since in the past, theater as well as unit commanders have counter-manded their own policies as well as war department pronouncements with regard to rotation and furloughs. Necessities of war.

I suppose you're wondering if all this is leading up to a gripe by myself about when I'll get home or when I'll be rotated statesward. Well, don't hold your breath until I gripe. I have no reason to.

My nineteen months overseas makes me very junior in the Pacific circus. I have almost no desire to return to the states until the war is entirely over. A furlough would not interest me unless I could visit some place I had not seen before.

I am quite satisfied with my life in the Army for the time being. A little more (but not too much) excitement would be welcome. A few luxuries such as ice cream, milk, and a decent place to raise hell would certainly help, but one ought not to have to go all the way back to the States for those.

All in all, I'll be damned glad when the War is ended and I am a civilian again; but until it is over I would just as soon sweat it out over here where there is at least a chance of my doing some good some time.

Speaking of going home—

I presume you realize that I have developed such a terrific phobia toward Maywood* that even your presence there would never force me to spend more than a couple of days in the place. And if you didn't live there, I would never approach within five hundred miles of the place.

Ah me! Happy memories of childhood! Oh to be able to recapture those mystic, hellish days!

As I'm sure I have mentioned before, I will settle, if I ever settle, in New York City or New England.

I want to see the rest of the world before I do any root-taking, however.

Pipedreams, probably. But I like the brand of opium.

Will include a request for a few items in case you should be able to get any of them—note separate sheet.

Glad to get Helen's address. She hasn't written me in one solid year. Don't

---

*Carson's hometown in Illinois.

really see why I should write to her, but I understand it is considered conventional to do so occasionally.

The Philippines are a first class pest hole when it comes to intestinal diseases. There are myriads of worms causing everything from almost certain death to mere discomfort; not to mention dysentery, flukes, mosquitoes, and what-have-you.

Fortunately, so far the men of my outfit and myself have escaped the host of pitfalls and are in quite good health. The heat makes life miserable at times, but we have our air-conditioned beach to escape to during the hottest part of the day.

Most of us have lost weight. (A few of the fattest have grown fatter and are much kidded on the point.) Few of my clothes fit very well, but I still must weigh close to 160 pounds.

A little snow would be much appreciated now. Can you arrange for some? Remind me to include that in my postal request.

As ever
*The Omnipotent One**

COUNTING POINTS

LETTER HOME FROM RICHARD CIPRA[2]

A soldier writes to his sister, tallying his points and anticipating his return home.

May 27, 1945

Lambach, Austria

Dear Eleanor,

We get to lick our own envelopes now,** so I am going to write one to see how it feels!!

We finally got some mail after waiting two weeks and four of them were from you. I also got the cigarettes. Thanks a lot, I can always use 'em.

Yes, I had 5 beans in a V-E Day pot, but as usual I lost!*** My corporal won the pot, which had $40 in it.

---

*An unusual way to sign a letter, but Carson always used this name when writing to his parents.

**This comment undoubtedly refers to the lifting of censors' reading of mail.

***The soldier had five dollars in a pool to guess the correct day that Germany would surrender.

Mom sent me Bernard's new address. So far I haven't heard from him. His Regiment sure sounds familiar, seems I've seen them around somewhere.

We are in the 3rd Army now. About the 4th of March we left the First Army front and joined up with the 71st Inf. Div. on the Seventh Army front for about two weeks and the 71st (and us) then left the 7th Army and went to the 3rd Army. We were with the 71st Div. on the 3rd Army front when the fighting stopped. We really had some good shooting* the last month before it all stopped!!

Gosh, how my boy "Joe" has grown! And Kay, she's a young lady already—and a good-looker, too. If this war lasts much longer they will be drafting Joe before I get to see him again!!

Anyway, I never got caught with my "points" down! I have accumulated a total of 90—if they do us any good!!

I got 50 points for months in service, 15 for months overseas, and 25 for 5 major campaigns (5 battle stars). I really am figuring on a furlough, if I don't get a discharge.

Oh yes, what were Joe and Kay playing when you took their pictures? Or were they just practicing!!

I can see my sister is just as good looking as ever, too, and really you're almost fat!! (I'm glad I'm not where you can get your hands on me!!)

By the way, do you know anything about a camera? I have a Zeiss Ikon, 120 folding camera that's a honey. It has a 3.5 lens and a shutter speed from 1 second to 1/400 of a second. I don't know much about the thing, but they tell me that's good!! It really is an expensive camera alright. I've only got two rolls of film for it, so I am not taking many pictures. I am saving a roll for the Statue of Liberty, when I see the old gal I am going to take a whole roll!!!

Well, I reckon I'd better quit for now. Maybe I'll have time for another one to-nite.

Thanks a lot for the swell pictures, also the cigs and newspaper clippings. Be sure and write soon.

Love,
Richard

A WAC WAITS FOR HER SHIP

FROM THE NOTEBOOKS OF JEANNE E. BETCHER[3]

American women who served abroad were just as anxious to get back to the United States as were their male counterparts. Here a

---

*He is in a tank destroyer battalion.

young woman in the Women's Army Corp, decorated for her service, lets her parents know that her return is not far off.

24 August 1945

Namur, Belgium

Dearest Mother and Father,

Hello, and how are you this grey day? It is having a time to clear up—the heavy, dark clouds are still sailing along in the sky.

Today's "Stars and Stripes" contains good news for the Wac—headlines "44 Point Wacs Start Home Tomorrow"—"2300 to Quit E.T.O. by End of September"—"The redeployment of all Wacs in the European Theatre of Operations with 44 or more points, which will return approximately 2,300 service women to the U.S. by the end of September, will begin tomorrow, it was announced yesterday by Lt. Col. Mary A. Hallaren, Theatre Wac Staff Director. Eight hundred (800) Wacs not classified as essential will report tomorrow to staging areas for both air and water shipment home. *The remaining 1,500 high-point service women,* including Wacs now in the *critical-skills* group, will ship home *before October."* (that means *me*)—hurrah, hurrah, hurrah.

That means that I will be coming home at long last in September sometime. Do not know whether we will be flown, or go by boat. No doubt the latter in view of the large number 1,500—and perhaps leave from England, if we sail on a large English liner.

Took this afternoon off, as my half-pass day for this week. Read a magazine, and then finished packing the box I have had under my bed, to send to you. Wonder if I will get home before the package arrives. Have everything pretty well in order—in fact, if they told me to get ready to leave tomorrow, I could be ready.

It will be three years on October 8 that I was sworn into the Army—and if I am in service at that time, will be able to wear a "hashmark" on my sleeve, denoting three years' service—but I believe I will be out of the Army by that time, and will not be permitted this hashmark. Do believe we will be discharged when we reach the States. Do hope so, for see no reason to keep us further in the Service. Just imagine, one month from today I may be at home. Can think of nothing else.

This afternoon after lunch, made myself some tea—and left the little stove on, and it heated the room. After supper tonight I shampooed my hair, and did a little laundry, and again plugged the stove on to the electric, and it is quite comfortable in the little room here. Am thinking, just before we leave here, of sending the stove to Mrs. Larrieu—it is heavy, but I do not believe it is five pounds. At least I will try and see.

Think this is all the news for now—so, "goodnight" sweet dreams.

Hope you are both in superb health. Am fine and dandy. With all my love, great hard hugs, million kisses.

Daughter Jeanne

P.S. Am enclosing a copy of my citation.

Jeanne Betcher earned her "hashmark" but was discharged shortly thereafter.

PASSING THE TIME

LETTER HOME FROM LOREN FRED[4]

Many of the troops were able to travel and see the sights of the Old World before they could be shipped home. Here a soldier describes his visit to a place not normally on the tourist routes.

26 July 1945

Btry B, 915th FA Bn

Fronberg, Germany

Dear Agnes,

I just came up to the office to write this letter—since I have been working in the supply room, I still come back up here in the evenings to write letters—when Cardinal came in. He is in charge of quarters downstairs, and I guess he heard me come in. He wanted to show me some pictures he had got back from Paris today. He had one of me which was taken while we were at Schwarzenfeld. It's a good, clear picture, and I thought you might like to have it. He said he would have to order some more anyway, so he gave me the one he had. We found the high silk hat in the house we were staying in, as well as the walking stick. Several of us had pictures taken, using those as props. The white instrument hanging around my neck is the exposure meter you sent me. Cardinal had the pictures ready to send home, I guess; he wrote the inscription on the back. How do you like me as a "dude"?

The second day of our tour began with 10 in 1 rations for breakfast. Even when we were on the tour, we had to have guards at night to watch the trucks, gasoline and food; all the names were put into a helmet and drawn for guard. I missed that, but I was drawn for KP—the only day during the trip that any-one worked KP. All the rest of the time we were in cities, and there was always someone around who was glad to wash the few pots and pans there were for something to eat. The KP I did that day was the easiest I ever had. At noon we had cold dinner, and there was nothing to do. At night there was very little work.

After breakfast we packed up, and the very first thing we did was ride out to the little town of Dachau not far from Munich. Near there was the Dachau concentration camp, the oldest in Germany. I used to think the names of these camps were given to them specially, but I guess they are named after the town they are near.

The camp is a very large place, with lots of brick buildings and quite a number of large wooden barracks. There really is very little to see except the buildings. Part of the camp now imprisons a large number of former SS troopers. We were taken on a tour of the camp by a former prisoner who was released by the swift approach of the Americans just before the war ended. He told us that all the prisoners were to be shot before the Americans got there, but there wasn't time. He never did tell us his nationality, but he was a political prisoner and had been in the camp over 3 years. During that time he had learned to speak English.

I have been surprised to find so many people over here who know at least a little English. Quite a number speak it quite well. Not long ago when I went to the circus, our truck picked up two Polish girls and boys, Jews, who were going our way. One of the girls had been in a camp of some kind here in Germany and had learned to speak English there. Some other prisoners had taught her. These people who have learned English speak it quite well and sometimes have difficulty understanding Americans because they use so much slang.

Back to the concentration camp, our guide took us to the old crematorium. It was a small building, with only one furnace. Two bodies could be burned at a time. Later there was such a rush that they began putting three bodies in each side of the furnace—six in all. After cremation the ashes were sent to relatives of the deceased, but when three were burned together there is no telling who got whose ashes—not that it would make much difference. Later on this still wasn't fast enough to keep up, so a new building was put up, which housed four furnaces. Here also three bodies were burned at a time. Even these furnaces couldn't keep up, so the time the bodies were left in was cut down, resulting in unfinished cremation. Later in the tour he showed us partially burned hands and feet in a dump in the camp. Some of the bodies and ashes were dumped there, some were scattered and buried in the fields near camp. After the rush got so great, ashes were no longer sent to relatives. In the basement of one building, we saw little jars of ashes that had been there since 1942.

In another building he showed us the false shower room. Here prisoners were crowded together under fake showers, thinking they were to be given a bath. When the room was full, a guard watching through a little glass window turned chlorine gas into the room. In a nearby room we could see where bodies were piled to await cremation. Blood and hair were dried on the walls.

Not far from there was the place where some of the prisoners were shot. They were forced to kneel while a guard shot them with a pistol. Later on this system was improved so that a board drain was built, over which the prisoners knelt. Blood ran through this drain into the ground, and the drain was washed off with water.

There was quite a large dog kennel, too. The guide said only very large dogs were kept. They were specially trained and could always distinguish between the prisoners and civilians or guards. When the liberators arrived, all the dogs were shot. When we were entering the camp, I saw a dog that looked as though he must have been the type used. I believe it was the largest dog I have ever seen, and I have seen some big ones. He must have been nearly three feet high, much bigger than the St. Bernard in the picture.

When we left Dachau, we returned to Munich and were supposed to make a tour of the city. We should have visited Dachau the night before, but we were late in getting there and had to wait until morning. Consequently, we didn't visit much in Munich. From what some of the other boys told us later, we missed several things but nothing unusually interesting, I guess. I don't think our officer knew exactly how to get out of the city, and we spent a little time trying to find the way.

One thing that interested me was to see the streetcars in operation there. They were also running in Nurnberg.* There were a large number of knocked out cars on the tracks, but these had been pushed onto sidings, and the streetcars went around them. The cars are smaller than ours, with one long seat extending the length of the car, running down each side, instead of smaller seats facing forward as ours do. Usually there is one car pulling two others. Apparently they are made that way, too. The cars in the rear were not equipped to operate alone.

Up to this point, the trip hadn't proved especially interesting to me and most of the others. Getting lost the previous afternoon didn't help any. A few were sorry they had come. During the afternoon, though, the trip began to get more interesting. I'll tell you about that tomorrow. I didn't get far on the trip this time, even though I did get quite a ways on the letter.

With love,
Loren

---

*Nuremberg, in English.

> Wife, writing to point-deficient husband overseas: Having fine wish. Time you were here.
>
> —Eddie Cantor

OVERSEEING THE DEFEATED

LETTERS HOME FROM HENRY NOVAK[5]

Henry Novak had seen combat in the field artillery and was now waiting for the chance to go home. His unit was assigned to guarding former members of the SS, the most ardent and morally repugnant Nazis of all, as the GIs bided their time and accumulated points. He includes some frank observations about that duty and other experiences in his letters home to his waiting wife and infant daughter. Note also his strong views about striking workers back in the United States.

Friday May 25

Germany

Dearest Sis and Stevie Lee,

I have just come down out of the guard tower after spending two hours watching a big bunch of krauts preparing for bed. I'm in the guard house now writing and listening to the radio. I hope that you are both enjoying life as much as I am these days. Of course, I'd be thousands of times happier if I were with you. I received some clippings along with the May 1st "Perry News" tonite but no letters. I am enclosing three pictures in with these letters and three negatives. Two of the pictures are of Charlie and I with a couple of cows. In many of the farming communities over here they use cows for plowing land and hauling because the German Army took all of their oxen and horses. The other picture is of the ponton bridge over which we crossed the Rhine. The one negative is of Stan and I standing beside our new prime mover. The other two negatives are of me with the triplets who were evacuees and were living next door to us in Sachsenburg. Today, I took a roll of pictures of this prison camp and in a few days I should have some more pictures. I don't know if you ever saw anybody with or how they act but to me it's a pretty sad sight. Many of these prisoners have them and we are doing our best to delouse them. In the last war many of our boys had these so-called cooties and they called the method of finding them "reading your shirt." I saw many of the krauts doing just that today. They take off their clothes one piece at a time and go down each and every seam just as you would read the page of a book and pick off the lice. They also have them in the hair on their body. To me, it's comic to see a kraut walking along and suddenly grab himself wherever he has been bitten and then start probing. I can truthfully say that since we have been in combat I have never seen a G.I. with cooties. However, here we are susceptible to them because our guard house is a former "slave labor" barrack and it has plenty of them due to carelessness on the part of our officers. We are starting to get some SS troopers in now. They are the inhuman bad boys of the Nazi army. They even have swastikas or SS branded on their sides and their fellow soldiers hate them. These SS men are in for a long stretch of some sort of hard labor and if they even look crosseyed they can expect a bullet and I don't mean where it will *wound* them. From all indications the boys in our outfit who have 85 or more points are going to pull out soon. I might add while on the subject of cows working that on this side of the Rhine about 50% of the farm work and hauling is done by them. The way the superforts* are working out on Japan these days it shouldn't be too long until her industries are smashed and she crumbles internally. In my own mind or way of thinking unless the present system changes, I think our chances of *not* going to the Pacific are about 60–40. However, one never knows. Well honey, I guess that's about all for tonite. Take good care of yourselves and give our little dickens a great big kiss from Daddy. To the sweetest gal there is, loads of love, hugs and kisses.

Your loving daddy
Hen

Give my best to Ma, Jean and the folks.

Saturday May 26

Germany

My dearest and sweetest girls,

I hope that you, Mumie and Stevie Lee are both happy and healthy these days. As usual, I can't complain about much but I sure am missing you both very much. I received your fine letter of May 15th today. I'm glad everything is going well for you back home. Here, things never seem to change anymore. Today I had a first hand look-see on how the S.S. troops operated but this time they were on the receiving end. After watching what went on for awhile I had to turn away for fear of turning my stomach. I've seen boys killed and wounded,

---

*B-29 bombers.

heard stories and saw pictures but I just can't seem to be the guy that could torture another human being. We have a couple hundred of those "elite" storm troopers mixed in with high Nazi officials and Gestapo men. Our job is to take these birds on hard labor details and keep them busy. As far as we are concerned that's about all there would be to it. But with each detail of 40 men we get three non-coms form the regular German army (Wehrmacht) to keep them on the ball. These SS men are strictly killers and there have been cases where they have killed their parents to show that they are inhuman. They also have shot many of the Wehrmacht when they wanted to surrender. Well, these non-coms keep them on the ball—with rubber hoses and canes. If an SS, High Nazi or Gestapo as much as tries to take a deep breath for a break he gets the hose or stick and I don't mean lightly either. One of the non-coms told me that his mother had been or was a Jewess and three years ago before they (SS) hauled her away to a concentration camp they made her lick the steps in front of her home with her tongue. He thinks she is dead now. Today there were SS Men cleaning floors using only the breath from their lungs and on their bellies. To me, it is barbaric and I can't even watch it long but I also can't feel sorry for them because the punishment they are getting from men of their own nationality still doesn't come close to their reign of terror. Well honey that's a wicked story but it's glued in my mind. I guess I'm about finished for tonite darling except that I want you to know that I love you more and more as the days go by and am aching to get away from it all. Give our little dickens a great big kiss and loads of love, hugs and kisses to my little pugnose.

Your loving daddy
Hen

Give my best to Ma, Jean and the folks.

Request for Three Day Pass

1954 SINGAM SWITCHBOARD OPERATING DETACHMENT

APO 749

22 August 1945

Subject: Request for Three Day Pass
To: Commanding Officer, Camp Baltimore, Suippes Sub-Area, AAC.

Request Pfc Novak, Henry R., 33 706 421, of this organization be authorized a three day pass to Paris when available.

[signature]
Chester M. Rytlewski, Pfc
Commanding

Sat. Oct. 6th

Reims, France

My darling gals,

I'm tanked! I wish I were with you both at the present time and since I'm not, I hope you are in tip-top shape. I am O.K. except for being a little "inebriated." Isn't that a shame?! I didn't get any mail today and I sure do miss that. Jerry and John went to Brussels this morning to see what they can see. Of course, since they have already been there previously I'm quite sure what their object will be. They will be the type of gal that supplies that moment of exaltation and a few days later the boys are sweating it out. I layed around all day and tonite saw a very snappy movie, "Out of This World." That Cass Daley is a scream. After the movie Mac, Lollis, Campbell and I decided to drink a couple of beers. We bought sixty glasses, which just filled our table. We drank them and here we are. We're now waiting for Jerry and John to come back. Lollis is really tanked and is putting on quite a show. I forgot to tell you that the 552 is now in the vicinity of Verdun. There are all kinds of rumors flying around that maybe we will be home in November. I sure hope so. Lollis just said for me to tell you "that Hank is true to you, that he loves you very much and is anxious to come back home." My! My! I guess I better close because the boys are laughing themselves silly. A great big hug and kiss for our little rascal and until tomorrow loads of the best hugs, love and kisses to the sweetest little brown eyed gal ever. I love you so doggoned much.

Your loving Daddy
Hen

Give my best to Ma, Jean and the folks.

Sat. Oct. 13th,

Verdun, France

Hiya darlings!

I hope that you are both feeling fine and dandy these days. I am O.K. and am thinking about you both all the time. Everything was going along O.K. until we got the "S+S"* today and saw that the English are taking the Queen Elizabeth and the Acquitaine besides some Victory ships out of the redeployment pipeline. I don't know how much this is going to put us back if any but should it, I'll hate those Limeys as much as I do those striking bastards

---

*Stars and Stripes, the newspaper specially written and printed for servicemen and women.

back at New York. So far, there have been no orders to change our schedule. I took a good hot shower this morning and then wrote Gene a letter to let him know how things are going. This afternoon I took a roll of pictures (8) of the Verdun monument with Ches. I took one picture of a baby sleeping in his carriage. This evening Ches and I saw a fairly good movie, "The Falcon Goes to San Francisco." There was also a good short with Leon Errol. Well kids that's about it. Don't forget that great big hug and kiss for our Stevie, honey. Until tomorrow pleasant dreams and oceans of love, hugs and kisses for my dearest little brown eyed sweetheart. I love you, oodles and oodles.

> Your loving Daddy
> *Hen*

Give my best to Ma, Jean and the folks.

Sunday Oct. 14th

Verdun, France

My dearest and beloved gals,

I hope you are both enjoying the best of health these days. I'm O.K. but not very happy, especially after seeing the headline in today's "Stars and Stripes." "70 Pointers Taken Off Shipping List." Wouldn't that take the elastic out of your panties? Of course, we haven't received any change in our orders yet but that is enough to take the laugh away from a laughing hyena. Also on the front page was a picture of 60,000 dock workers listening to one of their "leaders." I wonder if he is any relation to Hitler, Mussolini or Tojo. You would have thought that all 60,000 of them were because when "S+S" came out today, all thru the building, the shout was unanimous, "What a spot for an atomic bomb!!" No kidding, Sis, when I get home Corbett and those Senators are going to get some scorching letters. The way these G.I.'s talk those Congressmen and Senators are sure going to earn their salt when we get back home. Yep, a lot of those strikers need to have a few G.I.'s around when they cause that kind of trouble. Then they would get their first taste of war and that's no kidding. I think Truman is taking things too easy with these strikers. I think F.D.R. would have kept the redeployment lines clear anyway. I spent a quiet Sunday here in the building except for a walk down to the Red Cross Club with Ches for coffee and donuts. Life gets more monotonous each day when the prospects of getting home next month grow dim. A guy just gets disgusted and loses what little faith he had in the War Dept. I would have much rather spent these last three months in Germany. There at least, I could have occupied myself arguing with the krauts against fascism and Naziism. Here we have fought against such things and back home men with bank

accounts filled with war wages are striking and causing violence with mob
hysteria, led by "little fuehrers." We also have a Senator named Bilbo "Miss."
who calls people wops, dagos and hunkies. Next we have some of those so-
called original "Americans" the D.A.R., which practice race discrimination.
My aching back, we sure are putting up with a lot. Maybe I'm nuts but things
don't seem to be going right at all. Maybe I shouldn't have told you to quit
writing yet but we shall see what we shall see. Well darlings I guess that's about
all I can think of today. Gosh! honey, I sure was hoping to get home next
month so that I could spend all the coming holidays with my loved ones. I
love and miss you both as much as ever. Keep our little rascal in trim with that
great big hug and kisses. Until tomorrow loads of love, hugs and kisses for
my beautiful brown-eyed little gal that I love so very much.

Your loving Daddy
Hen

Give my best to Ma, Jean and all the folks.

P.S. I read about 2 1/2 months of your old letters today that I have kept. I
have all of them from March until the end of Sept.

LIVING A LIFE ON HOLD

LETTERS HOME FROM WILLARD H. FLUCK[6]

*It took Willard Fluck eight months to make his way home after
victory had been won in Europe. These letters detail his saga,
typical of many hundreds of thousands of GIs.*

May 31, 1945

Near Paris, France

Dear Folks,

Hello again from your dearly beloved son. There isn't much new except that
I'm getting a two-day pass starting tomorrow. I've been lucky, having had two
twelve-hour passes there already. I don't remember just what (if anything) I've
already told you about France or Paris, but maybe you'd be interested in hearing a few observations.

Paris these days is lousy with soldiers, mostly American and French, since
all the GIs that can be given passes are given them. Since there isn't much food
in France, we eat at Red Cross Centers when on pass. There are a lot of them,
and they even sell ice cream and beer now. There are sightseeing tours which
take you to see all the famous buildings and all kinds of stuff like that there.
It's a modern city, but there aren't any real tall buildings or a lot of bright neon

signs or modern automobiles. Boy, you should see some of the cars they drive. I even saw a four-wheeled two-seated contrivance that was propelled by the driver by pedaling—like children's toy automobiles.

It seems to be a native custom when feeling the call of nature to find a side street, turn one's back to the lady friend (I don't believe it's considered polite to face her), and proceed to urinate against the side of the nearest building. And in one place I found a woman "porter" cleaning the men's toilet. I didn't ask whether men cleaned the women's. Ah yes, Europe is a great place. The weather has been swell, and I've already got quite a sun-tan.

I get a kick out of Paris's subways. You see GIs looking over maps and charts trying to figure out where they're going and what trains to take. You know, I think I'll get a job with the Chamber of Commerce when I get back and write travel books and make charts and travel catalogs.

I'm anxious to get some mail and see what's going on back home.

Well, I guess that's all for this time. I guess the girls (my dear sisters, that is) wonder why I haven't written. I will when I get my mail.

Gotta close. Take good care of yourselves.

Love
Bud

July 3, 1945

Ladenburg, Germany

Dear Folks,

I received your last letter—the one of the 26th—in six days. That's pretty good time. Sorry I couldn't get home for my birthday.

Now I've got six of your letters to answer yet. I guess I've already answered most of your questions. Thanks for the birthday card.

No, we're not allowed to talk to German people (legally). I do a little interpreting now and then though. A while ago a woman was around—we live in her house (some of our company do)—saying two rabbits and a chicken were gone from her shed. I'm sure none of our guys took them, but some of the civilians are real low on food, and they easily could have. That's the way it goes. These people think they have troubles. They're lucky. They still have a house and a shed to put animals into, and—they're still alive.

We still get a little training, but a lot of time is spent pressing pants and shirts and shining shoes. It feels sort of good to be a "garrison" soldier again instead of a "combat" soldier. And of course I spend a lot of time writing letters. I've answered most of them now, though.

You asked how we ate when we traveled for days. On the train are kitchen cars, and they cook two meals per day and serve them along the railroad when the train stops. The third meal is usually a "K" or "C" ration. Those are meals put up in individual boxes and tin cans. The army says we must be fed three meals per day—two of them hot meals if possible.

No, I didn't have a cake with candles on it, but I got my behind whacked good by the boys. There's quite a difference between that and having a cake, but it reminded me that I'm a year older.

Well, that about does it. Shall close. Stay well.

Love
Bud

July 24, 1945

Ladenburg, Germany

Dear Folks,

Once again this is your beloved son. I sure hope you're all well and fine. I am. I haven't written to you for quite a while, but I wrote to Roy on Saturday, I believe.

There hasn't been much happening lately as per usual. I went to a boxing show near Mannheim last night. I'm sure you'd have liked it, Pop. Billie Conn put on an exhibition fight as the feature attraction.* My buddy and I were lucky enough to get a front row seat right behind Conn's corner, so we saw everything.

Today I went to Mannheim again to work on another athletic stadium that is being built. We use prisoners to do the work, and believe me we don't coddle them. I happened to get a bunch of Hungarians today, so my German didn't help out very much.

Aside from that, life has been pretty dull. But I'm not complaining at all. Yesterday I pressed both my uniforms. It took four hours, but they sure look slick.

I'll enclose a few more pictures. Must close.

Love
Bud

Dec. 29, 1945

Camp Pittsburgh**
Rheims, France

Dear Folks,

We're still here, but at least now we know when we are to leave. We leave here on Jan 2nd for Le Havre and should get there the following day. There, it will be from three to five days until we get on a boat. If we get a large ship,

---

*Billie Conn was a light heavyweight prizefighter who had nearly won the world heavyweight championship from Joe Louis a few years earlier.

**The last camps in which the soldiers lived before their departure for the United States were often named after U.S. cities.

the trip won't take much over a week, but on a Liberty or Victory ship it will take twice that. That's the situation as it stands now. However, in the army anything can happen.

I guess the last of my mail has reached me by now, so I'll have to do without.

The weather certainly has been miserable lately. It rains almost continuously, and the mud is becoming ankle deep. The one consolation is that it's still fairly warm. From the looks of things, we'll have snow instead of rain very soon.

I've been wondering whether I have any civilian clothing anymore. From what we hear, almost all types of clothing are hard to get and expensive, too.

We've had several lectures on the merits of our government insurance. I've about decided to keep mine if I find the premiums aren't too high. But there's plenty of time to settle that later. What we want most now is that discharge.

Can't think of anything else right now. More later. Don't expect me before the end of January.

Stay well

Love
Bud

Jan. 13, 1946
Camp Wings
Le Havre, France
Dear Folks,

This time it looks as though we might be leaving. However, knowing the Army as I do, I wouldn't bet a dime either way. We're definitely supposed to board ship on the 15th—Tuesday. Allowing twelve days sailing time and four days to be discharged, we should make it home by the first of February. That's if the War Department doesn't decide to slow things down a little more.

Today makes one month we've been in these redeployment camps waiting to get a ship home. The actual processing takes perhaps five days. The remainder of the time was wasted. I shouldn't say wasted exactly, because I've learned to play chess and pinochle and several other card games and have read half a library of books in this past month. But even for a month, that isn't a helluva lot, is it!

In case you would like to know what my plans are for the future, for the immediate future I have no plans and for the later future I have more of the same.

This is my last letter from overseas. If I'm not home by Diane's birthday, you'd better write your congressman and find out where I am.

Stay well and don't work too hard.

Love
Bud

F our-year-old Judy sat stiffly on a railroad station bench in her best Sunday dress. She kept her hands folded tightly on her lap and her eyes straight ahead, strangely quiet.

"Isn't it a pity," her mother whispered to me, "that she won't remember him? It's just one of those things that war does," she sighed, "making strangers of so many fathers."

"Don't worry," I tried to reassure her, "Bud will understand."

The train rumbled in, the gates opened, and Bud came, tanned and grinning. He whooped when he saw us. Before we knew what was happening, Judy was on her feet—a pink-and-white blur as she raced to her father's arms. She got a strangle hold around his neck, then pulled back and gave him the most radiant, worshipful look I've ever seen, as she said, "Why, Daddy, you did remember me, didn't you?"

—Nelson Valjean, Saturday Evening Post

GETTING TO KNOW THE GERMANS

LETTER HOME FROM MILDRED KARLSEN[7]

The occupation troops' contact with the Germans occurred on many levels and took many forms. Confronting the belief in Nazism was among the more difficult aspects of the Americans' relationship, as this letter from a WAC makes clear.

22 July 45

Frankfurt A/Main

Dear Leona and Max,

I arrived here in Germany last Sunday and have been so busy ever since that I just haven't had time to write anybody. I don't know what to say to describe the place. You would never believe it. There isn't a building in Frankfurt which hasn't been bombed. The streets aren't cleared of the rubble yet and they're still digging people out. And what they ever started this for is beyond me. The country is beautiful. Cecil drove me around the first 3 days I was here and Germany is really nice. They just don't have any cities left. I've been swimming in one of the pools Hitler built for the youth of Germany and it sure is nice. There are pools and parks all over. We have them now to build us up!

Out here at the house where the General and Cecil live (I'm here now) there are 3 German women who do the cooking and cleaning. No wonder Cecil gained weight! What meals. They made thin pancakes for me just like Mom makes. I talk with them in my bum German. One is a real Nazi, but the other two hated Hitler, or so they say now. One is from Bavaria and I have a hard time understanding her. The highways are the best I've seen since the States and the flowers are prettier and the grass greener! Who does that remind you of? Seriously, I can't imagine why they start wars. I told that to the Nazi woman today. She speaks English and she said she knew I was her enemy when I talked like that. She lost her husband and still isn't convinced. Most of them try to be friendly now, but I don't trust them too far. We can't leave the area without an armed guard and Cecil always has his six shooter handy. He's stretched out next to me now snoring. I washed his shirt after dinner and right now I'm supposed to iron it. He always puts me to work—nice guy.

I also acquired a lovely set of dishes and am sending them home. I hope they don't break. It took about 2 1/2 hours to fly to Frankfurt from Paris.

I'll write you a good letter one of these days—right now I have work to do and I don't feel like writing anyway.

Hope the kids are all right.

Love,

Mil

P.S. Note the new address on the envelope and please write soon.

THE HORRORS OF WAR AND THE TRIALS OF OCCUPATION

LETTERS HOME FROM HAROLD PORTER[8]

Harold Porter witnessed the terrible and heartrending detritus of the Holocaust. As a medical technician in a unit that arrived at Dachau just as Germany surrendered, he was among the earliest

*Americans to behold firsthand the sufferings of the Nazi concen-
tration camp inmates. After caring for the emaciated and dis-
eased prisoners, he remained in Germany for much of the subsequent occupation and did not hesitate to share his observations
about German behavior, and the behavior of the occupying
forces, with his family.*

10 May 1945

Dear Mother and Father,

I've told you before about the thousands of dead bodies here. They are not
nearly so ghastly nor horrible as our patients, the "living corpses." Gandhi
after a thirty day fast would still look like Hercules when compared with some
of these men. They have no buttocks at all, and on some their vertebrae can
be seen rubbing on their stomach. It's unbelievable that they could still be
alive. And the odor of a ward is nearly as bad as the odor of the crematory.
All have raw ugly bed sores, puss dripping infections, scabs, scales, ulcers, bites
plus typhus, beri-beri, scurvy, T.B., erysipelas and 101 other symptoms.

We don't even think of them as human. If we did, we'd never be able to
do the work. They look like weird beings from Mars—with their shaven heads
(part of the de-lousing technique), knobby joints, huge hands, feet, and pop-
ping eyes. Many are toothless. They lie curled up in the oddest positions, and
when morning comes we go around and remove the corpses—still stiff in the
freakish pose they held when they died. Most have dysentery of the "continuous bloody dribble" type—and of course are unable to drag themselves to
the latrine. The alternative I'll leave you to imagine. (I certainly am thankful
I'm not a ward boy.) Those that are not gibbering idiots are dumb statues.
They die off like flies while I'm giving them penicillin. To enter a ward at night
is like hearing the "Inner Sanctum" radio program. There are weird wails,
sobs, groans, gnashing of teeth, and above it all the chant of men praying. I'll
never forget it as long as I live. I have picked up complete bodies in a blanket
with *two* fingers to carry them to the crematory.

This job could go on for ever; the number of patients for practical purposes is infinite. Normally we're a 400 bed hospital. We're prepared to take
over 1200 here.

I wear a mask, gown, hat and rubber gloves all the time, but you can bet
your life it will be just my luck to come down with something. The fellows
are volunteering for infantry duty in the Pacific, but no such luck.

More later.

Love,
Harold

12 May 1945

Dear Mother and Father,

A Belgian major who speaks perfect English and to whom I was giving penicillin to clear up a lot of nasty boils, told me about liberation day. He, an American officer, and eight British officers lived together and had a radio set, smuggled in by a bribed guard, hidden under the floor. They followed the news and estimated the day we would arrive. In preparation they had spread the news, formed committees to make banners, formed their own police and assassination force, and taught a lot of prisoners how to say "thank you" in English.

They expected us Tuesday. We came Sunday, two days early. The first Americans to reach the gates of the compound were kissed, torn to shreds, made to sign autographs, carried throughout the camp on the shoulders of prisoners—who were so hysterical with joy they were in tears.

Much of the station's complement of (SS troops) escaped, but nearly all the guards were caught at their posts. When the Americans first opened the gates, they gave automatic weapons to some of the inmates, and while half were celebrating their release, the other half went about massacring the guards. They not only killed them but clubbed them to pieces and desecrated them. This, and other variations of torture were still going on when I got here. Some guards tried to pose as prisoners, and perhaps some have succeeded. But we saw one who was forced to strip, was tortured with cold water, made to put on the prisoners' striped uniform, backed against a wall with his hands up, was stoned and eventually shot by an American who probably wanted to put him out of his misery. Even yet while rummaging through a building we came across the body of an SS trooper just as he was left by the freed prisoners who found him—usually with his head mashed to a pulp and often with his fingers whittled off if he wore rings.

Besides the bodies of SS troopers, the thousands of starved corpses, are also the carcasses of the guard dogs—huge mastiffs, wolfhounds and German shepherds used to guard the prisoners. Some of these were still alive and a few Americans are trying to make pets out of them—to the disgust of the prisoners.

The sun was hot again today—and you now what that means with all this spoiled meat laying around. This place is just one horrible nightmare.

Love,
Harold

27 May 1945

Dachau Concentration Camp
Dachau, Germany

Dear Father and Mother,

The Germans have descended upon us! Doing the same work that two of our
own ward boys did the first week we were here are now six enlisted German
medics, two German nurses, 2 German doctors plus 3 or 4 Russian or Yugoslav
utility men. All we do is supervise. We're supposed to explain things to them,
as they are going to take over. But only the officers speak English, and they
hob-nob with our officers—so we just sit back and let their enlisted men work.
They still wear all their insignia including campaign medals. The officers look
as if they had just finished posing for a fashion magazine ad. They sure have
smart uniforms, and they strut about like peacocks. And who do you suppose
they are? They are the same men (a field hospital) who occupied the building
we used in Sarrebourg! They left just a few days before we took over. They
have been medics since the beginning of the war and have seen service both
in Russia and Italy.

The officers seem interested enough in the work, judging by the questions they ask. The enlisted men are quick to do what they're told and are very
subservient, click their heels, jump to open doors for us, but don't seem to
take any more interest in their work than we do. Their nurses put ours to
shame. They plunge right in—even clean a fellow up when he couldn't hold
out til the bed pan got there. German nurses are *not* members of the German
army.

Not being able to speak German is certainly a handicap. All patients speak
and understand some German. I've tried to study a little now and then, but I
don't have the formal background I had in French. These language difficulties have led to some funny incidents. There are certain necessary terms in
regard to the body functions that are a "must" for every nurse and ward boy—
we soon pick up the Russian word, Polish, Yugoslavian, or Italian word for
urinal or bed-pan. At least we know what is meant when a patient uses these
words, so we soon add them to our vocabulary. One of our own doctors who
speaks fluent Polish came into a ward and heard a nurse using these terms—
which turned out to be terrible obscenities in Polish—words that just aren't
used in polite society. He got a big kick out of it. Some patients learn a little
English—and some learn a little French. Often you hear French, English and
German words used in the same sentence. "Bitte very much" is now the
accepted substitute for the former English phrase "you are welcome"—just
because one of our Yugoslavs started using it. Today a Hungarian patient came
into one of the wards and our doctor was trying to question him using his

limited college German. Finally the patient, after quite a bit of difficulty trying to understand the doctor, said, in perfect English, "You don't speak German
very well, do you?" It turned out he is a count who has studied at Oxford.
Seems there are quite a few of them here.

All the Belgians, Dutch and most of the French have left. Hungarians,
Russians, Romanians and Poles are the predominant nationalities now. There
are quite a few artists among them. We have had violin concerts by Polish
violinists in our day room, one fellow does caricatures, another crayon draw-
ings and some fellows are even sitting for oil portraits—done by a professor
of Art at the University of Minsk. The Gypsy children, for some reason or
other *all* seem to be able to play a violin or accordion—They have put on
some lively shows for us.

There is one German civilian doctor helping us who wears white buck-
skin shorts to work—held up by fancy tooled and braided suspenders. He also
wears knee length socks. This costume is not uncommon around here. Can
you imagine an America professional man dressing like that?

When a fellow dies, his corpse is placed outside the ward and collected
the following morning. The other night about three in the morning I came
out of a ward after giving penicillin. It was raining and thundering. The wind
was blowing—and our guards were fooling with some German "Screaming
Meemies" they had found. (These are rockets—our army has no equivalent.)
One of these went whistling overhead just as I opened the door. I jumped,
slipped, stumbled over one of the corpses and frightened away one of the
mastiffs that had been chewing on the foot. Boy, what a feeling!

The guards caught some hungry patients (all patients here are hungry)
making off with a bucket of human entrails outside the 127 Evac autopsy
tent. You guess what they planned to do with them. I know.

If we don't get out of here soon, I'm sure I'll get a psycho-neurotic disability discharge within a month. Things happen here that probably have never
happened before in the history of the world.

Love,
Harold

31 May 1945
Dachau Concentration Camp
Dachau, Germany

Dear Mother and Father,
Today was the day Marc Coyle and I were going to skip out and hitch-hike
down to Innsbruck, Austria for a day or two. We've changed our plans though
because it is raining.

Most of the girls in Dachau have put on Red Cross uniforms and are out here on the wards helping. With the German soldiers, nurses, doctors, detached service men, French nurses, and German Red Cross girls, we now have so much help that we get in one another's way. How the army thinks it can put a lot of girls working side by side with American soldiers and still expect to enforce the non-fraternization policy is beyond me. Now that the fighting is over, the average soldier wants to forget about the war as fast as possible, and the mere presence of civilians reminds him of home. A surprising number of the girls speak English. Perhaps their most outstanding characteristic is their smug ignorance. Someone has compared their attitude to that of a drunk who has awakened after a binge and wants to be told what he did when he was out. Their shock at discovering what went on here in the camp certainly seems genuine enough. And there is no doubt about it, they *are* good workers. Besides, the patients seem to prefer them to ours—but this is natural enough when the language situation is considered. You have no idea how exasperating it can be trying to care for a patient when you can't understand what he is talking about and he can't understand you.

Penicillin will no longer be given to any but American soldiers, so I'm out of a job. The 1st sergeant will discover this soon enough, but until he does I'm just going to rest and take things easy. If the weather ever clears up before we move, I'll walk or hitch-hike to the end of the Munich Street Car line and ride in. The city transportation system seems intact, but from what I've heard the city is pretty well wrecked.

From what I've seen, I would say that the suffering that the Germans put up with during the war was exaggerated in the U.S. These people around here lived the life of kings. About the only luxury they lacked was cars—and everyone had a bike anyway. They wear beautiful clothing—and even though their food situation was supposed to be skimpy, they're all much fatter than the French.

So much of what we see here is so different from what we expected. For instance, the Polish prisoners are probably the most violently anti-Jewish group in camp. Some of the German prisoners are still ardent Nazis, and of course, everyone hates and fears the Russians except half the Yugoslavs. The other half, plus the French, give the impression they would just as soon fight the Russians as the Germans. Italians also seem to have no friends.

Undoubtedly this beautiful mix up and internal friction was exactly what the Germans encouraged because it made the group as a whole easier to handle. All potential leaders within the compound were quickly eliminated. It's disgusting to find out how quickly some of the prisoners were willing to cooperate with the SS guards in torturing other prisoners—especially if it meant better conditions for themselves.

Most of them have degenerated to animals; they fight among themselves, plunge head first into garbage cans and eat like pigs. They steal from one another all the time. A group of them took some of our D.D.F. powder and, apparently thinking it was cereal, cooked it up into mush and ate it. They all died.

On the other hand, it is surprising to find there are quite a few who were able to maintain control of themselves during their imprisonment—and actually improve themselves by studying languages. Some men are fluent in 5 or 6 languages.

I've often thought that as far as personal comforts, rating, and pay are concerned, I would be much better off in the navy. But I've never regretted being in the army because as long as I'm not going to make a career out of the service, the educational value of the sights I've been exposed to in the army are far more valuable than looking at vast expanses of water ever would have been.

Love,
Harold

5 June 1945

Bad Mergentheim, Germany

Dear Mother and Father,

Letter 99 with its message from Madelon came yesterday. I have yet to receive number 98. No, you need only take the rifle. Leave the relic behind. But, I suppose you will have left by the time you get this so there isn't much use of my saying what to take and what not to.*

I've sent some literature, postcards and pictures of this town and of our hotel. They describe the place better than I can.

So far, I haven't had much rest with all the cleaning up we've had to do. On top of this I stand guard from 4:00 to 8:00 both morning and afternoon at a medical warehouse near here. This won't last much longer—I hope. It is light til 10:30 at night here and dawn comes at 3:30 in the morning. But there is a curfew for all soldiers and civilians at 9:00, so there's not much to do then but write letters or drink at our own bar.

For the most part the civilians ignore us or treat us indifferently—somewhat like the Germans were treated in Holland, I imagine. When you walk down the street, some cow away from you, others look very bitter or sneer, the ex-soldiers and returning soldiers (of which there are lots) stay shy of us

---

*Porter's parents were moving from Michigan to Colorado.

entirely. Many stare right at us with a frown on their face, and we stare right back—It's sort of like the old childhood game of trying to "out stare" the other fellow. There is no regional costume here as in Dachau—except possibly red aprons on the rural girls. The townspeople, being unusually wealthy in peace-time, still have beautiful clothes. There are lots of women dressed in mourning clothes, lots of nuns, monks, and divinity students—as there is a theological school here. Like the rest of Germany that I've seen, everyone is devoutly religious, and religious reminders are everywhere.

There are two exceptions to the attitude I've described above. The first is that of the children. German children are certainly the most beautiful in the world—particularly the little girls. Of course healthy bodies and good clothes do wonders for their appearance. The skinny, pale little French with their rickets and T.B. were certainly a contrast to the children here. Most are blonde with blue eyes—the little girls with pig tails or with a peculiar bun knotted right on top. It's with the children that the non-fraternization policy breaks down completely. They run out, take hold of your hand, and walk down the street with you. Almost all the guards in town constantly have swarms of children around them. And there are so *many* children—half the town seems to be between the ages of 2 and 8. About 25% of them are children of unwed or widowed mothers.

The second exception is with the older girls—17 to 25. Most will do anything to attract an American soldier—despite the terrific stigma it puts on them as far as the rest of the civilians are concerned. There has been such a shortage of eligible men for so long in Germany that sexual morality as we know it in the States is all Topsy Turvy here. The M.P.s have a terrific job trying to enforce the non-fraternization policy as far as the girls are concerned. To infantrymen in particular, anything in civilian clothes, particularly girls, makes him homesick. Besides they seem to insist that the right to German women is one of the rights they won by winning the war. The M.P.s have given up in disgust—and usually turned to fraternizing themselves—even the officers. But it's strictly illegal, which means that most of the rendezvous must take place in the surrounding woods—or else you have to get in the girl's house by nine and not show yourself on the street before 7:00 the next morning.

Civilians were banned from public swimming places—so the soldiers went outside of town and swam in the river so they could be with the girls. Now, children and girls are tacitly permitted to swim in the same places and at the same time with American soldiers. Men are strictly forbidden to enter public swimming places.

My room-mate is very fluent in German—and so far our fraternization has been of the legal variety—with the Gypsy acrobatic girls of the visiting circus. They're Hungarians, but speak French, German, and even some

English—as they've worked for Ringling Bros in the States. Amazing characters! But the show moves on tomorrow, so we'll have to find something else.

Love,
Harold

9 June 1945
Kurhotel Viktoria
Bad Mergentheim

Dear Mother and Father,

Enlargements of pictures taken at Dachau are being exhibited around the town with signs in German saying "Who's Guilt?" and "You knew about this, yet did not protest." Hush and I have been spending the evening mingling with the crowds as they watch the posters. He eavesdrops on the conversation and translates for me. One of the most consistent exclamations on the part of the Germans is that they did *not* know what was going on in these camps. I think this true to a greater extent than the allies are willing to admit—although certainly not true to the extent that the Germans claim.

The non-fraternization policy has degenerated into pretty much of a farce—particularly as far as the girls are concerned. The M.P.s, being on the streets after the curfew hours, are fraternizing more than the infantrymen. We even have girls in our bar and in our ball room—infractions which would result in confinement, fines, and a court martial of our officers if the rules were enforced.

The German girls are certainly different from the French. They're not nearly so vivacious, gay or nonchalant. The French are gay and impulsive; the German girls serious, but sentimental. They are not so spontaneous, but more logical. To me, the French are enigmatic. I like the French, but find myself temperamentally much more like the Germans. The girls around here are mostly blue-eyed blondes with pigtails or wrap around braids. They wear no perfume and no make up, but have a natural beauty that seems to be lacking in the Americans. They're not as dainty, as chic or as coy as the French, but are much more curvaceous—slightly too hefty for my tastes. Most of them—especially the former hotel employees, speak English. In the town proper few costumes are worn—but the farmer girls dress up, particularly on Sunday. With its present policy, it seems to me the army has got itself into the embarrassing and difficult position of trying to legislate against human nature.

Thanks for the pictures—letters 98 and 100 came yesterday. I know just how Madelon feels with the heavy helmet on. But the fact that I had mine on when some bricks and plaster fell on me during an air-raid is the reason I'm still here. We don't wear them anymore though.

Harold Porter pointing to "Whose Guilt" poster in postwar Germany. (Courtesy of the Dwight D. Eisenhower Library, Sonya Porter Collection.)

An official report is being written upon Dachau, and in the course of the interviews the war crimes commission has been holding some amazing tales have come to light—so bizarre that I hesitate even to tell anyone because I wouldn't be believed. Lately I've been swimming and reading. Right now I'm leaving for the 83rd Division library.

Love,
Harold

12 June 1945

Kurhotel Viktoria
Bad Mergentheim

Dear Mother and Father,

Letters 101 and 102 came this morning. Switzerland is still neutral and any American crossing the border is still interned and will be until a peace with Germany is signed. I'll see if I can get a music box here however. Aunt Kathleen writes to me too and complains of homesickness. It certainly must be something if she weighs only 105. I don't see why she worries over Lera. Isn't Lera old enough to know her own mind? It should be a warning to you not to indulge in any concern over the love-lifes of your children because I, for one, am quite apt to be utterly unpredictable. Seriously though, after what I've seen of personal troubles and ruined lives at Dachau, Aunt Kathleen's worrying over the religion of a prospective son-in-law seems quite petty and insignificant. Catholicism, here in Germany anyway, has nothing at all to do with everyday living, and I doubt if it will be any more important in Lera's life unless she allows it to be.

I have just now returned from a two hour discussion in our auditorium of "Fraternization." It will probably be a topic of discussion as long as we have troops in Germany. I understand it is being debated back home too. Most of our men, having seen Dachau, are thoroughly in accord with the policy as a policy, but in practice it is something else. If you're not in Germany, it is a wonderful idea. Certainly the civilians have come to look upon our attitude as one big joke. The army is being very haphazard in its enforcement. The 63rd Infantry Division (5 months in action) is notorious for its flagrant violation. Most of the division is resting in this town—and a large part of the men are sleeping with German girls or German widows. This was quite surprising to us at first, but now our men are doing the same thing—only not quite so openly. It seems odd to hear an infantryman praise the Germans and speak of them as superior to the French. The German women take the attitude that we have killed their husbands and their brothers so it is our duty to replace them with ourselves—certainly a queer twist of logic that only a German mind could invent. One thing is certain: the policy is not working—although everyone agrees that it is a just and necessary policy. If it weren't for the German girls, it would be easy to enforce.

Personally, I haven't made up my mind on the matter. It seems ridiculous to keep the policy if it isn't going to be enforced, and enforcing it is an impossible job, as I see it. We have already been so wishy-washy and undecided on what we are going to do with Germany now that we have beaten her, that I sometimes wonder if we have beaten her. We had no policy for Italy, and now

Transport deck covered with troops and military band. (Courtesy of the Dwight D. Eisenhower Library, Harry J. Cordell Collection.)

we have none here. One faction seems to take the attitude that the German attitude can be changed—that they can be re-educated and that we would gain more in the end by associating with them and teaching them the American way of life. Personally I don't think they can be re-educated and that we are wrong to proceed on the policy that they will ever be any different than they have been—for several generations anyway. The coming war between Russia and the US is the latest topic of civilian interest, but we have been pretty well prepared to expect this. Even the Poles in Dachau were looking forward to the day when we would fight the Russians.

Several of the fellows have received clippings of columns written by news-papermen who were with us at Dachau. If you see any, I wish you would send them to me.

The Seventh Army is to be one of the Armies of Occupation, but that doesn't mean we couldn't be transferred from the 7th Army at any moment. Officially, we are still awaiting orders.

Love,
Harold

22 June 1945

Bad Mergentheim Germany

Dear Mother and Father,

Several weeks ago we were told that the German Marks issued by the German government were illegal. So I, along with everyone else, threw away several hundred dollars worth of marks I'd found on bodies. Now it turns out that the Germans are willing to accept them and the Army doesn't seem to care who has them. I only have about $6.00 worth of small bills left plus a few large denomination notes which no one can change. The only thing we can't do with German marks is convert them to U.S. money and send it home. Unlike France, the monetary exchange works in our favor here. A haircut costs 10¢, beer 2¢, wine 10¢, a shave 4 1/2¢, shoes (some of the fellows have had cobblers make shoes from leather taken from Dachau) cost $1.30. The only trouble is there is nothing to buy. We have to pay for our laundry with candy, cigarettes, and gum, because people don't seem to care for money. This trading is illegal, but it's the only way we can get our laundry done.

More and more German soldiers are being discharged from the army every day. Already we've had several embarrassing incidents where returning Germans have found their wives with Americans. For the most part though the ex-soldiers are the meekest and best behaved of all the civilians.

Some of our doctors are moving into the home of a German Army doctor. I was assigned to a detail to help tidy up the place. The Doctor's wife and two daughters were there helping us. They all spoke English and seemed like typical Americans. As usual the fraternization ban was ignored and everyone got along fine. Cpl. Hush and I cleaned out her son's room, and kept lots of books and literature we found. He is 23 years old, was active in the Hitler Youth from 12 til 17, and since then has been an SS trooper of the same regiment that provided the guards for Dachau. His mother freely admitted all this and told us how proud she was of him—stressing the honor connected with being in the SS. She does not know where he is now, but expects he'll be discharged soon. Judging from the literature we found around the house, the whole family were ardent Nazis. Both daughters were members of the German Maiden Bund—a group of girls devoted to providing carnal entertainment for German officers. This was the most thoroughly and hopelessly conditioned Nazi family I've come in contact with so far.

A bunch of Life magazines have just arrived, and we've been sitting around picking out errors in their stories. It's surprising how inaccurate some stories are. For instance, in the May 28 issue, the picture on the bottom of the first article of the "werewolf shadow" is not that at all, as everyone over here knows. These shadows plus the words PST! and FEIND HÖRT MIT! (The enemy is with us) appear all over Germany—on buildings and on billboards. It is just part of an intensive campaign to keep civilians security conscious, much the same as similar posters around U.S. ports and army camps.

Another issue features an article on the typical American girl, and a great argument has been going on comparing her with German and French Girls. The fellows arguing in favor of the German girls certainly are not without support. The caption of "Naturalness" on one of the pictures is quite a joke with the fellows here. If the German girls excel anyplace, it is there. By contrast the Americans are as artificial and painted-up as burlesque queens. Personally, I think the reason the German girls are receiving the acclaim they are is because they are here while the Americans are there. I've been getting a letter from a fellow I roomed with in Michigan who is now in Italy. All he does is rave about the Italian girls.

Fraternization with children is now officially permitted. With others the situation has changed slightly. The M.P.s decided that the waitresses and chambermaids that we employ will have to leave at 7:00. This eliminates our informal evening dances. On top of this we're constantly being subjected to posters telling us what fiends the Germans are, and reminding us of Dachau horrors. Horror pictures are the least popular and are soon torn down. No one wants to remember them.

Horses wear ear muffs here—red blue purple or green—and they're trimmed with fancy fringe. It seems they're supposed to keep fleas out; they certainly look odd.

Love,
Harold

GREETINGS FOR THE RETURNING SERVICEMAN

When the soldiers and sailors finally made it home, they were officially thanked and then sent back to civilian life with certain benefits and much advice.

Letter from the Secretary of the Navy[9]

July 9, 1946

Mr. Teddie Welch
Gen. Del.
Sallisaw, Oklahoma

My Dear Mr. Welch:

I have addressed this letter to reach you after all the formalities of your separation from active service are completed. I have done so because, without formality but as clearly as I know how to say it, I want the Navy's pride in you, which it is my privilege to express, to reach into your civil life and to remain with you always.

You have served in the greatest Navy in the world.

It crushed two enemy fleets at once, receiving their surrenders only four months apart.

It brought our land-based airpower within bombing range of the enemy and set our ground armies on the beachheads of final victory.

It performed the multitude of tasks necessary to support these military operations.

No other Navy at any time has done so much. For your part in these achievements you deserve to be proud as long as you live. The Nation which you served at a time of crisis will remember you with gratitude.

The best wishes of the Navy go with you into civilian life. Good luck!

Sincerely yours,
James Forrestal
Secretary of the Navy

Pamphlet from the War and Navy Departments, "Going Back to Civilian Life"[10]

Recognition of the achievements of the returning troops was widespread and sincere. Here a military publication compares the veterans to the Founding Fathers.

. . . Our country was founded by men and women, like you, who were willing to fight for its freedom. It has remained free because, when the need arose, new generations were willing to fight and, if necessary, to die for what they loved.

By your service in this war you have done your share to safeguard liberty for yourself, your family, and the Nation. You have helped to preserve that liberty for generations to come. . . .

CIO Publication, "When You Come Back"[11]

Organized labor solidified the gains it had made under the New Deal during the "truce" with management in the war years, but it braced for a resumption of the struggle when victory was achieved. Here is an excerpt from a union publication aimed at the returning serviceman.

"How does Army cooking rate with your mother's?" asked Marty, the night he went over to meet Joe's boy.

Tom laughed.

"It's funny the way a GI feels being home again," he said. "Soft beds and sheets, no guns to clean, no sweating out orders. But I feel scared, too."

"Why scared," asked Marty, "after all you've been through?"

"Things are simpler in the Army," continued Tom. "When there were problems, we were all in the same deal together. Here, a fellow seems more alone. Nobody seems to give a damn, except his family . . ."

"That's where you're wrong, Tom," said Marty, lighting his pipe. "We're all learning to work together. If we work together, there's no problem we can't solve."

"I was telling Tom what you told me about jobs for all," put in Joe. "But he doesn't entirely agree."

"In the service," Tom explained, "most of the men think there'll be a scramble for jobs after it's over and those that get there first get jobs and as for the rest—well, it's just tough . . ."

"You know," Tom continued, "most of the ten million men in the service have been through plenty hell since they left home. Been away from their wives and families. Had to learn how to live different lives. Plenty of them have seen poverty and starvation and buddies blown to pieces just after they may have bummed them for a butt. I can't put it into words: but these men just won't be satisfied with 'No Help Wanted' signs. They feel that asking for a job isn't asking for such a damn lot. Slogans won't cut much ice . . ."

Marty blew a cloud of smoke at the ceiling, then said: "When our union uses the slogan 'Jobs for ALL,' we don't do this, Tom, to kid anybody. We do it because jobs for everybody are possible. We say that—if we take advantage of the opportunity facing us—there can be jobs for every ex-GI and anybody else who wants them."

"What do you mean by 'opportunity?'" asked Tom.

"Every family, every store, every business, every nation in the world needs equipment of some kind," explained Marty. "We're coming out of this war with the greatest opportunity a country ever had to supply everyone with a good job and build prosperity. Here, let me read you some figures." And Marty fished out of his pocket a clipping from which he read:

"About one-third of all homes in the United States are in need of major repairs."

"About one-third of all homes have no baths."

"About one-third are still without electricity."

"Almost 95 million people do not have a good diet."

"Almost 40 percent of all draftees are rejected for physical reasons."

"One-half of all our school buildings are one-room schools."

"We need 16,000,000 new homes."

"We need increased food production."

"We need more hospitals and clinics.

"We need more projects to provide inexpensive electricity."

"We need more school buildings."

"You can see," concluded Marty, "what our own needs are. That's what I mean by 'opportunity'."

"And that doesn't include," added Joe, "the fact that people in nearly every other country in the world need what America makes. Tractors, cars, generator, electrical equipment like we make in the shop. Countries like England, China and Russia will be wanting to rebuild. And that means more jobs."

"That makes sense," admitted Tom. "When the time comes everybody will be just bucking for a chance to start making things civilians want. And that means a hell of a lot of jobs."

"We can have prosperity like the world's never seen," said Marty. "But labor, veterans, farmers, industry and government have all got to work together just like they did during the war. They have to keep cooperating, or else . . ."

"Why shouldn't anyone want to cooperate?" asked Tom. "A person's ripe for a psycho-ward not to see that."

"Reactionary interests spread the idea as much as they can that there's sure to be a depression and breadlines," said Marty. "They figure that during a depression workers will take jobs at any pay. Then the unions could be busted and wage standards shot to hell."

"I guess something like that happened after the last war," said Tom. "But people won't stand for it this time. I know the GIs won't."

"Of course they won't," said Marty, "if we all work together. But do you know, Tom, what 'divide and conquer' means?"

"That's what Hitler tried to do," answered Tom. "He got the people of every country he invaded fighting among themselves over phony issues. Then he stepped in. Every GI knows that."

"If the small group of fascist-minded people we have in America can't find an issue to get people quarreling about," said Marty, "they'll invent an issue. And since they control plenty of newspapers and radio stations, they try to influence people."

"Maybe they won't get away with it," said Tom. "We GIs are learning the difference between latrine rumors and the facts. In the service we read how unions were always striking and war workers were wearing silk shirts to work. But most of us didn't really believe those things, even when we blew our tops about them."

"Fact is," said Marty, "the number of hours lost by strikes since Pearl Harbor was only one-tenth of one percent of time worked. But that isn't what the newspapers printed!"

"They didn't print Government figures either which showed the average take-home money made during the war was less than $45.00 a week," pointed out Joe.

"Oh, some GIs were fooled," said Tom. "But men in service know people back home couldn't be producing equipment like they were, if they were striking every few minutes. It just didn't make sense."

"Unions are doing their part," said Marty. "We've gone down the line joining the fight for everything that helps GIs. That includes working to raise base pay and family allotments, to pass the soldier-vote bill, the GI Bill of Rights, and laws to guarantee jobs during the time shops are turning over to civilian production."

"Unions like the UE* started in where the GI Bill of Rights ends," said Joe. "Good as the GI Bill is, it only goes part of the way. The fact is that only one vet in every five has a legal claim to a job and then only for a year. The union is the best guarantee of getting seniority rights and security."

"You have to tell GIs all this," said Tom. "They don't read about it in the papers. The best news I've heard since my sergeant took me off K.P. is what you've told me about jobs for everybody. It makes sense."

"The unions don't pretend to be able to do the job alone," said Marty. "We've accomplished most when everybody in town works together. These days no one group of people can do a damn thing alone."

"And that's where GIs like Tom come in," said Joe.

"Hell," said Tom, "What can a lousy P.F.C. like me do to help?"

"There's plenty ex-GIs can do," said Marty. "You can work in your home town, in your church, your union, your veterans' organization to get everybody to understand what the hell unity really means as far as jobs and prosperity are concerned."

"It's GIs like you, Tom," said Joe, "who can help straighten people out who think that this is the time to start their own private war against their neighbor because he happened to be a soldier or a sailor or a civilian during the war; or because his skin is light or dark, or because he is a Jew or not a Jew; or because he has a foreign-sounding name."

---

*United Electrical, Radio and Machine Workers of America, CIO.

"GIs aren't coming back home the kids some of them were when they left," Tom pointed out. "These men were smart enough to learn soldiering and lick the Nazis and Japs. To do this they had to learn to work with all kinds of people—black and white, Americans, Russians, British, Chinese, northerners and southerners, farmers and city people. When you're in the service, everybody looks the same in a pair of fatigues. I think these GIs are going to be damned hard to fool when they get back . . ."

"You can say that again," said Joe.

"Well, it's getting late," said Marty. "But before I leave, I want to invite you to visit our union headquarters and meet the members of our UE Veterans' Welfare Committee. They'll be able to answer more of your questions. Maybe help you get the kind of job you want."

"Thanks," said Tom, shaking hands. "First I'm checking in with my draft board and then my next stop is union headquarters."

A corporal entered company headquarters on a Marine base and announced: "Corporal Jones has the first sergeant's permission to speak to Lieutenant Johnson, Sir."
"What can I do for you, Corporal," inquired Johnson.

"Sir," said the corporal, standing properly at attention, "I am about to receive my discharge. I have been watching the lieutenant, sir, since I have been in his platoon and have been favorably impressed."

The lieutenant stiffened.

"I am head of a construction and engineering firm on the West Coast," continued the corporal. "If the lieutenant contemplates a return to civilian life, I would be pleased to offer the lieutenant a job in my organization."

HONORING THE WORLD WAR II GENERATION

AMERICAN LEGION PUBLICATION, "AUGUST 14! VICTORY DAY FOR WORLD WAR II"[12]

The American Legion attempted to have August 14, the date of the Japanese surrender ending all hostilities in World War II, declared a national holiday. Here is an excerpt from an American Legion publication on the topic.

Annual observance of August 14th as "Victory Day" of World War II is being urged by The American Legion. It has called on its 58 Departments and 14,857 posts to take the lead in all communities in celebrating this anniversary this year to establish it as an annual observance.

August 14, 1945, marked the capitulation of Japan, bringing to a victorious and final close the greatest war ever fought in freedom's cause. More than 300,000 gallant American fighting men and women gave their lives to bring about the total defeat of Nazism, Fascism and Nipponism.

The day marking the complete military triumph for America and the nations allied with her in the global war of liberation ranks, therefore, with the most important dates in human history.

The building of a new world in which all mankind hopes peace will be enduring and war forever outlawed dates from August 14, 1945.

The American Legion is urging annual observance of August 14th as "Victory Day" of World War II for the following purposes:

1. To give thanks for the great victory we have won.

2. To pay tribute to the memory of the heroic dead who made the victory possible.

3. To give recognition to the sacrifices and the devotion of the men and women who served and still are serving in the nation's armed forces.

4. To keep alive the recollection of the war efforts and sacrifices on the home front—the civilian defense activities, the black-outs, the rationing, the record-breaking production of war workers.

5. To rededicate all loyal Americans to the unfinished task of translating our military victory into lasting peace.

The American Legion has caused to be introduced in Congress legislation to designate August 14th of each year as "Victory Day" of World War II and have it set aside as the official national holiday commemorating the successful termination of that greatest of all wars.

The American Legion bills pending in Congress are H. R. 4185 and S. 1464.

Though the formal instrument of surrender was signed by Japan September 2, 1945 (V-J Day), that date often falls on—or too close to—Labor Day to permit a separate and distinct observance.

Each department of The American Legion is asked to urge the governor of its state to issue immediately a proclamation designating August 14, 1946, as "Victory Day" and calling on all communities in the state to participate in fitting ceremonies and exercises commemorating the winning of World War II.

All the departments are asked to urge all their posts to take the lead in arranging local celebrations of "Victory Day." With two-thirds of American Legion membership now composed of World War II veterans, it is fitting that this organization should be a leader in appropriate observations of this anniversary.

■ SOURCES

1. Bruce Carson to Family, April 29, 1945, "Bruce Carson Letters 1945 (1)" File, Richard Lowitt Papers, World War II Participants and Contemporaries Collection, Dwight D. Eisenhower Library, Abilene, Kansas.
2. Richard Cipra to Eleanor Lewis, May 27, 1945, "Letters—Richard Cipra, 1945" File, Elmer Lewis Papers, World War II Participants and Contemporaries Collection, Eisenhower Library.
3. Notebook, by Jeanne E. Betcher, "Jeanne Betcher—Notebook, 1945 (4)" File, World War II Participants and Contemporaries Collection, Eisenhower Library.
4. Loren Fred to Wife, July 26, 1945, "Letters (1)" File, Loren Fred Papers, World War II Participants and Contemporaries Collection, Eisenhower Library.
5. The documents in this section are from Stephanie Salada Papers, Private Collection, Pittsburgh, Pennsylvania.
6. The letters in this section are from Willard H. Fluck to Parents, May 31, 1945, "Letters 1945 (1)" File; July 3 and 24, 1945, "Letters 1945 (2)" File; December 29, 1945, "Letters 1945 (3)" File; and January 13, 1946, "Letters 1946" File, Willard H. Fluck Papers, World War II Participants and Contemporaries Collection, Eisenhower Library.
7. Mildred Karlsen to Sister, July 22, 1945, "Scrapbook (4)" File, Mildred Karlsen Morris Papers, World War II Participants and Contemporaries Collection, Eisenhower Library.
8. Harold Porter to Parents, May 10, 12, 27, and 31, 1945, "Letters May 1945" File; June 5, 9, and 12, 1945, "Letters June–July 1945" File; and Harold Porter Papers, World War II Participants and Contemporaries Collection, Eisenhower Library.
9. James Forrestal to Teddie Welch, July 9, 1946, "Mary Blosser—Documents" File, Mary Blosser Papers, World War II Participants and Contemporaries Collection, Eisenhower Library.
10. War and Navy Departments, "Going Back to Civilian Life," August 1945, "Miscellaneous Pamphlets" File, Mrs. Frank Kozak Papers, World War II Participants and Contemporaries Collection, Eisenhower Library.
11. The United Electrical, Radio and Machine Workers of America, CIO, "When You Come Back," 1944, "American Legion Publications (2)" File, World War II Participants and Contemporaries Collection, Eisenhower Library.
12. "August 14! Victory Day for World War II," prepared and distributed by National Public Relations Division, American Legion, n.d., "American Legion Publications (3)" File, World War II Participants and Contemporaries Collection, Eisenhower Library.

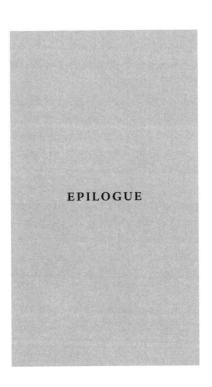

EPILOGUE

IN AUTUMN 1945, THE AMERICANS WHO HAD WAGED THE GREATEST WAR IN THEIR nation's history returned to peacetime pursuits. The soldiers and sailors straggled home, never quite knowing when they would make it back, never quite knowing what to expect when they did. The wheels of war industry slowed, then stopped, as the factories switched over to full-scale civilian production once again. Women, despite their having had a taste of financial and social independence, returned to the kitchen and the nursery. Rationing and price controls gradually disappeared. Some veterans went back to their old jobs, some found new ones, some went to technical school or college under the provisions of the Servicemen's Readjustment Act, better known as the "GI Bill of Rights" or, commonly, the "GI Bill." Uniforms and blackout curtains were put away. The great battles, the evils of Nazism, the proper functions of the United Nations Organization, and even the mighty atomic bomb faded into the background as Americans tried to pick up the pieces of their old lives.

None would succeed in doing so, because their old lives were irretrievably gone. The America on which Japanese bombs had fallen on that Sunday morning in 1941 had passed into history, transformed by the years of struggle. Organized labor would be challenged in the years ahead but for now was solidly entrenched. The New Deal programs were also by now part of the American landscape, and not even Republican victories in the next several years, including, finally, a recapture of the White House in 1952, would threaten that Rooseveltian legacy. African Americans had served their nation well and were finding an ever louder voice in their calls for equality. And the depression-era economy that had been rejuvenated by the government's massive wartime spending continued to boom with peacetime consumer spending.

For the generation who actually waged World War II, however, in the factories, corn fields, highways and railroads, mines and shipyards, as well as on its battlefields, there was not much of a pre–Pearl Harbor life to resurrect anyway. When war had come to the United States, they had been in school or not far removed from it, no longer quite children but not yet full citizens of the adult world, just beginning to come to terms with employment, courtship and marriage, civic responsibility, career planning, parenthood. That natural process had been disrupted and distorted by the war. Families and relationships were sundered, the lure of good wages pulled people to new regional and urban environments, higher earnings provided financial security and bred profligate spending, and societal mores evolved to reflect the newfound mobility and social fluidity of wartime America. In short, the World War II generation would never perceive or behave toward one another in quite the same way again. Moreover, because the nation's war aims of undoing a decade of fascist aggression and eventually extirpating the bellicose ringleaders had been convincingly achieved through overwhelming military victory, Americans would never view the rest of the world, or their own place in it, in quite the same way again either. The experience instilled a variety of values and lessons on the World War II generation. For one thing, the war had been fought with remarkably little resistance and dissent in the United States. To be sure, the nation had had draft dodgers, conscientious objectors, pacifists, and slackers, but, in the context of the history of American wars, these dissenters were at record low levels. Well under 1 percent of those who registered for selective service were officially classified as evaders, and most of those were simply men who had made technical errors in their registration. Conscientious objectors totaled 43,000, less than half of 1 percent of the 10 million persons drafted, and even then 58 percent of the objectors served in the armed forces in noncombatant roles. There were a few noted pacifists, such as Montana Congresswoman Jeanette Rankin and the actor Lew Ayres, but pacifism never posed any serious or even organized threat to the war effort. In sum, the American war effort was remarkably well supported by the citizenry and became the most resolute affirmation of patriotic values in the nation's history.

As Americans, for the second time in as many generations, rejoiced at their reunions with returning servicemen and grieved for those who would never come back, the desirability of preventing a third, and likely worse, world war became more pronounced. It is safe to say that, after two major conflicts in the past quarter century, most Yanks were not eager to go "over there" again, but they had come to believe that they did have some responsibility for policing world affairs to relieve their children of the need to repeat the experience. So Americans at last embraced the internationalism of Woodrow Wilson, which they had rejected in its League of Nations version after World War I, in the form of the United Nations Organization.

In the long run the UN proved too unwieldy for maintaining world peace. However, the postwar United States, determined to learn the lessons of history, had come to eschew the isolationism that, in their view, had allowed the cancer of fascist aggression in the 1930s to grow into a malignancy requiring extended, painful, and expensive surgery to excise. Further, the Americans who had struggled so mightily with Hitler, Mussolini, and Tojo identified in Joseph Stalin's regime a new strain of the now familiar totalitarian expansionist threat. The result was the widely supported policy of containment, that is, the attempt to combat Communist expansion wherever and in whatever form it might take, from direct, conventional aggression to low-level insurgencies or even general anticapitalistic propaganda. Believing that failure to stand up to such aggression anywhere might launch a process of insidious Communist expansion that would knock down popular governments like dominoes, Americans supported intervention, on varying levels, in numerous contested regions and nations around the globe. First formulated by the Truman administration, the policy of containment became the cornerstone of American diplomacy for the cold war. In this way the high price of Kasserine, Omaha Beach, and Tarawa led to the smaller but politically troubled bloodletting at Pusan and Tet, Pork Chop Hill and Khe Sanh. It was the price of assuming some responsibility for the global balance of power.

World War II had also wrought a monumental change in the national economy. The lean years of the Great Depression had seen a devastating combination of industrial stagnation, as the investment capital of the prosperous 1920s had gone into unbridled stock speculation and faulty foreign loans and into agricultural overproduction, driving farm prices down and impoverishing the 40 percent of Americans who still depended on the fruit of the land for their livelihood. The result had been unparalleled unemployment, declining incomes, and penury. But the war solved the problem of overproduction by creating ceaseless demand for goods and services of every stripe and pattern, agricultural and industrial. With fifteen million citizens taking up arms, labor, once so abundant, became scarce enough to drive up employment, wages, and consumer buying power.

Despite the economic transformation, Americans learned they must sacrifice, not only their sons and brothers, but also the many pleasures and goods their improved earnings might have purchased in more peaceful times.

Shortages and rationing thus extended what had already been a decade of deprivation for another five years. Income went into savings, particularly in the form of war bonds, because now there was so little for consumers to buy.

American industry's reconversion to civilian goods production, which began well before the war ended, ignited an explosion of spending that forestalled the widely anticipated postwar recession, such as had befallen the nation in 1919. Furthermore, the GI Bill softened the impact of the restoration of the millions of servicemen to the labor pool by sending hundreds of thousands of the returning veterans to the classroom over the next several years. The loan benefits of the bill also boosted residential construction, a major stimulus to the economy. When organized labor weathered the storm of management's postwar attempts to reclaim ground lost to the unions during the war, job security and higher wages for blue-collar workers ensured the continuation and, indeed, expansion, of the domestic market for consumer goods. Soon after the war, the Marshall Plan provided an additional boost with its loans to foreign nations on the mend and its incentives to buy American-made machine tools, farm equipment, and other capital goods. The U.S. economy embarked on a quarter century of sustained growth, the longest such period in its history.

The radical impact of the war on the economy meant more, however, than mounting bank accounts and an improvement in the quality of the American lifestyle, notable consequences of the war in themselves. Raised in poverty and coming of age in a time of sacrifice, the World War II generation interpreted their newfound prosperity as proof of both their invincibility and their righteousness. The sheer mass and quantity of U.S. weapons and equipment had overwhelmed German professional skill and fanatical Japanese bravery, and even the fighting forces of the other Allies had gained a material advantage over the fascist enemies thanks to the "arsenal of democracy." Yankee production may not have won the war all by itself, but to the Americans who witnessed the final military inundation and collapse of the Axis powers and then administered the occupation amid the rubble of the defeated nations, it was hard not to conclude that Seattle shipyards, Detroit assembly plants, and the steel mills of Pittsburgh had been the cornerstone of victory.

American affluence was evident in more places than the actual field of battle. Everywhere American fighting men journeyed in their pursuit of global victory, they encountered peoples less educated, healthy, prosperous, and well fed than themselves. Even the citizens of the industrialized and technologically advanced Allied nations such as Great Britain envied the U.S. fighting men their hearty and plentiful rations, their abundant equipment, their durable and immaculate uniforms, and their excellent medical care. The

Americans in turn had noted, in the lands they helped to liberate, the under-fed bodies, modest housing, and ubiquitous shortages of every sort of basic necessity. The GIs who tossed Hershey bars to emaciated street urchins and doled out Lucky Strikes to the ragged paupers of three continents never for-got the contrast between their own opulence and the omnipresent want in the eyes of all the foreign peoples they encountered, friend and foe alike.

To the World War II generation, there was more than chance or simple difference in economic fortunes behind the incontrovertible evidence of American plenty. U.S. abundance seemed elegant and indisputable proof of the superiority of American values. Allied Supreme Commander Dwight D. Eisenhower's depiction of the U.S. effort against Nazi Germany and Fascist Italy as a "crusade in Europe" sums up this view rather well. The enemy, whether bombastic Italians, cruel Germans, or the infuriatingly swaggering Japanese, were evil incarnate. That the Allies would sooner or later wreak divine retribution on such moral pestilence was never seriously doubted, for God would strengthen the hand of the enemies of Satan.

To the World War II generation, the fact that the "arsenal of democracy" rescued impoverished Melanesians and quaint Dutchmen and childlike Filipinos and all the other downtrodden casualties of Axis villainy suggested that there were indeed distinctions among the "good" nations, too, with God smiling most upon his favorites. And, besides the fascists' victims, U.S. production had also saved America's allies in arms. Be they primitive Russians, overrefined English, or defeated French, they could not have vanquished the fascist tide without Lend-Lease and other such assistance. Americans at that time, then, saw their success as the product of their industrial might, something no other nation could hope to match. Would God ever have bestowed such wonderful power on any but those of whom he most approved? In the turbulent 1960s, the children of the World War II generation would mistake this materialistic emphasis for misplaced values rather than an affirmation of Americanism and would accordingly rebel against it, but then these younger people had never experienced their parents' genuine fear of perverted fascism, their great sacri-fices to squelch it, or their well-earned pride in producing the tools of victory.

The power that the Almighty had bestowed upon America seemed limit-less to those who wielded it. The United States had underwritten and engi-neered a victory in the most massive struggle in human history. In addition, by 1945 America's war machine, whether one was considering the frontline GI or the master strategists in Washington, had risen to prominence and could match that of any other nation. And then there was the atomic bomb, yet another sign of divine favor but also a military trump card that conferred unbounded leverage in international affairs. The United States, it seemed, could shape the world as it thought best, surely part of a heavenly plan for bringing peace and justice to the beleaguered planet. This faith in the nation's unlimited and righteous power, too, played a role in the subsequent U.S. involvement in Korea and Vietnam.

World War II thus underlay the worldview of the generation who led the country through the long, frightening years of the cold war. The foreign policy of George Bush was as profoundly affected by the world war as that of Harry Truman had been forty-five years earlier. Only with the electoral defeat of World War II veteran Bob Dole in the presidential race of 1996 did this generation pass from center stage in American politics.

What made the effects of World War II on that generation so profound was the combination of the depth and the breadth of the war's impact. All wars result in some deaths, separations, and maimings and the interruption or perhaps shattering of some lives. But World War II extended these experiences to the entire populace. Even those families fortunate enough to escape the loss of loved ones nevertheless felt the omnipresence of the war. Scrap, paper, and war bond drives were regular occurrences, jobs became plentiful, consumer goods became scarce, young men donned uniforms and disappeared from communities, lifestyles changed because of the shortages, and one could not listen to the radio, open a magazine, go to a movie, or walk down the street without some reminders of the war's presence. World War II touched a whole generation of Americans as no other military experience, before or since. Only the Civil War can lay claim to such ubiquity, but even so, in the 1860s there were many citizens for whom the conflict was far off and vague, while they continued on with their lives in the farmlands and small towns distant from the action.

Because of this kind of pervasiveness, along with the widespread support for and dedication to the war effort, for the United States World War II was a uniquely shared experience. No other generation of Americans has been touched so thoroughly by a military ordeal. Save for a nuclear exchange, no other generation will be so affected in the future.

The reason is that warfare has changed. Since World War II, the weapons have grown more terribly awesome in their range and destructiveness, so much so that the worst nuclear, biological, and chemical weapons mutually deter their employment. "Conventional" military technology is similarly advanced, to the point that overall destructive non-nuclear capability has risen despite the shrinking numbers of military personnel. Mobilization for war, even a major war, would not affect the American people in the twenty-first century to nearly the same extent that it did in the 1940s. Social and economic disruption and metamorphoses in a non-nuclear confrontation will never again match the unprecedented levels they reached in World War II. With less personal involvement and risk, patriotic commitment to the cause is not likely to reach those remarkable levels either. World War II, as much as any other major event generated different experiences, and hence different perceptions and memories, for its participants. Thus, there are, among the generation who waged and endured and won the war, many World War IIs, all of them "true" or valid. Furthermore, memory has made even more versions, built around or starting from a truth, but now in a form different from the way others remembered it, today or even shortly thereafter, as they discussed the war in their diaries and reports and letters home. Besides the effect of the simple passage of time, the participants remember now, as human nature compels them to, through the prism of Vietnam, the civil rights movement and feminism, the fall of the Berlin Wall, grandparenthood, and everything else that has occurred in the decades since Japanese and Allied representatives signed the instrument of surrender in the late summer stillness of Tokyo Bay.

The Americans who waged World War II were as flawed and imperfect as any generation, but their circumstances compelled them to some extraordinary experiences and achievements. When we recognize their imperfections and shortcomings, their accomplishments become not less but rather all the more remarkable and admirable. They shaped not only their world but ours, for their influence reaches through the Cold War and postindustrialism to us in the twenty-first century. Archie Bunker is off the air now, but his reruns are worth watching. After all, he was in the Big One.

INDEX

Refrigeration, and domestic conservation efforts, 224–25
Refugees, French, 139
Religious faith: American Legion on,
16, 17; among Germans, 258; at
front, 79, 90, 92, 94, 95, 98; in naval
combat, 73, 75, 76, 77, 127, 128, 129,
130; in rear, 153; about righteousness of U.S. cause, 277; in U.S. culture, 216, 261
Retreat, 49
Richards, Esther, 96
Richardson, Martha, 136, 181
Rickert, Mirriam, 196
Rifle, M1 Garand, 38
Riordan, Chas, 88–90
Romance(s): anecdotes about, 183, 186;
begun in correspondence, 178–79;
described in correspondence,
180–83; and sorrow, 183–85; sustained in correspondence, 186–89,
198–202
Roosevelt, Franklin Delano: on
American role in War, 4; death of,
170; evaluations of, 170, 171–72,
245; length of presidency, 212; mes-
sage to departing troops, 58;
Mothers' Mobilizing Against War
petition to, 9; New Deal legacy of,
273–74; in North Africa, 78
Rosie the Riveter, 122
R.O.T.C. training, 48
Royal Air Force (RAF), letters home
from, 63–72
Rydziel, Stanley, 131
Rytlewski, Chester M., 243

Sailors' experiences, 202f; of casualties,
75, 130; during induction and training, 33–38; at Iwo Jima, 123–27,
127–31; on merchant vessels,
132–33; in Pacific theater, 72–77
Sanitation, domestic conservation
efforts and, 224–25
Saturday Evening Post, 250
Scott, Don, 154

Secretary of Navy, letter thanking ser-
vicemen, 265
Sergeants, in cavalry, 46
Servicemen's Readjustment Act (GI
Bill), 273, 276
Seventh Army, 262–63
Sexual conduct: American Legion on,
15, 197–98; in Australia, 169; of
German women under Nazism,
263; of German women under
occupation, 258, 261, 263; prostitu-
tion by European women, 113; sol-
dier's rape of local women, 169; in
Women's Army Corps, 151–52. See
also Venereal disease
Sheetz, Carrie, 96
Sherrod, Robert, 131
Shilven, Mary Jane, 93
Ship building: shipyard worker's letter
to son, 192–97; types of ships built,
192–93; volume of, 191
Shipyard worker's letter to son, 192–97
Shore, Dinah, 139
Siegfried Line, 104, 105
Sightseeing: in Belgium, 244; in
England, 63; in France, 140, 154,
244, 246–47; in Germany, 238–40,
251; in Italy, 92
Sigman, Blanche, 96
Silverman, Saul, 196
Sixties generation's view of parents, 277
63rd Infantry Division, 261
Slanina, Fred, 195
Smart, Louise, 136
Smoke boats, 129
Soldiers: average size and weight, 10;
character types and backgrounds,
46; as citizen-soldiers, 11–12, 56, 60;
cost of feeding and clothing, 10 (see
also Logistical support); everyday
life for, 13f; injury and disease of,
101; Roosevelt's message to, 58. See
also specific topics
Souvenirs of war: for airmen, 61; combat troops, 80, 81; from Iwo Jima,
126; in North Africa, 79; official pol-